"McKittrick writes without rancour, scrupulously faithful to the facts and sensitive to social currents. Perhaps the most important quality his writing possesses is that of detachment, but a detachment made humane by a gentle strain of Ulster irony."

Irish Echo, New York

"Widely acknowledged as one of the foremost commentators on the conflict, his knowledge and understanding shine through, and the reader of this book is always sure of being both informed and entertained."

Books Ireland

"He has provided a clear and succinct overview of an extremely complex situation."

Academic Library Book Review

DAVID McKITTRICK was named Correspondent of the Year by the BBC's *What the Papers Say* in February 1999, and two months later was named Journalist of the Year in the Northern Ireland Press and Broadcasting Awards. As Ireland correspondent of the London *Independent* since 1986, he has won several other media awards, as well as the Ewart-Biggs Memorial Prize for the promotion of peace and understanding in Ireland. A frequent broadcaster who has reported on Northern Ireland since 1973, this is the fourth collection of his journalism to be published by Blackstaff Press. He is co-author with Eamonn Mallie of the 1996 book *The Fight for Peace*.

OTHER BOOKS BY DAVID McKITTRICK

Despatches from Belfast (Blackstaff Press, 1989)
Endgame (Blackstaff Press, 1994)
The Nervous Peace (Blackstaff Press, 1996)
The Fight for Peace (with Eamonn Mallie; Heinemann, 1996)

Through the
MINEFIELD

DAVID McKITTRICK

THE
BLACKSTAFF
PRESS
—
BELFAST

First published in 1999 by
The Blackstaff Press Limited
Blackstaff House, Wildflower Way, Apollo Road,
Belfast BT12 6TA, Northern Ireland

Typeset by Techniset Typesetters, Newton-le-Willows, Merseyside

Printed in England by Biddles Limited

A CIP catalogue record for this book
is available from the British Library.

ISBN 0-85640-652-X

*To Pat, for her
support, patience
and love*

CONTENTS

PREFACE   xiii

The nightmare slide to war   1

How Major stumbled into peace   4

Sinn Féin's fatal dilemma   6

Extremism is likely to win again   9

Reluctant runner dogged by rejection of ceasefire   11

Blasted from both sides   15

The men behind the wire   19

Why did they do it?   22

Orange Order's trail of troubles   26

Ulster looks into the abyss   33

Back to square one   35

Women find men behaving badly   40

Twenty-five years of Ireland's Dr No   42

The bombs that blew away peace   47

Double standards for terrorists   50

The IRA's grand strategy   54

Voters dream of day when hope and history rhyme   57

Labour's Irish question mark   62

Blair milks good will in Belfast   68

Northern Ireland changes colour   70

From killer to victim: Basher's death sums up the futility   74

Blair sets Ulster its biggest test   76

Ulster rides a rollercoaster of relief and fear   81

Mistrust mars Ulster hopes   83

Will he stick his neck out for peace?   85

A happy ending for Ulster?   90

Unionist standard-bearers square up to Sinn Féin   94

Behind every seat at the peace table stands a ghost   96

A bunch of toughs, a bottle of Guinness, aristocratic sex,
     and the odd de Valera lecture on Irish history   98

Does Ireland's destiny lie with a woman from the north? 101

One woman shows southerners they have new friends
  in the north 105

"King Rat" foresaw his death 108

Guns get into the Maze because it's an extraordinary kind
  of a jail 111

Inside the Maze 114

Extreme loyalists who have chosen to let their guns do
  the talking 117

Back to the butchery in Ulster. Can Mo Mowlam save
  the day? 120

Ripples still spreading from Bloody Sunday 123

Fatal ill-luck of friends across Ulster's divide 126

Ulster moves towards its Mandela moment 129

The long road to peace: how blood enemies learned
  to talk 132

A rare moment to celebrate as Ulster's old absolutes
  crumble 138

Unionists march towards bitter future battles 140

Nothing will ever be the same again 143

The people choose a different future 147

The new front line 149

At last, Trimble has a big idea to sell to Ulster 152

Architect of the peace process 155

Peace in Ulster may be on course but the champagne
  is still on ice 158

A day of confrontation, a night of terror – the fear is back 161

Is Drumcree the Orangemen's Alamo? 165

"If this is peace, what's war?" 169

Terrible beauty as victims are buried 173

Can good emerge from the evil of the Omagh bomb? 175

The bomb that united them 178

Omagh's legacy of sadness and hope 181

A new home for old foes 184

The man who puts terrorists back to work 187

The prize fighters 189
Defiance that led to death 194
Collins is borne past the graffiti of hate to his grave 196
Does peace have a chance? 198
Brave children's farewell to mother 202

CONCLUSION 204
INDEX 206

PREFACE

The years from 1996 to 1999 have been a time of momentous political breakthroughs and awful violence, a time when hope co-existed with horror, a time when the possibility of a new start for Northern Ireland came into view. Even to mention some of the events of that time is to reawaken a great many memories: the IRA bombing of Canary Wharf; the departure of John Major and Sir Patrick Mayhew and the arrival of Tony Blair and Mo Mowlam; three separate Drumcree crises; the death of Billy Wright and the wave of loyalist violence that followed; the Good Friday agreement; the referendums; the Omagh bomb; the new assembly; the Nobel Peace Prizes.

The journalism here appeared first in the *Independent* and the *Independent on Sunday*, representing the fourth Blackstaff Press collection of our coverage of Northern Ireland, the Republic and Anglo-Irish relations. If daily reportage is the first draft of history, then this might be called a second draft, in that the book consists of key articles selected from around 700 pieces of journalism from this period.

The articles have been tidied, edited and in some cases shortened to prevent repetition. With a few exceptions they appear in chronological order, to convey the sense of how major incident was followed by momentous development, and how nobody ever knew quite what would happen next.

Much thanks is due to colleagues, friends and sources, most of whom would be horrified to be named. I owe much to "the Greek" and to some of Belfast's best journalists such as Eamonn Mallie, Fionnuala O Connor, Deric Henderson, Brian Rowan and Ed Moloney for their advice, guidance, argument and analysis. Fionnuala read a draft and offered many helpful suggestions. The people at Blackstaff Press were as professional as ever, and as devoted as ever to accuracy, truth and fairness. The same goes for colleagues at the *Independent*, such as David Felton, Jan Thompson, John Price and Matt Hoffman: Matt in particular did so much to improve these pieces.

DAVID McKITTRICK
BELFAST
APRIL 1999

Northern Ireland had known real optimism during the IRA ceasefire which lasted between August 1994 and February 1996 but when the IRA broke it, by bombing Canary Wharf, fear and confusion returned. Two London newsagents died in the docklands bomb, then an IRA man was killed when his bomb went off prematurely in the centre of the city. For a grim moment hope seemed overtaken by despair.

20 FEBRUARY 1996   THE INDEPENDENT

The nightmare slide to war

They seem to be watching peace slip away. The IRA is once again bombing England, and before long will surely be bombing Northern Ireland. Then the loyalists will begin again, and a new cycle will be set in motion. Another generation seems destined to know terrorist death and destruction. The mood in Belfast is closer to despair than to mere dismay. Two weeks ago the peace looked to be holding; today people are trying to come to terms with what looks like a return to the worst of the bad old days.

It is all happening with the inexorability of a nightmare. Bit by bit the pieces are falling into place, one step leading to another, the elements that sustained a quarter-century of violence slotting into place all over again. And, as in a nightmare, there seems to be no way of stopping the process.

Ever since the first IRA bomb was detonated at Canary Wharf, there was a set of four steps with the potential to restart the troubles. The first step was the Canary Wharf attack itself, which proclaimed in the most brutal way the IRA's readiness to resort to the use of force. The next point was whether this was to be a one-off or the beginning of a campaign. The further attacks which have

1

taken place have established that Canary Wharf was the start of a series. The third point rests on whether the IRA is intent on reopening its campaign in Northern Ireland. All the signs are that it will do so and that we are in the middle of a phased escalation, with attacks in Belfast next on the agenda. If and when this happens, the fourth step will almost automatically be a resumption of loyalist violence.

It has to be remembered that violence from the extreme Protestants had for a number of years claimed more lives than did the IRA. During the ceasefire they have shown an encouraging interest in politics, but there is little doubt that if the IRA start again they too will go back to war. No one seems to know how to halt the four steps and stop the slide to war: perhaps something will prevent it, but no one can see what it might be.

Offering concessions to Sinn Féin president Gerry Adams, in the hope he could dissuade the IRA from more bombings, would amount to blatant appeasement of terrorism and would undermine democracy. Offers which might conceivably have been made before Canary Wharf are now impossible because of the nakedness of the IRA's political blackmail.

The idea of attempting new rounds of political talks which exclude Sinn Féin has been tried so many times in the past without success that it has no credibility. A new IRA campaign will mean new security measures, but the lesson of the last 25 years is that while the security forces can contain the terrorists they cannot defeat them. The old stalemate could quickly be re-established, where neither the authorities nor the IRA can achieve a military victory. It was the logic of this reality that led Gerry Adams to think of taking a political path towards a negotiated settlement. The IRA now seems to have rejected his logic.

At this moment the IRA leadership has not put before its own people, the 11 per cent of the Northern Ireland voting population which regularly supports Sinn Féin, an alternative vision of the way ahead. They can scarcely believe that another five or ten years of bombing will blast the British out of Ireland. If they do not believe that, however, then logic dictates that there will at some stage in the future be another attempt at a negotiated settlement. But everyone can see that a resumption of violence puts back the chances of another invitation to the conference table. To most people it makes no sense.

In the republican ghettos of Belfast, however, it makes sense enough. These are people with low expectations and a high toleration of violence, people who have become acclimatised to shootings and bombings on their streets. The lesson of the ceasefire, as far as they were concerned, was that the British are not yet ready to do business with their republican leaders. A Sinn Féin councillor explained yesterday: "The most common thing said to me during the ceasefire was, 'The Brits are rubbing your noses in it.' There's two different things here. Do people want to go back to war? No. Are they prepared to go back to war? Yes. They don't want war, they want peace, but they're not going to back down."

These are people whose life experiences are so removed from those of conventional society that they think differently from everyone else. They think they gained less from the ceasefire than the rest of society, concluding they got no new political recognition and certainly no new jobs. So they are fatalistically resigned to fighting on. For many of them the breakdown of the ceasefire is a disappointment but not a calamity. For the rest of the people of these islands, however, it is a catastrophe which will result in the loss of lives, and the loss of much of the hope that Ireland could at last look forward to a future without the shadow of violence.

The breakdown of the ceasefire gave Northern Ireland an uneasy springtime. A murderous feud spluttered on inside the Irish National Liberation Army, claiming two lives, while an internal loyalist argument killed another. But the IRA did not relaunch a full-scale campaign of violence within Northern Ireland, and nor did loyalists.

In February the British and Irish governments announced that all-party talks would start on 10 June, Sinn Féin to be admitted if an IRA ceasefire had been reinstated and if they passed several other tests. In March John Major announced that an election would take place in May. At a time when the peace process was in deep trouble, the prime minister claimed credit for launching the whole exercise.

How Major stumbled into peace

After February's IRA bombing in docklands which killed two people and caused such widespread damage, John Major made a broadcast to the nation in which he asserted: "In 1991 I began a new search for peace." If by this he meant the path which led to the December 1993 Downing Street declaration and the 1994 IRA cessation of violence, he is on decidedly shaky ground in implying ownership of the process.

The prime minister's devotion to seeking peace in Ireland is not in question: he has put more time and effort into that usually thankless task than any other modern prime minister. His personal commitment to the search ranks with that of Gladstone and Lloyd George. The criticism is not one of lack of commitment but lack of a compass. The outside world may have the impression that Major's hand on the tiller has been sure, determined and resolute, but this is not borne out by the private documentation. Rather, the picture is of a government which has often stumbled along, unsure of its bearings, divided in its counsels and unclear in its aims.

In October 1993 Major was asking the then Taoiseach Albert Reynolds to drop the process of drafting the declaration – "After giving it very careful consideration, with all the intelligence at our disposal," he wrote, "we have very reluctantly concluded that it will not run at the present time... I know how disappointing this will be to you. I look forward to considering other options."

The fact is that during most of the peace process, Major did not actually believe it would end in peace. It was in essence an Irish nationalist process revolving around Gerry Adams, Sinn Féin and the IRA, Albert Reynolds and Social Democratic and Labour party leader John Hume, together with Catholic priests, who, acting as catalysts, helped bring these different elements together for talks. This hidden network of contacts, particularly those between Gerry Adams and John Hume, helped produce new thinking among participants. Some of those who met republicans later said they could see, as they looked into the eyes of Adams and the others, a growing appreciation of views from outside the hermetically sealed republican underworld.

The giant conceptual step eventually taken by the republicans was to call a halt to terrorism, and to do so without any promises from the British government. Instead, the cessation would be called on the understanding that an end to violence would mean the beginning of a powerful new nationalist political coalition. This was followed, in August 1994, by the huge practical step of the IRA cessation. While many outside observers have assumed that this can in large measure be attributed to John Major's intricate behind-the-scenes manoeuvrings, there is a case to be made that it all happened despite the government's stance rather than because of it.

The government, for a time under Margaret Thatcher and subsequently under John Major, had its own secret lines to the IRA and Sinn Féin between 1990 and 1993. But the striking feature of the voluminous documentation available is that throughout those three years the two sides never actually got down to real business. They meandered in circles, becoming bogged down in procedural issues, and at no point was there a comprehensive exploration of the issues and the positions of the two sides. This contact with the British first puzzled the IRA, then exasperated them, then left them convinced that London was not serious and was acting in bad faith. The IRA concluded, in fact, that the British were even more treacherous than they had always assumed, a judgement which did nothing to speed the arrival of the cessation.

In August 1994 Major, having listened to the advice of his ministers and his intelligence agencies, did not believe the IRA was about to declare an open-ended ceasefire. Taken by surprise by the cessation announcement, his handling of subsequent events was less than sure-footed: the government often seemed to regard the whole thing as a greasy ball rather than a golden opportunity. In the autumn of 1995 the same people who had advised him that there would be no ceasefire were telling him that there would be no resumption of violence. This catastrophically inaccurate assessment led Major to believe he was free to push and pressurise Sinn Féin as much as he wished.

In this the government, and the intelligence people, got the republican psychology wrong. The democratic instinct rightly recoils from the notion that terrorists should be rewarded because they decide to stop using murder. But this was an instance where huge benefits could have been gained not by rewarding the republicans but by convincing them that their entry into mainstream politics was assured. The government never conveyed any sense of this to the IRA. Instead, the impression was given that Britain was intent on turning the cessation into a surrender. The IRA took the British demand for de-commissioning of weapons to be an insistence on capitulation. The months of stalemate which ensued were followed by the docklands bomb.

The republican mindset is a complex and often subtle one: they misread the British but, even more frequently, the British misread them. One Dublin source said with some bitterness that the British "didn't know why the ceasefire started and don't know why it finished".

Martin McGuinness of Sinn Féin has made it clear that the chances of an early IRA ceasefire are bleak, but the fact that the peace process so often came to life again when it had seemed defunct means that hope of its revival springs eternal. In the meantime some lessons can be learnt from the past six years. One is that clandestine talks can sometimes bear fruit. Another is that the government is unlikely to make the right moves in relation to the republicans until it becomes more successful at getting inside the republican brain, studying how these people think, and working out how best their sensibilities can be managed.

Renewed bombings in Britain suggested the IRA had given up on what was seen as a weak Major government, dependent on unionist support. But although nationalists were critical of John Major, Sinn Féin and the IRA faced hard questions both within and outside their own community.

14 MAY 1996   THE INDEPENDENT

Sinn Féin's fatal dilemma

The republican movement is, as the Americans say, between a rock and a hard place, poised in some anguish between peace and war; and it is the Americans who are helping to keep that pressure mounting all the time. The noises from Washington over the weekend, pressing for a new ceasefire, are a telling reminder that if bombing continues the republicans can expect only isolation – no more visas for Gerry Adams, no more chats in the White House, no more access to the corridors of power.

The republicans are probably more worried about the loss of transatlantic influence than they are afraid of the 10 June negotiations starting without them. The Clinton administration has significantly enhanced the standing and prestige of Sinn Féin: the loss of it would be sorely felt. The republicans also stand on the verge of losing large swathes of Irish-America, that powerful element which, quite independently of Clinton, has much valuable political clout and finance to offer. Even the most pro-republican Irish-Americans are now absolutely adamant that without a ceasefire nothing can be done for Sinn Féin.

The isolation incurred by a refusal to cease fire would be domestic as well as international. Neither British nor Irish ministers will meet Sinn Féin until there is a new cessation, and almost everyone in Ireland will support the two government's insistence that without a ceasefire Sinn Féin will not be allowed into the 10 June talks.

There is another point of pressure on the republicans to give peace another chance, and it comes from their own people, those 11 per cent of Northern Ireland voters who regularly support Sinn Féin. The IRA may bluster that it is prepared for another 25 years of violence, but the people of the Falls Road and Ardoyne are plainly horrified at such a prospect. Gerry Adams, in the years he spent pushing towards the 1994 ceasefire, in effect put his movement into negotiation mode: the concept of victory was quietly discarded from the republican lexicon and replaced by that of peace.

His argument that the British could not be defeated militarily has permeated the republican psyche, and helps explain why so many republicans were dismayed when the IRA attacked docklands in February. No one in the IRA has publicly mapped out a route to victory; the feeling is general that going back to violence would alienate the Americans and all the other elements who stuck their necks out in the cause of bringing Sinn Féin into politics, and in the end would not work. In fact, from a republican point of view, returning to violence could be the most dangerous course of all. No one doubts that the IRA is still a formidable killing machine but in the long term it needs a purpose and a realisable goal to sustain it. Fighting on against a backdrop of growing lack of belief and apathy among its supporters would invite eventual defeat for the IRA.

To the republican mindset, therefore, the most likely means of progress lies in a revived peace process. Although the docklands bomb was a shattering blow to the previous process, the dust cleared to reveal a near-universal belief, among republicans and non-violent nationalists alike, that the way ahead lies in another such process. For nationalists, a new paradigm has been firmly established.

The reader may well wonder why, if this is so, the republicans are not therefore hastening in the direction of a new ceasefire. Such a development, in advance of the 10 June talks date, is not out of the question, but at the moment it has to be said that the odds seem stacked against it. This is principally because the republicans suspect the British have a completely different paradigm in mind.

Sinn Féin will only press for a ceasefire if it is convinced the 10 June talks will represent real peace negotiations and would not simply be a de-commissioning conference. Republicans look at unionist leaders David Trimble and Ian Paisley and conclude that they will do real political business only under intense pressure. They think such pressure can only come from the Taoiseach, John Bruton, and from John Major. They believe Bruton, whom they see as placing too much importance on unionist interests, cannot be relied upon. And they have the deepest suspicions about John Major's intentions. There is, of course, nothing new in this, since it is axiomatic to republicans that all British governments are perfidious. Although both London and Dublin have given numerous assurances that the talks will be for real, and will not simply consist of republicans being harangued to hand over weaponry, republican suspicions remain.

If another ceasefire is engineered and the talks then turn out to be a charade, the credibility of the Adams leadership would be gone. To take a chance and go for it, he needs some cast-iron assurance that they will not get bogged down on the de-commissioning issue. But he needs to be certain of British intentions and no one in Ireland, unionist or nationalist, is ever certain of that. The talks have been arranged in such a way that they could indeed be the wide-ranging negotiations Sinn Féin wants. But they might instead turn out to be based on the preference of some British policy-makers for an approach of containment.

The approach of keeping the lid on held sway for many years in security terms, and in the last few years also became visible in the political sphere. Important government elements shied away from the peace process. This had at its heart the concept of all-inclusive talks leading to a far-reaching negotiation, amounting to nothing less than a historic renegotiation of the political arrangements of 1920–21.

Many on the British side were temperamentally more comfortable with the modest approach of locating an element of middle ground, however small, and incrementally building it up. The aim of this approach is not to draw the republicans into politics but to freeze them out and eventually defeat them. London's emphasis on the de-commissioning issue is quoted by many republicans to support the theory that this is John Major's real intention.

For the government the issue is a delicate one. Ministers clearly wish to maintain the pressure for de-commissioning. Yet if republicans are convinced this will be the centrepiece of the talks then there will be no ceasefire. That in turn means there will be no republicans at the conference table, which means that talks on de-commissioning would be largely academic.

President Clinton, John Hume and Dublin are hopeful that a new offer of entry into politics will at some stage bring about another ceasefire. The republicans, not yet convinced that John Major wants to bring them in from the cold, are torn between talks that could be a trap and more violence which could bring eventual ruination.

In May 1996 the election campaign for a new Northern Ireland Forum for Political Dialogue was a lively affair with clashes between David Trimble and Ian Paisley; and as polling day approached the Democratic Unionist party seemed to show more spirit than the Ulster Unionists.

30 MAY 1996   THE INDEPENDENT

Extremism is likely to win again

Sadly for the British government, the plain fact is that elections in Northern Ireland produce, more often than not, bad news for those who hope for harmony, agreement and reconciliation. Very often they have generated messages unwelcome to London, and today ministers must have the sinking feeling that the same thing may happen again.

This election was billed as the gateway to talks, an expression of the democratic will which would serve as a preliminary for far-reaching peace negotiations. But that was when there was an IRA ceasefire: now there is none, and unless one appears, the talks set for 10 June look like being severely limited in their scope. Worse than this, from London's point of view, is the fact that support for the extremes seems to be holding up well. Democratic Unionist party leader the Reverend Ian Paisley is on the electoral rampage, while there is no sign that Sinn Féin is losing ground. This is not a promising basis for talks.

The election was asked for by David Trimble, the newish and electorally untested leader of the Ulster Unionist party, and was called despite angry nationalist protests. His unionist opponents sense some dismay in the Trimble camp that they, rather than he, will benefit from it – "We're making Trimble tremble," one of his rivals gloated.

The results may yet confound everyone, but it has to be said that most of the electoral surprises of the past have not been pleasant ones for the government. Not a single poll is remembered by the moderate centre as a success: rather, it has been a story of a steady diminution of the middle ground. Elections tend to expose the grim geology of Northern Ireland politics, with a smallish island layer of middle-ground moderation forever pressed between unionism and nationalism. And Paisley is always around to provide spectacular, and generally highly effective, vulcanism.

Countries like South Africa can find elections uplifting and even joyous occasions, but in Northern Ireland the prevailing sense is of voters trudging to the polls to do their tribal duty, an exercise in keeping the other side out rather than an affirmation of faith in democratic processes. Unionists have traditionally liked elections, confident as they are that on a straight headcount they always win. But of late unionist politicians complain that some of their people have become cynical and disillusioned with elections, and increasingly stay at home.

Nationalists, by contrast, have become increasingly organised, with both Sinn Féin and John Hume's SDLP building formidable machines. Two years ago Hume startled Paisley by almost matching Paisley's traditionally gigantic European vote; Sinn Féin, meanwhile, notch up the highest percentage vote of any party in Belfast city council. Things change slowly, but they do change.

The history of elections reflects the history of the troubles: the 1969 victory for Bernadette Devlin, which showed nationalists could win elections; the meteoric rise of Ian Paisley, who captured a Westminster seat in 1970 and has held it ever since; the fragmentation of unionism; the rise of Sinn Féin as an electoral force in the early 1980s. Soberingly, there have been two by-elections resulting from the murders of politicians.

But very often the real focus of events has lain elsewhere – in Anglo-Irish relations, in Washington, most of all in the terrorist war in the backstreets. Elections themselves have made no apparent contribution to banishing the gunmen. But this time there could yet be a happy ending. Once the election is out of the way some means might be found of reassuring republicans that the talks will be for real, and not simply about IRA arms de-commissioning. There

10

might then be another ceasefire.

The days leading up to 10 June are likely to be hectic, with mounting pressure from London, Dublin and Washington for a renewed ceasefire. If that should be successful, then even the sternest critics of the election will conclude it was a worthwhile exercise.

The May election brought the politicians on to the streets in search of votes. The campaign showed loyalist paramilitary parties beginning to learn political lessons.

29 & 31 MAY 1996   THE INDEPENDENT

Reluctant runner dogged by rejection of ceasefire

Bobby Lavery, councillor and reluctant election candidate, stands at the top of the New Lodge with a small band of determined-looking men ready to brave the steady downpour and canvass for Sinn Féin. The biggest sign locally says "No return to Stormont rule". He is a reluctant runner because he regards the election as an unnecessary thing, a stalling tactic by Britain, "an absolute utter farce". He would have preferred a nationalist boycott, but with election day looming Sinn Féin has to try its hardest to demonstrate that its support is not on the ebb. He recounts that on one doorstep a woman, an acquaintance of his own family, said she wouldn't vote for Sinn Féin. When he asked her why not, she said simply: "Ceasefire's broke." So do the majority of people want another cessation?

Lavery, whose son and brother were shot dead by loyalists, replies: "Well, it would be silly for anyone to say they don't want a ceasefire, because anybody that wants to live for the rest of their lives in a situation of killing is crazy. The question I keep getting asked is – is there going to be another ceasefire? I think it's one of the silliest questions I ever heard, because there's nothing more certain than there'll be another ceasefire.

"The pertinent question is when – will it be soon? The answer to that lies with the army council of the IRA, and to a greater extent with John Major. This de-commissioning – the British, first and foremost they want surrender; just like the generals of old when they handed over their sword, they want republicans to show that symbol of defeat and hand over something.

"Now there's no way they're going to get that. Unfortunately John Major is in a position where he's almost totally dependent on unionist votes, so I don't think you'll see any major movement this side of a British general election."

A brief drive away is a loyalist area where David Ervine and the Progressive Unionist party are trying to do what Sinn Féin did for republicanism, and graft a new political dimension on to loyalist paramilitarism. Doing so means persuading Protestants to switch away from mainstream unionism: an Ian Paisley poster, in suitably lurid orange, serves as a reminder that old voting habits die hard.

Ervine's canvassers gather in a little club decorated with Union Jacks, pictures of the Queen, and scenes depicting Protestant gallantry in the First World War. They pile into a minibus and drive to Orangefield to spread the message. "It's all extremely heartening," he says. "A lot of us are new to knocking on doors, but we're very encouraged by the responses. Nobody is slamming doors in our faces." If his party finishes in the top ten it will be admitted to talks, where it will face demands, perhaps led by UUP leader David Trimble, for a speedy hand-over of loyalist weapons. "I've only had one question about de-commissioning, only one," says Ervine. "That was from a man who felt loyalists shouldn't de-commission until the IRA do."

Less than an hour later Trimble, on a public platform in the town hall in Ballymena, the buckle in the Bible belt, urges his audience to spurn such parties. "We have seen some rather unsavoury people strut across the political stage," he declares. "I hope the electorate cuts them down to size on Thursday." The Ulster Unionist leader said there would not be an election had it not been for his party, though he admitted the system being used was not what he had wanted. He compared it to the *Star Trek* cliché – "It's the elections, Jim, but not as we know them."

But, having brought the elections about, there are signs that his party is anxious that it will not do as well as it had originally hoped. The main reason for this is that seasoned electoral warhorse Ian Paisley who, although he turned 70 last month, is tramping the campaign trail with undimmed energy and gusto.

12

Outside the hall a racy jet-black jeep pounds round the Ballymena streets, loudspeaker blaring. Even before the meeting is over the driver, Ian Paisley's son, Ian Junior, knows that fewer than 50 people were at the meeting: a total of 38 were in the audience. Leaning through the car window, young Ian delivers a snappy seminar on how to get unionist votes. "Trimble fails to clarify his positions, whether it's on social issues or constitutional policy. They're a party of generalities – they don't have a specific tight position on most of these things. That makes it very difficult for them to come across with a consistent message.

"I think the electorate's sophisticated, but I don't think they're sophisticated to the extent that they can appreciate all the minutiae and innuendo." It was a simple, direct message from a party, expert in harvesting votes, and hopeful of harvesting many thousands this week.

If manpower and methodical organisation are the keys to success in elections, then in West Belfast at least Sinn Féin are set to do well in the Northern Ireland poll. Outside polling stations in the republican heartlands of Ballymurphy and Springfield sat little caravans containing two or three Sinn Féin workers. Many voters made their way to them before going into the polling stations, standing in a queue to hand in their voting cards.

Inside the caravans Sinn Féin workers had large pieces of cardboard with voting registers Sellotaped to them, street by street. As the people handed in their cards their addresses were found in Glenalina Park, Britton's Parade and Ballymurphy Crescent, and carefully underlined. Other mysterious marks were added with a green highlighter.

The caravans, festooned with posters, pictures of Gerry Adams and tricolour flags, provided a splash of colour on a dull, wet day. But security precautions were in evidence too: the registration numbers were covered up with black bin bags.

Up in Andersonstown came the media event of the day as Gerry Adams arrived to cast his vote at Holy Child primary school. Locals craned their necks for a glimpse, but he was engulfed in a scrum of American, European and Japanese camera crews. If he said anything of significance in the scrum he said it to America, Europe and Japan, not to Belfast.

Across the peaceline in Protestant Ballygomartin a middle-aged woman emerged from Forth River primary school complaining of the long list of Unionist parties on the ballot paper: "Talk about confusing in there," she shook her head. "Progressive Unionists, Ulster Unionists and all the rest – I knew beforehand who I wanted to vote for but still it was confusing. When I saw that big list I was thrown a bit."

Here there are no caravans and fewer workers. There are two men from the new Ulster Democratic party dressed, oddly enough, in identical dark green double-breasted suits, and a small bouncy woman from the Progressive Unionist party, which is said, in the latest journalistic euphemism, to be familiar with the thinking of the paramilitary Ulster Volunteer Force.

She turned out to be Tracey Gould, an executive member of the PUP. "We need your vote to get us round the table," she tells those on their way into the polling station. What makes her think talks would work? "Because I think the smaller parties like us are more realistic about what we need to do. We need to respect each other's culture – gone are the days of the old Stormont and the old power base, the Protestant superiority."

Half a mile away in Woodvale heads turned at another polling station as bagpipe music was heard. A car with an excellent loudspeaker system zoomed round the corner, pulled up at the station and out jumped the Reverend Eric Smyth, the Paisleyite lord mayor of Belfast. He helped out an elderly man and then zoomed off again in another jaunty skirl of pipes.

Some PUP people shook their heads in wonder as they heard of Sinn Féin's level of organisation. "I suppose we'd be organised too if we had a million dollars from America," one woman said ruefully, contemplating her handful of leaflets, damp from the Belfast drizzle.

Sinn Féin and Ian Paisley were the May election's success stories, while there was little comfort for David Trimble's Ulster Unionists. But one underlying message nonetheless sustained a slender hope of eventual progress: it was clear there was no appetite for going back to violence.

Blasted from both sides

"There's absolutely no doubt about it," the republican activist remarked just before the election results were declared. "The August '94 ceasefire was the most popular thing we ever did in 25 years." When the results came through he, like the rest of Sinn Féin, was stunned by their unprecedented vote, a vote which seems to denote overwhelming republican approval of the last ceasefire and a heartfelt wish that there will soon be another.

The overall results of the election mean the Irish peace process has just taken yet another dramatic and unforeseen new turn. It has moved in a direction which paradoxically makes eventual peace more likely, but the prospect of agreement less so. London, Dublin and the Northern Ireland parties are still struggling to come to grips with results which have significantly altered the landscape within both nationalism and unionism. It shattered a number of illusions and showed up both new difficulties and new opportunities. Most of all, and best of all, it has severely limited the IRA's military options, making it next to impossible for the organisation to return to full-scale terrorism. But it has increased Sinn Féin's political options, greatly strengthening Gerry Adams's hand in his quest to lead republicans into politics.

In the short term, the signs are that it will not produce an IRA ceasefire in time to allow Sinn Féin entry to the political talks due to open on 10 June. But the vote, as a massive endorsement of the peace process, means that the chances of another cessation – hopefully a final one – within months are now very high. The question is really not if but when. The peace process is, however, a long game, and there will be many more twists and turns ahead.

From the start the whole idea of an election rested on dubious logic. One unstated purpose for it was an attempt by John Major and his Northern Ireland Secretary, Sir Patrick Mayhew, to exert a measure of control over a process which was not of their making. Once again, however, results which they must regard as undesirable indicate that this goal has eluded them.

One stated justification for the contest was that it would provide a mandate for the various elements. This was always slightly puzzling, since repeated results, from 10 elections in 15 years, show that party fortunes rarely fluctuate by more than a few percentage points.

The main reason advanced for the contest was that unionists had indicated that they would, after an election, be prepared to talk to Sinn Féin, even if no IRA arms were de-commissioned. This too is now in question, however, partly due to a toughening of the positions of rival unionist parties during the election campaign.

Before the election, British policy-makers believed they could ride two horses at once, and could straddle both the main theories on how progress might be made. One theory was that republicans were ready to move away from violence, and could be drawn into the political processes. Others believed there was more merit in the less dramatic path of concentrating on the middle ground, and building incrementally on it, from the centre out.

Many in government believed both approaches could be pursued simultaneously. Some, including senior ministers, had become so intellectually committed to the second theory that when the IRA cessation came along in August 1994 they had much trouble, psychologically and temperamentally, in coming to terms with it. Some never have. One minister recently explained that it had been shown around the world that the way to resolve conflicts was to bring the centres together: once they could be induced to work together, the extremes began to crumble.

This perspective helps explain why some in government would shed few tears if Sinn Féin were not represented at the 10 June talks. The problem for adherents of this theory, however, is that it has been dealt a devastating blow by the election, in which the major victors were Sinn Féin and Ian Paisley. Simultaneously the centre has been whittled away. The centrist Alliance party, which could once command 14 per cent of the vote, went down to 6.5 per cent, leading to a revival of the caustic jibe that parties positioned in the middle of the road often get knocked down. None of the other parties which tried to appeal to both sides scored more than one per cent.

But even more than this, it is the state of play within unionism which has dealt the centre-out theory such a cruel knock. Discounting the peculiar results of European contests in Northern Ireland, the major unionist grouping, David Trimble's Ulster Unionists, collected its lowest-ever share of the vote. In six previous elections it always scored at least 29 per cent: this time it took only 24 per cent.

Paisley's support, meanwhile, showed a solid increase, while a further 9 per cent of unionist votes were scattered among Robert McCartney's UK Unionists and the two fledgling parties, led by David Ervine and Gary McMichael, which have evolved from loyalist paramilitary groups. Most observers have welcomed the respectable loyalist showing as one which will encourage them into politics and away from paramilitarism.

Unionism, in other words, has ceased to be a two-party movement and has fragmented into five parts, two large and three small. Trimble must be uneasily aware that, for the first time, his party does not represent a majority of unionist voters, and that the combined votes of Paisley and McCartney came within 13,000 votes of his total.

Paisley and McCartney do not harbour any desire to form some new centrist coalition with John Hume and the SDLP: nor, for that matter, does Trimble. According to the centre-out theory such intra-unionist divisions can create opportunities for dividing the unionist bloc, but this has not been so in the past. The experience of the unionist fragmentation of the 1970s is that Ian Paisley, when armed with a strong vote as he is today, can exercise a strong influence over other unionist parties. Unionist leaders who contemplated a move to moderation came to dread his anathema, and learned to stay within the fold.

The unionist splintering arises from a mixture of personalities, policies and indeed from a range of fundamentally different views of the future. On one wing are the fledgling loyalists, who fought on a pro-talks ticket; on the other are Paisley and McCartney, who do not want to negotiate with Sinn Féin; and somewhere in the middle is Trimble, who might be drawn into negotiation, though only under stringent conditions. Translating this into terms of the wider population gives a snapshot of the spread of opinion among unionists generally. It suggests that 46 per cent of unionists supported the Paisley–McCartney line, 11 per cent went for the pro-negotiation loyalists, and 43 per cent favoured the less clearcut Ulster Unionist approach.

By contrast nationalist voters displayed an extraordinary unanimity in favour of the peace process. John Hume and Gerry Adams, whose names will forever be linked in the expression "Hume–Adams", both received massive personal endorsements. The SDLP's overall vote dropped by a fraction, while Sinn Féin's rose to its highest-ever level: one voter in seven supported the republicans. Many may consider this a cause for deep depression, and indeed it may be wondered how votes for a party closely identified with the IRA can possibly be construed as support for peace. The answer lies in the way Sinn Féin fought the campaign, emphasising peace at every turn, and in the message republican canvassers received on the doorsteps.

That message was one of huge support for the last peace process, and for the idea that a new one should now be constructed. The regular Sinn Féin vote turned out but so too did many people who had never bothered voting before, or who had refrained from supporting the party while IRA violence was at its height.

When the bomb which killed two people and ended the ceasefire went off in docklands in February 1996, it seemed the IRA might be intent on a return to full-scale war. But the general republican reaction to that bomb, expressed in the first instance privately and now publicly in this election result, amounts to an impressive utilisation of what used to be called "people power". The general republican community, which for so many years either tolerated or actively supported the IRA campaign, has now told the army council that those days are over. One canny west Belfast woman summed it up: "It was a statement of trust in Adams, a vote of confidence in how he handled the peace process. It was also two fingers to the Brits for messing it all up. It was a vote against a return to war. There would be horror if the IRA started up again without a very, very good reason. Something pretty horrendous would have to happen to justify it."

One of the key points at issue between those who favour the peace process and those who prefer the centre-out approach is whether unionism or republicanism is the more flexible. The peace process was posited on a belief that republicans were more ready for movement, a belief which was apparently vindicated by the August 1994 ceasefire but was then dented by its collapse. This election has been damaging for the centre-out theory, however, in that it produced no sign that unionism is ripe for reaching agreement with nationalists.

Unionist Ulster may be uncertain of the way ahead, but nationalist Ireland is united in concluding that any talks which do not include Sinn Féin are, in the words of one Irish government adviser, not worth a penny candle. Nationalists have, in other words, discarded the centre-out approach as futile.

But the Sinn Féin mandate was not a directive to pursue peace at any price: rather, it has given the republicans space and eased the pressure on them. It has curtailed their military options but increased their political options. They appear to have decided to observe the talks and assure themselves they will amount to real negotiations before opting to join them. They will have the luxury of watching how London, Dublin and the unionists conduct themselves before making a judgement on whether the game is worth the candle.

David Trimble, who asked for the contest, has been weakened by it. The British government, which called the election, has had to watch in dismay as the centre contracted and the extremes profited. Gerry Adams, who had declared himself implacably opposed to the election, has ironically emerged as its chief beneficiary. And the peace process, which has so often seemed defunct, somehow moves mysteriously on, in a way which no one really fully understands, full of surprises, keeping alive the hope that a lasting peace can yet be attained.

With talks between all parties at Stormont due to begin, time had run out for a ceasefire to allow Sinn Féin to the table, though there was still hope that one might follow later. Then three days before the Stormont start date Garda officer Jerry McCabe was shot dead while escorting a mail van in County Limerick. A statement from the IRA denied involvement but few believed them. The first day of talks was largely a contest between image-makers.

11 JUNE 1996   THE INDEPENDENT

The men behind the wire

Up close it didn't feel like the stuff of history. It seemed like confusion, a disorganised mêlée in which, not for the first time, the republican and loyalist publicity machines bested the government's spin doctors. John Major did his best, on the first day of potentially momentous talks in Belfast, to strike a note of realistic statesmanship: he had no illusions, he said, about how long, difficult and demanding the process might be. But the propaganda battle honours of the day went to Gerry Adams and Ian Paisley, who grabbed the headlines with their finely calculated grandstanding. Adams was pictured worldwide as the potential peacemaker barred from the conference chamber; Paisley, who cares little for the wider world and concentrates on his domestic market, was able to project himself locally as the union's fiercest defender.

Inside Castle Buildings in suburban east Belfast, the parties and the British and Irish governments finally convened for what might or might not turn out to be all-important talks. The presence of John Major and the Taoiseach, John Bruton, was meant to send the message that this was the real thing. But as so often before, Paisley, veteran of a thousand demos, protests and headline-grabbing manoeuvres, took the proceedings by the scruff of the neck. George

19

Gerry Adams and Martin McGuinness demand entry to talks

Mitchell, the former US senator asked by the two governments to chair much of the talks, was, Paisley declared, "fully in the republican camp. If he's in, I'm out."

A Mitchell–Paisley meeting was hastily arranged, but the DUP leader emerged from it with his earlier opinion intact. Thus it was that John Major, having made his opening speech, handed over the proceedings not to Senator Mitchell but to the Northern Ireland Secretary, Sir Patrick Mayhew. Doing so averted a potential Paisley walkout, but it also introduced a new element of uncertainty as to Senator Mitchell's role in the whole process. Then, with Sir Patrick in the chair, Paisley and others tried to unpick the agenda thrashed out last week by London and Dublin. Major's forecast that it could be long, difficult and demanding already rings true.

The Major and Bruton speeches were meant to be broadcast live on BBC but, half an hour before they went on air, somebody in the government pulled the plug and the live coverage was aborted. The government was worried, the rumour went, about the possibility of Paisleyite heckling. The cameras focused instead on Gerry Adams who, as promised, led a large Sinn Féin team up to Stormont to demand entry to the talks. The largest media posse ever seen in Belfast recorded Adams encountering gates secured with a padlock. They then filmed him circumventing this obstacle and making his way up to another set of gates. Here the cameras, which came from Japan, Norway and many other countries, dwelt on him long and lovingly. It went on for so long that one government press officer completely lost his cool and, abandoning the subtler points of news management, simply grabbed one television camera and wrenched it off the amazed cameraman's shoulder. "Get off," said the shocked cameraman, but when he refocused the press officer tried to pull the wires off the back of the camera.

But the Sinn Féin retinue moved remorselessly on through the gates and headed for the conference centre itself, hampered by a crowd of perhaps three hundred media people, Adams speechifying all the way. Bereft of pictures of the two prime ministers opening the talks, the cameras instead feasted on the strong simple image of republicans being denied a place at the table.

It was at the third and final fence that the Sinn Féin crew became, in the words of the old republican tune, the Men Behind the Wire. The rousing drinking song is particularly apposite for Adams himself, for he was once interned and then convicted of attempting to escape from lawful custody.

On this occasion, however, he was trying to get in rather than trying to get out. A government official appeared on the other side of the chain-link fence, and several exchanges followed. When it was finally established that, as everyone had expected, the gate would not be opened, the Sinn Féin delegation peeled away to give an impromptu press conference followed by dozens of interviews. Martin McGuinness remarked that it was the biggest media scrum he had ever seen. "I can't believe how stupid they are," one Sinn Féin member said in wonderment of the government. "Do you know," said another, "that the Northern Ireland Office has over 40 press officers? Think of the damage we could do with that."

Gerry Adams and Ian Paisley presumably went home last night, put their feet up and reflected on a good day's tactical work. The government people, licking their wounds, presumably reflected that Rome wasn't built in a day, that the worst of the pyrotechnics might be past, and that, hopefully, tomorrow is another day.

Even the most resolute of those who still hoped the peace process might be rescued were shaken when the IRA wrecked the centre of Manchester with a huge bomb on 15 June 1996. On the same day a statement admitted they were also responsible for killing Garda Jerry McCabe.

16 JUNE 1996   THE INDEPENDENT ON SUNDAY

Why did they do it?

There were times, during the 1970s and 1980s, when incidents such as yesterday's horror in Manchester were actually quite popular among many of those who live in the backstreets of Belfast's republican ghettos. In those days the feeling was widespread among republicans that such bombs gave the British a salutary taste of the Northern Ireland war, and demonstrated that the conflict was not confined to the island of Ireland. But yesterday, when the first news flashes about the bombing came through, it only took a few phone calls to people living in west Belfast to establish that many republican sympathisers were experiencing the same sick, sinking feelings in their stomachs as non-republicans. This time there was little trace of the old grim satisfaction of a blow being struck against Britain. Instead, it was summed up by one man who said, "Oh, Christ no, not again." This change in sentiment will serve as little consolation to those whose faces were flayed by flying glass in the centre of Manchester. But it will provide some measure of hope to those who fear that another 25-year cycle of death and destruction is in the making.

The bombing showed, yet again, that the republican movement in general and the IRA in particular is a completely unpredictable entity. In recent weeks there had been the usual range of reports and speculation about their intentions. Some predicted that a ceasefire could happen in advance of the talks which opened in Belfast on 10 June; many hoped another cessation was possible within weeks or months, if the IRA became convinced those talks were

HOWARD BARLOW, *Independent*

Sheer destruction: the mess the IRA made of Manchester city centre

for real. Only a few thought that such an attack was on the cards.

Most, in other words, regarded an attack such as yesterday's as almost inconceivable, going as it does against the flow of opinion within the republican movement generally. One huge unanswered question is whether the bombing signifies the beginning of a sustained IRA campaign in Britain or is simply one of an occasional series designed as cruel reminders that the IRA, though inactive in Northern Ireland, has not gone away.

What the bomb certainly signifies, however, is that a serious struggle is going on for the heart of the republican movement. The IRA army council, which must have ordered the Manchester attack, has military control over the gunmen, the bombers and their supplies. It appears to contain military purists, impatient with the peace process which has dominated Ireland in recent years and happier with the old simplicities of fertiliser and Semtex. They literally call the shots: IRA volunteers are subject to their discipline and must carry out their orders. Failure to do so, it is widely understood, may result in death. One of the old certainties was that the army council was in charge of everything. Its word was law: volunteers did what they were told and Sinn Féin, which in the old days was merely a useful propaganda accessory to the IRA, responded to its directions.

But on both fronts things have changed. The military discipline was thrown into question when, earlier this month, armed raiders shot dead a detective in Limerick. This sent a shockwave through the Irish Republic whose largely unarmed police force, the Garda Síochána, enjoys an extraordinarily high level of public support. The IRA said at first that none of its members had carried out the killing, a statement which was taken seriously by the Dublin government and others, since such IRA denials have in the past proved reasonably reliable. But it soon became obvious that a west of Ireland IRA unit was indeed involved.

Just yesterday the IRA issued a second statement, now admitting its members were responsible but denying the killing had been authorised. No one is quite sure what this means. The murder could have been a direct challenge to the IRA leadership, or a botched raid that went wrong: it could have represented an outright rejection of the whole philosophy of the peace process. Either way, it left a police officer dead and introduced serious doubts about what is happening within the IRA.

Now the Manchester bombing has posed the most fundamental of questions about the state of opinion within the republican movement as a whole. The army council is formally in charge, but there are increasing signs that the movement at large is looking for leadership not to the IRA but to Gerry Adams and the others who lead Sinn Féin. They built a modernised concept of republicanism with a new vocabulary in which victory took second place to peace. And, crucially, they constructed a plausible alternative to the campaign of terrorism, in which Sinn Féin would wield influence by forging new links with constitutional nationalists in Ireland, north and south, and in the United States. The record Sinn Féin vote in last month's election was viewed in Belfast as a comprehensive endorsement of the peace process approach. The Manchester bombing therefore flies in the face of that overwhelming wave of support for negotiation in preference to violence.

Northern Ireland tasted peace during the last ceasefire, and relished the taste. Few if any new jobs came to the ghettos, but the quality of life improved dramatically if only because the chances of attack from extreme loyalists, and of street friction with the security forces, faded away. Besides, the theory that the British and the unionists were not to be defeated militarily but were more likely to be outmanoeuvred by a broad nationalist coalition took firm root in the ghettos. But while Adams decisively won the wider debate, he seems to have lost the argument with the army council.

The signs are that the Sinn Féin leadership want to be in talks and in the political processes. They will not admit it publicly, but they are likely to be dismayed by the Manchester attack. Like their voters, they have come to believe that such acts of violence are counter-productive. The differences between Sinn Féin and the army council are so enormous that in any other organisation they would have produced a split. Sinn Féin wants to win friends and influence people, while IRA bombs produce only isolation at home and abroad. But republicans are determined that there will be no formal split and so they stay together, even though in reality there is a yawning gap of analysis.

Such bombs will clearly keep Sinn Féin out of the talks which opened in Belfast this week. Furthermore, it will certainly endanger lives in Northern Ireland, for while the IRA may have no intention of resuming its campaign in Belfast, there have been signs of restlessness within the extreme loyalist groups. Those organisations specifically warned in March that further IRA attacks in Britain carried the risk of loyalist retaliation with the danger of swift escalation. All this is obvious to the IRA, to Gerry Adams, and to almost everyone in Belfast: it is a scenario which sketches out how a city whose people do not want war could yet be plunged into further conflict, against the wishes of almost everyone.

The gulf between the Adams approach and the actions of the IRA is clearly very wide, yet there is one point of agreement between them. A number of leading Sinn Féin people have said publicly that the present British government is too dependent on unionist good will in the Commons lobbies to enter into serious negotiations with republicans. The IRA must believe this too, for with this latest bomb it all but rules out Sinn Féin entry into the present negotiations.

The larger question is whether the bomb means the IRA is writing off the Major government, or putting paid to the entire peace process. Perhaps they believe that the peace process can be revived next year, when they would hope to do business with a new, stronger British government; or perhaps they are regressing towards their old former position. The first scenario would mean that the peace process could yet again be resurrected, as it has been after so many apparently fatal blows. The second scenario would mean that a streak of near-nihilism is prevailing over the wishes of the republican community as a whole, and that the bleak prospect of more such bombings lies ahead.

Summer added traditional trouble to the political gloom. In 1995 a compromise had been reached in the case of the Orange Order parade, held on the Sunday before the Twelfth, to the little church of Drumcree outside

Portadown. Friction had developed because the marchers insisted on an age-old route homeward through what had now become a solidly Catholic district, Garvaghy Road. After protesters stood quietly to allow the march past, as agreed, they were angered when local Ulster Unionist MP David Trimble said there had been no compromise and held hands aloft with the Reverend Ian Paisley to applause from Orangemen in the centre of Portadown.

The 1995 episode became known as Drumcree 1. As Drumcree 2 loomed, the air was filled with what turned out to be amply justified apprehension.

---

8 JULY 1996 & 11 JULY 1997   THE INDEPENDENT

Orange Order's trail of troubles

The strength of feeling the Orange Order generates, on both sides, is difficult for outsiders to comprehend, as a London newspaper noted in 1920: "The thrill which the genuine Orangeman finds in demonstrations cannot be communicated to the most impressionable stranger, however devoted he may be to the British empire. The relief which Ulster still feels at the liberation bought on the Boyne 230 years ago is unfathomable to an outsider; but these things are all very real to Orangemen."

The Order has gone through many phases in its history – some more respectable than others – but for more than a century it has functioned in

The politics of the metronome: Orangemen on the march

essence as a pan-Protestant front, helping to unify various strands within unionism. Although its leaders deny any suggestion that it is anti-Catholic, it has been consistently anti-ecumenical and opposed to religious integration. While its regulations tell its members to abstain from uncharitable words, actions, or sentiments against Catholics, they are also pledged to "resist the ascendancy of that church" by all lawful means. They are also warned not to attend "any act or ceremony of Popish worship", and a number have been expelled or otherwise disciplined for doing so. On the other hand, the Order contains a great many clergymen and devout Protestants who genuinely regard it as the essence of law-abiding Christianity and good order. One of its most hallowed texts sets out the ideal Orangeman: "He should cultivate truth and justice, brotherly kindness and charity, devotion and piety, concord and unity and obedience to the laws; his deportment should be gentle and compassionate, kind and courteous."

It has sometimes been difficult to discern such high-minded sentiments, for example when Orangemen triumphantly hold up five fingers as they parade past a spot where five Catholics were shot dead. Previous marching seasons have produced widespread disorder, and while other elements bear some

27

responsibility for these disasters, it is the Order's metronomic determination to march past hostile Catholic areas which has time and again occasioned serious disturbance. It was in fact ever thus, for throughout its two-century history the Order has left behind a trail of troubles.

In 1864, after Belfast was racked with riots which over 18 days left 12 dead and 100 injured, an official inquiry reported: "Belfast is liable to periodic disturbances on occasions well known as the Orange anniversaries. If the celebration of these anniversaries be attended with such risk, we might well ask why any party should obstinately adhere to it.

"Can neither the discouragement of the powerful and influential nor the adverse opinion of the wise and good induce those who indulge in such vain and mischievous displays to remember the claims of citizenship, or charity, or of civilisation?"

One of the factors, however, in helping the Order sustain itself through the recurring bouts of criticism is the fact that those in authority have traditionally alternated between criticising it and co-opting it into the system. There is an extraordinary historical pattern of the Order sometimes undermining the stability of the north of Ireland and sometimes acting as one of its most fundamental props.

This was the case right from the Order's foundation in the last years of the eighteenth century, not far from Drumcree in County Armagh, then as now one of bitterest of places. It was forged in the crucible of sectarian conflict there from precursors such as the Peep o' Day Boys. Set up after a gang of Protestants had bested a gang of Catholics in a clash fuelled by land hunger and sectarianism, the Order helped drive 7,000 Catholics out of the county in just two months. Catholics were threatened: "Now Teak this for Warnig, For if you Bee in this Contry Wednesday Night I will Blow your Soul to the Low hils of hell And Burn the House you are in."

Such methods, coupled with its rapid growth, initially alarmed the government, but with republican rebellion in the air the authorities swiftly moved to co-opt the Order as a counter-revolutionary force. A magistrate spelt out the official calculation: "As for the Orangemen, we have a difficult card to play; they must not be entirely discountenanced – on the contrary, we must in a certain degree uphold them, for, with all their licentiousness, on them we must rely for the preservation of our lives and properties, should critical times occur."

So it proved. The landed gentry moved quickly to assume leadership of the Order, instilling discipline and deference into what had originally been denounced as "lawless banditti". In Napoleonic times 25,000 regular troops were augmented by 20,000 yeomen, almost all of them Orangemen, who played an important part in putting down the United Irishmen's rebellion of

1798. The brutality employed was legendary, a British officer noting: "Hundreds and thousands of wretches were butchered while unarmed on their knees begging mercy; and it is difficult to say whether soldiers, yeomen or militia men took most delight in their bloody work."

The subsequent history of Orangeism continues the pattern of duality, alternately undermining authority and upholding it. At one stage its Grand Master was the Duke of Cumberland, but then it was banned in 1825 because of worries of the extent of its penetration of the army, which was found to contain many Orange lodges. In the north of Ireland it remained in existence despite the ban, though for much of the nineteenth century it was deserted by the upper classes and had little prestige. Freed from its deferential posture, the century experienced what might be called the golden age of the Orange riot.

In 1813 Belfast experienced its first religious riot when an Orange procession marched into a Catholic street. Two were killed and four injured, but this turned out to be a minor affray compared to what was to follow: 1829 brought major disorder in 11 different locations, with at least 16 deaths. Back in County Armagh the first service at Drumcree had taken place in 1807; the first arrests were in 1833, while the first Catholic death, in 1835, was followed in 1869 by the first Protestant fatality.

Riots were by now commonplace, a pro-Orange observer giving this floridly graphic description of the 1873 Boyne commemorations in Portadown: "A most wanton and unprovoked attack, dastardly and despicably sneakish, was made upon the Orangemen from the backs and windows of the houses with stones, brick-bats, large pieces of broken crockery, all of which were thrown with a violence and continuity perfectly compatible with the skulking pultroonery that dictated such a plan for waylaying a number of peaceable men whose only crime was that they were Protestants and loyal subjects."

But it was Belfast which saw the worst of the violence with repeated riots during the marching season, most of them following Orange demonstrations, 12 major disturbances taking place between 1813 and 1886. Several of the subsequent government inquiries showed that most of the city's policemen were Orangemen. Six commissions of inquiry were set up to report on the causes of rioting. The reports of all six blamed two main factors, poor policing and Orange parades. One report said: "The celebration of that [Orange July] festival is plainly and unmistakably the originating cause of these riots", adding that the occasion was used "to remind one party of the triumph of their ancestors over those of the other, and to inculcate the feelings of Protestant superiority over their Roman Catholic neighbours".

In the 1880s, however, contact with the upper classes was re-established when the threat of home rule appeared on the horizon. The Tory Lord Randolph Churchill famously said that if Gladstone "went for home rule, the

Orange card would be the one to play. Please God it may turn out the ace of trumps and not the two."

This was the beginning of an alliance between Tories, the unionist business classes and the Order. As in the late eighteenth century, Orangemen were once again co-opted as part of a wider game. Orange lodges provided the framework for a citizen army, the Ulster Volunteer Force, whose threat of force played a large part in persuading London that the largely Protestant north should be exempted from home rule. They drilled in the Orange halls, then in their tens of thousands, at the urging of their new leaders, joined the British army to fight in the First World War. Thousands of their number lost their lives at the Somme and other battlefields. Many were cut down at Thiepval wood, on the anniversary of the battle of the Boyne, one witness recounting: "As they scrambled over the parapet they shouted the old battle cries 'No surrender' and 'Remember 1690'. Many wore Orange ribbons and one sergeant of the Inniskillings had on his Orange sash."

The new state of Northern Ireland, having been established with such a large contribution by the Order, from the outset took on a distinctly Orange coloration. An Orange lodge was established within the new police force, the Royal Ulster Constabulary, while Orangemen made up the bulk of a new militia, the B Specials. In many areas the B Specials were based in Orange halls.

Politically too Orangeism became an integral part of the state, James Craig, Northern Ireland's first prime minister, declaring: "I have always said I am an Orangeman first and a politician afterwards." A majority of Unionist cabinet ministers and MPs between then and 1972 were members of the Order; most Unionist party meetings were held in Orange halls, while ministers used Orange platforms for important speeches. The power of the Order during those years has been described by two senior Methodists: "Membership was an indispensable condition of political advancement. It protected the employment of Protestants by its influence over employers, which is a polite way of saying that it contrived systematic discrimination against Catholics. Local authorities were dominated by members of the local lodges."

This close identification of unionist governments with the Order tended to fortify the deep belief that Orange marches had a special status. During this period Orange marches were rarely rerouted while nationalist or republican parades, which were in any event much less frequent, were often subject to restrictions or bans. Major Orange occasions thus became what one commentator described as "effectively a ritual of state". Yet extraordinarily, even with such influence at its command, the impulse to march could on occasion overwhelm all other considerations.

More than once the unionist government banned marches on public order grounds only to back down under Orange pressure. The most notable example of this came in 1935 when, at a particularly tense time, the government banned all processions. Faced with angry Orange opposition, the government relented and exempted Orange marches from the ban. In the subsequent rioting 11 people were killed, hundreds injured, more than 500 families driven from their homes and more than 2,000 Catholics expelled from their workplaces.

In modern times, even as the authorities grapple with the marching problem, they also continue to rely on the Order for manpower. No figures are available for the numbers of security force personnel who are Orangemen, but the Order has made it known that around 13 per cent of RUC officers killed in the troubles, and around a quarter of Ulster Defence Regiment victims, were members.

Today, as the shadow of the Twelfth of July looms once again, the government would dearly love the Order to call off or reroute its more contentious marches. If it does not, then the authorities can opt for bans or rerouting, yet they are all too painfully aware that these can lead to major trouble. This government, like all the others down through the centuries, knows that taking on the Orange Order means confronting one of Northern Ireland's most powerful pressure groups, and touching the deepest and most sensitive nerve of the Protestants of Ulster.

In the event Drumcree 1996 was worse than even the most worried had thought possible. On 7 July a confrontation began between Orangemen at Drumcree,

31

County Armagh, and police after RUC Chief Constable Sir Hugh Annesley announced they would not be permitted to take the Garvaghy Road route back to Portadown. Separated by a barbed-wire fence erected by the army, Orangemen taunted and threatened police. More Orangemen arrived to swell the protest and army reinforcements were called. Disturbances began in other parts of Northern Ireland as crowds poured into Drumcree, among them leading loyalist paramilitary figures.

On 8 July a Catholic taxi driver from nearby Lurgan, Michael McGoldrick, was shot dead after picking up a fare at a bar in a loyalist district. Senior police officers privately expressed the view that "King Rat", mid-Ulster loyalist Billy Wright, who lived in Portadown, was behind the killing.

Disorder spread in hundreds of co-ordinated incidents. Loyalists, many wearing Orange sashes, blocked hundreds of roads, and airports and ferry ports. Rioters burned business premises, buses were hijacked and there were reports of looting. In total police fired some 700 plastic bullets.

In the end police reversed their original decision, saturating the Garvaghy Road to allow the Orangemen through.

Ulster looks into
the abyss

Words such as "watershed" and "momentous" have been used so often in relation to Northern Ireland in recent years that their meaning is in danger of becoming devalued. But there is little doubt that the events of last week merit both of those terms and more. Furthermore, the watershed is one of a most disastrous kind.

The sight of riots, petrol bombs and destruction is bad enough, but the long-term consequences of what has happened will be even worse. The rule of law has been fundamentally and perhaps fatally undermined. The government gives every appearance of either not understanding what is happening or of being in denial. The impression given by Sir Patrick Mayhew, in a series of slightly giddy television appearances, was that the problem lay among three elements: unionists, nationalists and the RUC. There was no evident recognition that in the course of the week a large amount of authority had been transferred from the government to the men on the streets. Sir Patrick told one incredulous interviewer to cheer up.

What began at Drumcree on Sunday last as a problem over a march, developed, as thousands of Orangemen took to the streets in an effort to bring normal life to a standstill, into a fundamental issue of the rule of law. The eventual decision to reverse the original ruling and allow the Orangemen to march along the Garvaghy Road was defended by Sir Hugh Annesley and Sir Patrick on purely pragmatic grounds. If the RUC had not forced the march through, Sir Hugh argued, the security forces could have been overwhelmed and many deaths might have followed. There was no other option, Sir Patrick explained breezily.

This frank recognition of realpolitik ignored what many nationalists saw as the moral dimension. The authorities had thought it right to ban the march; their minds had been changed not by force of argument but by a wave of civil disobedience that stretched from peaceful demonstrations through hijackings and intimidation to serious assaults and a murder. Moderate nationalist Ireland, political and spiritual, watched in horror as the two men, and later John Major, spelled out that the government had in effect no choice but to bow to the disorder threatened by the big Orange battalions. This section of opinion has spent a quarter of a century arguing with republican extremists that Britain is neutral in the dispute. The government has, however, just conceded what the hawks in the IRA argue: that Britain responds primarily to violence.

David Trimble, leader of the Ulster Unionist party for less than a year, has just moved away from the strict parliamentarianism of his predecessor, James Molyneaux, and regressed to an earlier and more primitive form of unionism, the sort identified with Carson and Craig in the home rule crisis of 1912 and after. In other words, he is not just head of a small group of MPs but can also command a highly effective Orange street force.

The psychological mindset of most of the leaders of unionism and Orangeism is that if they eschew negotiation, stand firm and face down their opponents they are likely to get their way. They will now be confirmed in this belief. With Drumcree under his belt, Trimble may enter a more parliamentary phase; but from now on all will be aware, to quote Theodore Roosevelt, that while he may speak softly he carries a big stick.

After the loyalist general strike of 1974 it took British governments 11 years before they dared take an action strongly opposed by unionists and sign the 1985 Anglo-Irish agreement. Now a new armlock has been placed on British policy-makers.

The week had another terrible effect in that it set back for years the prospects of some agreed new settlement. Dublin and moderate nationalists have spent a decade and more working on the theory that while the union with Britain is here to stay for the foreseeable future, the consolation on offer to Irish nationalists is the construction, slowly but surely, of a fairer Northern Ireland in which both unionism and nationalism can be respected. That theory has been dealt a shattering blow.

Priests, bishops and nationalist MPs are all now saying the same thing: that the RUC, probably with government approval, showed itself one-sided both in its strategy and in the behaviour of individual officers. In 1969 the television pictures of officers clubbing Catholic civil rights campaigners led to the first serious trouble. In 1996, nationalist leaders watched with something close to disbelief as policemen did not move in on Orangemen blocking roads but waded in, with unmistakable energy and even enthusiasm, to shift Catholics sitting down on the Garvaghy Road.

The RUC, the most important institution of the state, had gone up in the estimation of many nationalists over recent years for its increased profession-alism and, often, its attention to political sensitivities. It is no exaggeration to say that almost all of this has been lost in the course of a single week, leaving many nationalists speculating darkly that there may have been some form of mutiny threatened within the force by officers who would not contemplate taking on the Orange Order. Most Orangemen clearly believe that they have won a great victory. Certainly their march got through, nationalists were humiliated and unionism and Orangemen demonstrated real muscle.

But in the process the underlying instability of the state was exposed, the very fabric of society was ripped and damaged, and the most fundamental questions were posed about the reformability of Northern Ireland. It seems hardly credible that a place which last year had the hope of a bright new future could so swiftly be transformed into a political wasteland, its economic prospects dashed, its image defaced, its communal relations in ruins. Even in Ireland the prospects have rarely seemed bleaker.

By the end of summer fresh resentment overlaid old grievance. A pall of pessimism hung over Northern Ireland.

25 AUGUST 1996   THE INDEPENDENT ON SUNDAY

Back to square one

In the sixteenth century an English civil servant wrote: "It is a proverb of old date, that the pride of France, the treason of England, and the war of Ireland, shall never have end. Which proverb, touching the war of Ireland, is like alway to continue, without God set it in men's breasts to find some new remedy that never was found before." The quill which he presumably used has today been replaced by a word processor, yet the sentiment he expressed is very much alive in Belfast today. The events of the last six months, principally the breakdown of the IRA ceasefire and July's Orange march confrontation at Drumcree, have sent almost everyone back to the drawing board in search of "some new remedy that never was found before".

They conduct their reassessments not in a spirit of enthusiasm but under a

The brethren: Orangemen pray for deliverance

deep pall of depression and apprehension which has enveloped not just the political classes but also most of the population. Just about everyone expects that it will get worse before it gets better; many say, sadly and bitterly, that it never will get better. The fact that this month's Apprentice Boys march in Londonderry passed off relatively peacefully brought some immediate relief, but it has not dented the widespread underlying sense that recent times have been politically, socially and economically ruinous.

A flavour of the legacy of the summer was conveyed by Norman Jenkinson, one of Belfast's least excitable newspaper columnists, who wrote: "From towns and villages all over this province come sad reports of sectarian damage to property, of intimidation, of the boycott of businesses, of accusations, of recriminations.

"Human stories of villages and townspeople who once lived in peace with one another, if not quite on close terms, now keeping their sullen distance. Heartbreaking accounts of communities torn apart by their Christian differences, living in fear for their futures, for their local economies.

"Communities ripped asunder by one week in July, some of their peoples seething with fury at what they see as their humiliation, some heady with the narcotic effect of perceived victory. Drumcree was a catastrophe for religious tolerance and it is doubtful if anything can be salvaged from it. Good people will try, but then good people are not the problem."

John Alderdice of the determinedly optimistic Alliance party has spoken of "a depth of sectarian division more widespread and corrosive than for some time". A nationalist leader said privately: "In all my years I have never seen so much bitterness and hatred, on both sides." Another political figure added: "It's bad, bad, bad and worse. My non-political friends are saying, 'What hope is there?' They're just deflated. A lot of them are talking about emigrating."

It is against this sombre background that, on 9 September, multi-party talks will be reconvened at Stormont following a summer break. Even before Drumcree, few believed they would succeed; now, with such a dearth of political and communal good will, hardly any participants or spectators believe tough issues such as de-commissioning and policing can be cracked, let alone the wider questions involved in mapping out a new future.

Yet one paradox in all this is that the poisonous atmosphere and lack of political momentum have not produced a reversion to full-scale terrorism. There has certainly been violence, including isolated murders, punishment beatings and general summer intimidation, as well as a number of major IRA bombing attacks in England. But in Northern Ireland the paramilitary campaigns which used to claim up to a hundred lives a year have not returned. No one knows quite why this is so, or how long it can last.

On the extreme Protestant side the loyalist ceasefire, declared in October 1994, has proved more durable than almost anyone expected. Punishment beatings have continued, but the UVF summarily expelled from the organisation the mid-Ulster unit which killed a Catholic man during the 1996 Drumcree stand-off.

Not only did the loyalist ceasefire survive the collapse of the IRA cessation in February of this year, but the political spokesmen of the paramilitaries have taken a consistently more conciliatory line than the mainstream unionist parties. There have, however, been periodic bouts of concern for their cessation and at this moment there are reports that it is under serious strain. It could well break down if, for example, the minor loyalist parties were to be expelled from the Stormont talks, or if the IRA were to escalate its violence.

No one can be sure what the IRA will do. There is no IRA ceasefire in effect, yet no IRA bombs are going off in Belfast: the last policeman and soldier to die were killed in the spring of 1994. The IRA campaign has so far been directed exclusively against England. The republican terrorists have the capacity to begin again in Northern Ireland, and it is anyone's guess why they have not. Perhaps they are waiting for the right moment; perhaps they intend to make Britain their principal battlefield. They will certainly be aware that, even though many young men are available as potential recruits, there is still little or no appetite in the wider republican community for another quarter-century of war. The difficulty for the republicans is that they are presently in distinct need of a new master plan. The peace process collapsed, they would argue, because of the British government's failure to call all-inclusive talks: entry into talks was in fact elevated to Sinn Féin's central demand.

This would presumably also be the centrepiece of any revived peace process, yet Drumcree has convinced most republicans that talking to unionists, as led by David Trimble and Ian Paisley, would be a waste of time. In any event, most republicans always believed unionists would only ever negotiate under steady pressure from London; and Drumcree seemed to establish that London has not the capacity to exert such pressure.

A republican movement which doubts that either terrorism or a new peace process can achieve its aims is clearly a movement in trouble. With no clear avenue of progress visible, the IRA may opt to wait for the next British election to see what business can be done with a new government. But in republican terms the IRA cannot simply do nothing, since that would give the impression of weakness. The logic, tragically, is thus: that it will use bombs in Britain in an attempt to keep Northern Ireland high on the British political agenda.

It is not just republican theorists who are going back to square one, for it was a summer which had no winners. Drumcree challenged and undermined many other long-held assumptions. Constitutional nationalism, for example, is now questioning whether Northern Ireland can ever be turned into an equitable modern state. Many now complain that unionism has proved itself irredeemably sectarian.

In the Republic, public opinion was appalled during the Drumcree crisis by the actions of the unionists, the RUC and the British government: the seething anger generated by the television pictures is difficult to overestimate. Those in the south who hoped it was all over are facing up to the painful notion that it may never end, and already there are signs of that emotion developing into a "plague on both your houses" syndrome.

That mirrors a sizeable section of opinion in Britain, where the dashing of the high hopes generated by the peace process has unsurprisingly produced dismay and disillusionment. For the government, next month's talks, no matter how unpromising they may seem, represent pretty much the only show in town. With no new IRA ceasefire in prospect, its ambition may be largely limited to crisis management and to ensuring the talks do not break down in acrimony.

Unionists too are reviewing their position. The fact that the marching organisations prevailed in many instances is a source of satisfaction to many. There is a widespread sense that at Drumcree Protestants finally took a stand

and showed their determination not to be pushed around. But others in the unionist community worry about the cost and the damage, in terms of community and political relations, the grievous blow to the standing of the RUC, and economic prospects. "As a political tactic it was disastrous," said a senior churchman. "Sinn Féin was on its knees, but Trimble succeeded in giving the republicans new legitimacy."

At Drumcree and elsewhere the Orange Order, in close association with the Ulster Unionist party, flexed its muscles and demonstrated a new strength. Any government will in future have to think twice before embarking on a course which might incur Orange wrath and get the roads blocked and barricaded again. But Drumcree won no new friends either for unionism or for Northern Ireland in general, and has increased the tendency in London, Dublin and Washington to think of it as an impossible place, and a problem which, no matter how much energy and good will is devoted to it, might have no solution.

Hope is in such desperately short supply that almost the best that can be said is that Northern Ireland has survived other black moments in the past, and that progress has unexpectedly been made. This is a dangerous, unpredictable time with no obvious solution in sight: if things are to improve, it will be due to "some new remedy that never was found before".

One of the most interesting political innovations of 1996 was the emergence of the Northern Ireland Women's Coalition. Although it attracted only a small vote it nonetheless won places at the talks table and in a new body established by John Major, the Northern Ireland Forum for Political Dialogue. The forum turned out to be a sideshow, Sinn Féin boycotting it from the start and the SDLP quickly withdrawing from its proceedings, complaining of heavy-handed unionist domination.

The Women's Coalition persevered, however, declaring itself committed to a new consensual politics transcending unionism and nationalism. Many of its members were experienced public figures playing important roles in the vibrant community and voluntary sectors to which women tended to gravitate in preference to mainstream politics. They soon discovered that politics was a rough old trade.

9 SEPTEMBER 1996 & 24 APRIL 1997   THE INDEPENDENT

Women find men behaving badly

Since her election to the forum Monica McWilliams, a senior lecturer in social science noted for her expertise in researching violence against women, has gained new insight into her speciality. She has had a finger jabbed into her arm by a member of the Reverend Ian Paisley's Democratic Unionists, and been pushed against a wall in a corridor by a senior member of the Ulster Unionists. In the forum Paisley has described her arguments as "red herrings – stinking, rotten red herrings". Her speeches are interrupted by shouts of "silly women" and "stop wasting time". One Ulster Unionist member publicly told her to sit down and shut up. It has been a rough and unchivalrous baptism for a cross-community group of women who came into electoral politics on a tide of hope and idealism.

"We've had to find a lot of courage to deal with it," says Monica McWilliams. "When you're facing angry faces shouting insults at you, it takes an inner courage to maintain a calm and make your points over that level of acrimony. We're representative of both communities – that confuses them, they don't like it, and it makes us the brunt of hatred, the brunt of venom. It has been quite devastating in the forum to witness raw, naked sectarianism."

In a debate on animal health, members had some difficulty in making out her words. As she spoke Paisley's son, Ian Junior, kept up a commentary: "Mooo," he intoned. "Mooo, mooo, mooo. Moooooo." It was a fairly typical day in the forum. Iris Robinson, wife of DUP MP Peter, said of the Women's Coalition: "They are doing their best to destroy anything that smacks of unionism or Protestantism. Thank God only 7,000 idiots voted for these women."

According to Monica McWilliams: "It is a very nasty place to be at times. There have been days when I put my hand on my head with despair. The level of sectarian commentary is as raw as anything you'd hear in a street fight. Everything is completely segregated. In the early days, if we walked into the ladies' toilets any unionist women walked out. The only improvement is to the extent that they now remain in the toilet." She exempts from such criticisms nationalists and republicans – who in any event stay away from the forum – and the smaller parties who are associated with loyalist paramilitarism. She says it is members of the DUP, the smaller UK Unionists, and to a lesser extent the Ulster Unionists, who behave badly towards the women.

She says: "Ian Paisley Junior says that if we can't stick the heat, we should get out of the kitchen. We can stick the heat – we actually want to be in it, the heat is what this is all about in terms of negotiations. But this is something else: we've been called traitors because we've said we're for inclusiveness. It's not just that it's an adversarial style: this is very sectarian, sometimes it's sexist, and it's personal insults as well. We've been humiliated publicly. A lot of these guys who are calling us traitors, and making us out to be something we're not, have minders, security people, police escorts. A lot of our women live in quite dangerous communities, and some of them have had difficulties because of this stuff. It can be dangerous."

The summer marching season was a bad setback. "It really created a terrible situation," she says. "It really shows us that the society is fairly dysfunctional at the moment, that we're not living in a normal society. I felt completely devastated – you have high expectations and then you get an awful fall. I had thought that the potential for creating some kind of accommodation was there, but clearly that was not the case." Like many of the other participants, she will go to the talks today with more hope than confidence of success. "Although I'm very pessimistic at the moment, I feel I have to retain the optimism that there is a possiblity that we can work towards some sort of inclusion. I'm trying to be optimistic, because I think if you just lived with thorough pessimism there would be no glimmer, there would be no reason for continuing. I have children, I want to live in this country."

In the midst of the gloom, one political figure went about his business with his customary grim enjoyment and commitment. Democratic Unionist party leader the Reverend Ian Paisley tried to have the two small loyalist parties expelled from the Stormont talks because the paramilitary groups for which they spoke had threatened to kill "King Rat", Billy Wright. The Paisley argument was that allowing the loyalist parties to stay at the table without condemning the Wright threat would make it easier for Sinn Féin to join talks without an IRA ceasefire. It was advanced with all of his traditional gusto.

20 SEPTEMBER 1996   THE INDEPENDENT

Twenty-five years of Ireland's Dr No

This is the 25th anniversary of the Democratic Unionist party, the grouping fashioned by Dr Ian Paisley as a weapon to ensure that Protestants and Catholics in Northern Ireland should not reach an accommodation. It has served brilliantly in its mission of helping to keep the two traditions apart. Today, at the age of 70, he is in the thick of the multi-party talks at Stormont, as fundamentalist a Protestant as ever, as central as ever to the Northern Ireland political scene, and once again functioning as an obstacle to agreement.

Ian Paisley was ordained a minister in the 1940s. By the 1950s he was

Never, never, never: Ian Paisley in his 70s, as firmly against accommodation as ever

figuring in bitter religious controversies; by the 1960s he had become a formidable street demagogue. Age may be slowing him down a little, but his record of 26 years in the Commons and 17 in the European parliament serves as a standing rebuttal of the proverb that travel broadens the mind. He still says today what he said in the 1960s: that Ulster is in peril from the IRA and the Vatican, that Northern Ireland Protestants cannot trust British governments, and that they had better take action to safeguard their heritage.

The tragedy is that one of the brightest, most subtle, most perceptive and best-organised minds of his generation should have opted, at every key juncture in his long career, for confrontation rather than accommodation. There do seem to have been a few points at which he privately contemplated making deals, but he never did and now, at the age of 70, he never will.

It has been an extraordinary career – in politics, in the pulpit, on the streets, in jail (twice, for protesting); a career packed with incident and drama, with a thousand demonstrations, diatribes, walkouts and calls to arms. The reason why he is the Doctor No of Irish politics is because Ian Paisley is not a politician with a sideline in religion; rather, he is a fundamentalist evangelical minister who is also in politics.

In his memoirs Maurice Hayes, a retired Catholic civil servant who has known Paisley for more than three decades, gives a thumbnail sketch of this larger-than-life, multifaceted character. "He is a complex personality," writes Hayes. "I have often thought there are about six Paisleys. Two of them are very nice people, two quite awful, and the other two could go either way. What I have to report is that he never told me a lie, never breached a confidence, and that as a constituency MP he worked unceasingly for all his constituents regardless of religion. True, he could be, and was, a rabblerouser. He very often filled the atmosphere with an inflammable vapour that other people could and did ignite ... In public he often appeared a driven man. In private he could be affable and very amusing. He did not, I think, use his church as a platform ... from which to gain political power. Rather, he entered politics to secure the fundamental religious values to which he is attached."

The Free Presbyterian church, of which he is moderator for life, has a much smaller membership than the votes he amasses but it is the core of his being. It includes a particularly concentrated element of the Irish Protestant preoccupation with Catholicism, the predominant religion of Ireland. His preaching style is melodramatic, his vocabulary unchanged since the days when James Callaghan accused him of "using the language of war cast in a biblical mould". Congregations continue to be bombarded with talk of the papal Anti-Christ in the Vatican, the maws of Rome, the mother of harlots, the blasphemous mass, and to be warned of Irish Catholicism's "continuous and concentrated campaigns to eliminate the Protestant community".

The distinguished Methodist Donald Soper once called this style cabaret, describing Belfast as a city of many religious nightclubs. It is certainly true that many of the old dears who come to see Paisley clearly enjoy the performance hugely, to the extent that it can seem as much entertainment as worship. It is also true that Paisley's technique of thrilling and frightening his listeners with the demonology of Rome, along with the fear of damnation, can lead to him being viewed as an evangelical Protestant version of Vincent Price. But it is a fundamental error to conclude from his extravagant theatricality that his religion is not genuine. Nothing could be further from the truth. He is remarkably learned in his theology. His Protestant faith is deep, sincere and unshakable: so too is his conviction that the Pope is in league with the devil. He told John Paul II that, to his face, confronting him on a visit to the European parliament by shouting repeatedly: "I renounce you as the Anti-Christ."

He once outlined his philosophy to his flock in his huge Martyr's Memorial church, the Belfast headquarters of a church which has branches in England, the Republic and Canada: "You've got to take your stand, you know. There's not going to be any compromise. If you compromise, God will curse you. If you stand, God will bless you. That's why God has blessed this preacher and this church."

As in religion, so in politics. When he looks at non-unionists in Northern Ireland he sees not nationalists or republicans but, primarily, Catholics. He puts his religion before his politics – and indeed higher than the crown, for he has made it clear that if the British monarchy ceases to be Protestant then his loyalty to it will cease.

It is small wonder, given this deep-seated aversion to compromise, that he caused so much grief to British politicians. Reginald Maudling found him "one of the most difficult characters anyone could hope to deal with. I always found his influence dangerous." William Whitelaw marvelled at his "unrivalled skill at undermining the plans of others. He can effectively destroy and obstruct, but he has never seemed able to act constructively." James Prior thought him "basically a man who thrives on the violent scene. His aim is to stir the emotions of the Protestant people. His bigotry easily boils over into bombast." Meetings Paisley held with Margaret Thatcher and John Major have ended in something close to uproar. It is an indication of the complexity of the man that Maudling, Whitelaw and Prior, while criticising him so sternly, also commented wonderingly that in private he could be charming, friendly and engaging.

Part of the exasperation of British ministers springs from his proficiency in the politics of alarmist denunciation, for he continually portrays British governments as conspiratorial and treacherous, forever engaged in sell-outs, betrayals and treachery. But another reason is the charge that he has so aggravated already dangerous situations, in a variety of ways. One ex-minister said: "It's all very well to say he's giving voice to genuine Protestant fears and worries, but it's more than that. He feeds the paranoia and reinforces it. He amplifies it."

A frequent criticism centres around his recurring forays into the murky underworld of extreme loyalism, when he goes beyond rhetoric and makes an alliance with men in masks. In doing so he has displayed less consistency than he does in matters religious. In 1974, for example, he co-operated with the largest paramilitary group, the Ulster Defence Association, to stage a loyalist general strike. The following year he denounced them as loyalist killers engaging in crimes "just as heinous and hellish as those of the IRA". But two years later, in 1977, he was back in close alliance with them to stage another stoppage.

He has also, on up to a dozen occasions over the years, called for Protestants to form a "third force" to take on the IRA. Sometimes these calls have involved shows of force: in 1986, for example, 4,000 men staged a nocturnal parade through the County Down town of Hillsborough, many of them masked and marching in formation. On another occasion journalists were brought to a County Antrim hillside at dead of night to find 500 men drawn up in military formation brandishing pieces of paper. Paisley explained these were gun certificates, declaring: "I will take full responsibility for anything these men do. We will stop at nothing."

Critics say such behaviour can help provoke impressionable Protestant youths to join paramilitary groups and become involved in actual, rather than rhetorical, violence. There is evidence that he can have a similar effect on the republican side.

In the 1970s a Protestant minister asked IRA leader Dáithí Ó Conaill about a rumour that the IRA would try to kill Paisley. The minister recalled: "Ó Conaill just simply told me: 'There's no way we would kill Ian Paisley. Paisley is the best recruiting sergeant we've got.' Ó Conaill said of Paisley's threats that the Protestant people would take the law into their own hands: 'When the Catholic community hears that, a chill goes down the spine of every Catholic in west Belfast. And after that we have no trouble getting volunteers, safe houses and money.' "

But despite his flirtations with the forces of darkness, the political Paisley has not always seemed so hardline. At times in his career there have been a couple of curious episodes where he has surprised, and unnerved, opponents by taking an unexpectedly moderate line. With hindsight, however, these look like mere tactical sallies designed to eat into support for the Ulster Unionists, the largest unionist party. The fact that it is the largest unionist party is one of the banes of Paisley's life, since it means that his DUP is forever number two. Yet the gap between the DUP and the UUP is not as big as most people assume; and herein lies Paisley's deeper political significance.

Because David Trimble's UUP has nine Westminster MPs while Paisley has only three, many casual observers tend to assume that the DUP is something of a fringe element. The statistics confound this. In Westminster elections Paisley takes on average 12 per cent of the vote, but this is not a true measure of his support, since in these contests many unionist voters cluster around the UUP as the party most likely to win seats.

When the results of other elections – for councils, assemblies and Europe – are analysed, Paisley's support soars. In this year's forum election Trimble took 46 per cent of the unionist vote: Paisley took 36 per cent and one of his close associates another 7 per cent. Paisley voters are by no means all evangelical, but they are certainly voting against compromise.

In other words, Paisley is not some peripheral phenomenon: he can credibly claim to speak for 4 out of every 10 unionist voters. This level of support is not enough to take control of unionism but it is certainly enough to exercise a powerful inhibiting influence on the Ulster Unionists. Any unionist leader contemplating an accommodation with nationalists knows that doing so would produce a furious Paisley onslaught.

To put it at its bleakest, Paisley's level of support, together with his forcefulness and political skills, could be enough to ensure that, as long as he is on the scene, there will never be political accommodation between unionist and nationalist. His lifelong preference for conflict over compromise means he would regard this as a victory for his fundamental religious values, and doubtless means he will be proud to have that as his epitaph.

Reprinted in the Belfast *Irish News*

On 7 October a bomb attack on army headquarters in the County Antrim town of Lisburn brought IRA violence back to Northern Ireland, fatally injuring 27-year-old Warrant Officer James Bradwell. His death and the political deadlock meant that the year ended with hope in short supply.

26 DECEMBER 1996   THE INDEPENDENT

The bombs that blew away peace

The year 1996 has been an annus horribilis for Northern Ireland, a truly awful, dispiriting year. When it opened there was an IRA ceasefire and talk of real talks: as it closes the government and the republicans are back at loggerheads, with more bombs feared at any moment. Half a year's worth of political talks, sans Sinn Féin, have proved almost entirely unproductive, inducing even more cynicism in an already pessimistic population. The joy of peace has, in 12 months, been replaced by the fear of more war.

And yet it is still possible to hear, in republican and other circles, people saying in their flat Belfast monotone: "It's over." It is certainly a tense and dangerous time; there is, almost certainly, more death and destruction to come; yet overall the sense is still that the troubles are moving towards their end.

It is impossible to disprove the opposite theory, which is that the troubles are endless and that the future holds not only eternal deadlock but perpetual violence too. Yet even this terrible year had in it what can be seen as signs of hope for the medium-term prospects. They were, admittedly, small enough signs, and they were eclipsed by the many setbacks. The year opened well enough, just a month after the near-rapturous Clinton Belfast visit, when the IRA ceasefire still held. But in February the IRA blew up London's dockland, killing two men, and euphoria was replaced by dismay.

The rest of the year was punctuated by acts of violence. Among other attacks the IRA tried to blow up Hammersmith bridge in April, and in June killed an Irish detective and blew up Manchester city centre. In July it had 10 tons of explosives seized in London; in October it set off two car bombs inside army headquarters in Lisburn. A soldier died in the Lisburn attack and no one died in Manchester, but in each case it was only great good fortune which prevented large-scale loss of life. The Lisburn bombings in particular were aimed at causing as many deaths as possible.

Yet it is also clear that during 1996 the IRA was fighting, in its terms, only half a war, maintaining a level of activity which fell far short of its full capacity for mayhem. People have died and destruction has been caused, although the terrorists did not attempt to crank the conflict back up to pre-1994 ceasefire levels. The signs are that this restricted level of activity is intended to send a political message. The republicans also sent an explicit message to London via John Hume: the proposition that the ceasefire would be restored if immediate negotiations were guaranteed.

The SDLP leader met the IRA within weeks of the Canary Wharf bomb. Within a few months he and Gerry Adams had put together "Hume–Adams Mark 2", a draft formulation to be taken to John Major. Hume shuttled back and forward between Adams and Major, and in July the prime minister gave Hume the terms of a possible restatement. In October Hume gave Major another reformulation; a week later Major replied to it.

It did not offer the republicans immediate entry into all-party talks, stipulating instead that any new ceasefire must be followed by an indeterminate monitoring period. In November Major published this reply, and a week ago confirmed this was his "last definitive word on the subject before the election". This seems to have effectively closed the negotiation. Opinions will forever vary on whether the prime minister's attitude was dictated by high-minded considerations of national security and protection of the democratic processes, or by a rather more ignoble desire not to antagonise right-wing backbenchers and unionist MPs. But whether it was the first, the second or a combination of both, the real surprise was not that the republican overture had been turned down, but that it had been made in the first place. Sinn Féin and the IRA knew as well as anyone else that this was a weak government, its authority fast ebbing away: the chances of it embarking on an extremely hazardous new initiative in its twilight days was plainly remote.

But the republican approach was nonetheless made, despite all the previous accusations of British bad faith, despite the obviously unpromising circumstances and the high risk of failure. This strongly suggests that the republicans – like the rest of nationalist Ireland – have concluded that the way ahead is not through restarting all-out war, but rather through a revival of the peace process.

It is also not widely appreciated in Britain just how deeply traumatic the Drumcree summer marching crisis was for Northern Ireland, and just how corrosive an effect it continues to have on Protestant–Catholic relations. A senior figure in policing circles recently said privately: "We were on the brink of all-out civil war. We kid ourselves that we live in a democracy – we have the potential in this community to have a Bosnia-style situation." A senior Presbyterian minister summed it up as "Northern Ireland's Chernobyl, with almost a melt-down in community relations". If ever the IRA needed an excuse for a return to the bad old days of full-scale violence, Drumcree was it. Yet the republicans did not try to turn the clock back and nor – in another hopeful sign – did the loyalist groups. The loyalist hard men are still out there, but throughout the year their political representatives displayed both skill and commitment in the Stormont political talks.

That was not enough, however, to move the talks process along, and month after month has been taken up with apparently fruitless wrangling. The political processes look jaded, fatigued, stale: perhaps the election will galvanise everyone into a fresh start. After each of the year's bombings, and after Drumcree, many felt pangs of dread and near-despair. Yet none of the incidents completely extinguished hope.

The IRA ceasefire ended in 1996, but the peace process provided a model for an exit from the troubles. This is the difference between now and the 1970s and 1980s: in those days violence seemed endemic, literally without end. Today, despite the bombs, there is an assumption that it will, after the election, be tried again; that there is still a faint, flickering light discernible at the end of the tunnel; and that it is not illogical to be a short-term pessimist and a medium-term optimist.

Early 1997 brought more IRA attacks on army and police. When violence also came from loyalist groups, controversy arose from the government's reaction.

Double standards for terrorists

The tooth fairy made its first ever recorded appearance in Northern Ireland politics this week, brandished with biting wit by one QC against another. UK Unionist party leader Robert McCartney used the mythical creature to slice through Sir Patrick Mayhew's reluctance to blame loyalists for the two boobytrap bombs placed under republican cars last month. He combined scorn and bitter Belfast humour to challenge the Northern Ireland Secretary's obfuscations – "Do you think it was the tooth fairy that's planted the bombs? Do you think it's a band of tooth fairies that are breaking legs and crucifying people throughout Northern Ireland?" He was not the only one to believe that Sir Patrick was telling fairy tales with his assertions, in the teeth of all the evidence, that the loyalist ceasefire was intact. The minister's claims were greeted with general derision in political circles.

More amusement greeted the assertion of his deputy, Sir John Wheeler, who employed considerable linguistic ingenuity to describe the loyalist ceasefire as "partially intact". Yet this was more than just an opportunity to chuckle at a minister's public discomfiture. It was an episode which posed far-reaching questions about this government's approach to Northern Ireland and the peace process. It is worth asking how a minister came to be making statements which nobody in Ireland believes and how the government exposed itself to such ridicule. It is also worth looking at the likely lasting effects of the whole bizarre performance.

The dogs in the street knew loyalists planted the bomb which injured republican Eddie Copeland, and the device which a Londonderry republican spotted beneath his car. Loyalist sources said it; so did security sources; and so, in a radio interview, did RUC Chief Constable Ronnie Flanagan.

Sir Patrick's motivation in striking a pose so much at odds with reality was to avoid having the political representatives of loyalist paramilitary groups expelled from the Stormont talks. The arguments in favour of their ejection are clear enough.

On the other hand, fringe loyalists such as David Ervine and Gary McMichael have won widespread respect for their performance. They are articulate and, in the eyes of most observers, genuine when they say they want to move their associates away from paramilitarism and into politics. The two fringe loyalist parties, the PUP and UDP, have their own mandate, having won 5.7 per cent of the vote in last year's election. But it is also well understood that they have strong links with the paramilitaries and in effect speak for them. They were allowed to join the more orthodox parties at the talks because the loyalist ceasefire was still in existence and because they formally subscribed to the Mitchell principles of non-violence. In doing so they solemnly declared their "total and absolute commitment to democratic and exclusively peaceful means of resolving political issues". Yet they have repeatedly refused to condemn the bombings.

The boobytrap attacks were not the only departure from these high ideals. In the summer, when a renegade outfit from their ranks killed a Catholic, they issued a public death threat against two of its leaders. Like the IRA, they persist in carrying out frequent savage "punishment attacks" in the ghettos. Like the IRA, they have de-commissioned none of their weapons, and show no sign of ever doing so. In fact their ceasefire, declared in October 1994, makes it clear that their suspension of violence is highly conditional. It was, and is, conditional on two separate counts, being explicitly dependent on republican violence and on their judgement that the union with Britain is safe.

In sum, it is not perfectionist pedantry to conclude that the loyalist record of commitment to democratic means alone is far from perfect. There has been a fair bit of what Sir Patrick's deputy, Michael Ancram, described this week as "dishonouring of the democratic principle". If the Mitchell rules are to be strictly adhered to, it is clear there are telling arguments for their ejection. But it is also clear that ministers will do all they can to keep the loyalists at the table – warts, boobytraps and all. Their approach is not purist but purely pragmatic, for there are strong reasons for not banishing the loyalists. Principal among these is the saving of lives. The hard fact is that casting out the loyalists would almost certainly produce an escalation in violence.

Some of the political loyalists say privately that their presence at the Stormont table has helped steady the militants in the ranks, and that without this access to political life the ceasefire would have collapsed long ago. Their expulsion from the talks, they argue, would remove this crucial political constraint; the paramilitary bosses would abandon the experiment of giving politics a chance and go back to war, with a vengeance.

The IRA, with its recent stream of attacks, is either banking on such a violent loyalist upsurge or is at best indifferent to it. If both sides take to the field again together, the result is likely to be a new spiral of violence on a scale not seen for years. Such a scenario would mean not only loss of life but also greatly reduced chances of reviving the peace process or maintaining the talks process. This perspective was summed up by David Trimble who urged caution and warned: "We must not act in a precipitate way so as to bring about more violence." This approach, if applied to the IRA at any stage, would be instantly denounced by the government and unionists as crass appeasement: this time it was quietly accepted.

Another cogent argument is that the banishment of the loyalists would probably wreck the talks themselves. With Sinn Féin absent and the talks remaining deadlocked on the arms de-commissioning issue, the talks have little real public credibility as it is. A loyalist departure could finish them off. Even if it did not do so immediately, it would practically preclude the possibility of any eventual agreement in negotiations. McCartney and his close ally, Ian Paisley, have made it plain enough that they have no interest in reaching a deal with nationalists.

Trimble has shown no enthusiasm in this direction either, but for the talks to have even a notional chance of success it is necessary to envisage not a Hume–Adams agreement but a Hume–Trimble accord. Some in government cling to the hope that this might be possible on the far side of the general election. But for that to come about Trimble would need a top-up from other unionists to meet the official requirement of achieving "sufficient consensus"; and realistically the only candidates in sight to give him support are the fringe loyalists. If the loyalists go, they will therefore take with them most of the remaining hopes for a negotiated agreement.

Such considerations help explain why Sir Patrick, faced with such a dilemma, opted to try to keep the loyalists inside the tent. But in doing so not with some degree of frankness, but rather with an explanation which can only be described as credibility-free, he has probably stored up trouble for his successor. This is because his stance will be cited, for years ahead, in the never-ending and crucially important debate within Irish nationalism on whether Britain is neutral in Ireland, and whether it deals even-handedly with unionists and nationalists. Its importance lies in the fact that the IRA uses the assertion that the British are partisanly pro-unionist to attempt to justify its terrorism.

Those who contend Britain is neutral have taken a real pounding in recent months from their opponents, who argue that the government kept the republicans out of talks and refused to criticise Trimble and other unionist leaders associated with the summer's immensely damaging marching confrontation at Drumcree. Now, the charge goes, Sir Patrick has shown himself as determined to keep the loyalists in talks as he has been to keep the republicans out. Sinn Féin's press office on the Falls Road, aware of the government's vulnerability on this point, has all week been churning out press releases accusing him of hypocrisy and worse. Sinn Féin scent an increased vote coming from all this.

It is, in fact, next to impossible to deny that the government treats republican and loyalist terrorists in different ways. The IRA, seeking to overthrow the state, has killed around 2,000 people, almost half of them members of the security forces. The organisation ignites deep passions in the government, triggering a strong emotional charge among many policy-makers.

The loyalists, who say they fight to maintain the state, have killed around 1,000 people, most of whom have been Catholic civilians. The official mind sees them as less threatening, and is able to deal with their menace in a less heated, more clinical way. The 1994 IRA cessation elicited from the government, almost instinctively, a challenging and generally confrontational stance. A very different instinct was visible this week towards the loyalists: a sense that every effort had to be made to coax and help them make the transition from terror to talks.

Nationalist Ireland is very receptive to the concept of welcoming prodigals into the fold; Unionist Ulster less so. But both sides would have welcomed a more honest explanation of government policy than they had this week. No one likes condescension, or having their intelligence insulted.

But even so, the sense that the government has one set of standards for the loyalists and another for republicans has rarely been more heightened. During the peace process the republicans were handled as though radioactive; now the loyalists are benefiting from pragmatism in plenty. The belief that double standards are being employed, and the image of Sir Patrick and his tooth fairies, will take a long time to dispel.

The level of violence rose. On 12 February an IRA sniper killed a soldier, Lance-Bombardier Stephen Restorick, at a checkpoint in Bessbrook, County Armagh. In March loyalists killed a 44-year-old Catholic father of 10 children, John Slane, in the kitchen of his west Belfast home.

In the run-up to the Westminster general election the IRA began using small bombs and threats of worse to cause great disruption. On 5 April, Grand National Day, a threat of bombs on the course led to a last-minute abandonment of the race, and chaos.

7 APRIL 1997   THE INDEPENDENT

The IRA's grand strategy

Talking to republicans in Belfast at the weekend, one was struck again by how thoughtful and calculating they can be in plotting and planning their characteristic blend of politics, propaganda and the application of terror. What happened in England last week was violence, but it was anything but mindless. It will come as little consolation to all those whose enjoyment of a great sporting occasion was marred, and especially to those who spent an uncomfortable Saturday night in Liverpool recreation centres, but their discomfiture was all part of a grand plan.

Listening to the republican explanations and analysis serves as a reminder that these people see themselves as playing a vast game of chess. It is chess on a boobytrapped board, with pieces which may explode at any moment, but in their minds it nonetheless has rules and a purpose.

Last week's disruption was the equivalent of making a few seemingly inconsequential moves which suddenly develop into a full-blown attack. The railway and motorway disruption originally seemed to be of mainly nuisance value, but they paved the way for the evacuation of Aintree. That new tack has opened up a whole new vista of headaches for the security authorities. As one republican put it: "This is a lower-level military campaign aimed at disruption and sabotage more than the spectacular stuff. It is affecting tens of thousands of people, so it takes on a British national character." The fact that Aintree was in IRA terms a signal success probably means that more of the same will follow. A senior republican described it as a strategy aimed at maximum disruption and maximum publicity coverage with a minimum of threat to the lives of the civilian population. It is also aimed at the election campaign.

But what do they hope to gain from it all? Republicans explain that in the short term it means that they cannot be ignored in the election, and that it keeps Ireland on the agenda. In the longer term it "reminds the incoming government that the IRA's campaign can be effective and can hurt them economically".

Republicans view yesterday's defiant comments from John Major and Labour's Jack Straw with a pinch of salt. The two main British parties may say the disruption will set back Sinn Féin's possible entry into talks, but this tune will change, republicans claim, once the election is out of the way. They predict that the next government, especially if it has a working majority, will move to do business with them. They expect an interregnum, particularly if Labour get in – "new faces in town, they're not going to do anything too speedily".

The political talks are due to resume on 3 June. Republicans do not expect to be there, but they expect that within weeks of the election the new government will privately be putting out feelers towards them. "The British are not stupid people," said one activist. "They must know that republicans want to do business with them." It is clear enough that a second IRA cessation will be on offer; it is also clear that it will not happen unless the next government gives a guarantee that it will lead automatically to Sinn Féin's entry into multi-party talks. In other words, all this chaos is aimed at securing Sinn Féin's place at the conference table under the best terms possible. They forecast that the ill will generated by the wrecking of the Grand National will, post-election, have evolved into a sober realisation that the only way to cope with republicans is to sit down with them.

Republicans remark that, in the wake of major IRA bombings such as last year's attacks at Canary Wharf and Manchester, many British people taking part in television and radio programmes said the government should talk to them. This is an important factor tucked away in the minds of the men making those deadly little chess moves.

They did not say so at the weekend, but they will have at least two other factors in their minds. One is that last year MI5 and the other security people had one of their best-ever years against republicans in Britain, rounding up a gang which has been described as the IRA's "A-team" and preventing a number of major attacks. Aintree seems to indicate that the IRA has made a successful comeback. The other factor is that a campaign which concentrates on sabotaging normal life in England rather than on taking lives has all the appearances of being carefully fashioned to fit in with the election in Northern Ireland. Three of Sinn Féin's leadership team – Gerry Adams, Martin McGuinness and Pat Doherty – are in with a shout of winning 3 of the 18 Northern Ireland seats. But all three look like being close contests, and every vote will count. Some support would be lost if the IRA were to set about causing civilian carnage, but Aintree-style activities tend not to cost Sinn Féin votes. They could in fact even help Sinn Féin, since some floating voters who want another ceasefire will draw the message from this type of attack that republicans are intent on positioning themselves for a second cessation rather than on restarting the whole war again on its previous scale.

If Sinn Féin does win seats, it may well be due as much to highly localised factors as to the overall republican strategy. Nonetheless a win is a win, and even though republicans would not take their Commons seats, the election of two or three new Sinn Féin MPs would be a tremendous boost.

The republican strategy is thus gradually emerging into public view. Sinn Féin will try to win seats so that it can argue it has an increased mandate. The IRA will grab the headlines with attacks in England and Northern Ireland, but try to concentrate on spectacular acts of sabotage and hope to avoid electorally damaging civilian casualties. It is a cunning strategy but it has flaws. The 1994 cessation brought a great surge of international good will towards Ireland in general and republicans in particular, but much of it has drained away since the resumption of violence.

Asking the next government to trust in republican bona fides is asking it to take an enormous risk. Many of those who believed in the 1994 cessation will approach the idea of cessation mark 2 with great suspicion. It is obvious, now as then, that there are a great many in the republican ranks who would be done with war; but there are also many in there who envisage their way ahead as being through a mix of politics and bombs.

The second faction is presently in the ascendancy. The republicans will offer a ceasefire in return for guaranteed access to the conference table, yet this will be asking the new government to take on trust that the saboteurs of today will, overnight, turn into the democrats of tomorrow. Aintree may have illustrated that republicans still have the capacity to bring chaos to Britain, but it is also helping ensure that any post-election negotiations will take place in an atmosphere just as bereft of trust.

April saw the politicians back on the stump.

23 & 30 APRIL 1997   THE INDEPENDENT

Voters dream of day when hope and history rhyme

Martin McGuinness of Sinn Féin canvasses in the shadow of Bellaghy bawn, a fortified farmhouse dating back three centuries. The bawn is a metaphor of possession and dispossession: the election much the same story, a modern enactment of ancient quarrels. This is pleasant countryside with an unpleasant history.

The bawn was built on a jutting rise to house Protestants, sent in from England to subdue and hold this rebellious land for English monarchs. The records show that John Rowley and Baptist Jones were given 3,200 acres of south Londonderry countryside to hold for England during the plantation. No one here has forgotten that it was Catholic land.

Today's political equivalent is the seat of Mid-Ulster, which has a nationalist majority but which since 1983 has been held by the Reverend William McCrea. Crea, a follower of the Reverend Ian Paisley, is on the furthest shores of political loyalism: he is the extremist's extremist. His bawn is now under assault from Martin McGuinness of Sinn Féin and from the SDLP's Denis Haughey, one of John Hume's personal aides. The contest gives an insight into

57

Martin McGuinness canvassing in Bellaghy, Co Londonderry

the state of opinion within northern nationalism, and thus the prospects for a new peace process.

Seamus Heaney, a local man, wrote of a time when hope and history might rhyme. In Bellaghy there is both much hope and, if anything, a surfeit of history, and in this election they are inextricably entwined. Martin McGuinness's doorstep patter reflects what are clearly the twin aspirations of nationalist voters, a new peace process and a McCrea defeat. "This is a very important election," he says to a balding man who is still blinking from the surprise of opening his door to encounter the Sinn Féin leader on his doorstep. "We're trying to use this election to do two things. First, to rebuild the peace process – we see it as a new opportunity for a peace settlement with a new British government. And it's also the best opportunity nationalists will ever have to get rid of Willie McCrea as MP." The message is a concise blend of the aspirational and the tribal.

Denis Haughey, meanwhile, directs his fire against both McCrea and McGuinness. A lot of those who voted for Sinn Féin in last year's forum election, he argues, did so "as a very sincere, honourable, well-intentioned gesture to try to encourage the IRA to make the peace". But now they feel let down and will come back to the SDLP, he says. A successful vote for Sinn Féin would make peace less likely – "I think the IRA would conclude that they can win votes without delivering peace."

McCrea, meanwhile, concentrates on the defence of his parliamentary bawn. Quite a few on the unionist side have no great love for him, but at election times they turn up in large numbers to do their constitutional, political and tribal duty by voting for him.

This time his seat is in its greatest-ever peril, for three reasons. First, boundary changes have been unhelpful to him; second, he faces in Martin McGuinness one of republicanism's best-known celebrities; and third, his support for a loyalist paramilitary figure looks like galvanising nationalist voters into a determined attempt to unseat him. Last September he appeared on the platform at a rally in support of Billy Wright, a hardline paramilitary who has openly associated himself with loyalist violence. Wright is not now in a position to return the favour by canvassing for the MP, for he has since been jailed for eight years for threatening to kill a woman.

The balding man told me later: "McCrea went on a stage with Billy Wright. That's turned everybody against him." And yet many of those expressing abhorrence about Wright's alleged associations with violence are gearing up to vote for McGuinness, whose reputation is, to put it no higher, not that of a pacifist. This is partly because a lot of them are republicans who support or tolerate the IRA, but also because they seem to believe Sinn Féin when it says it wants peace. Something important has changed here, as can be seen both from the Sinn Féin message, and the message they are getting back on the doorstep. One of his election workers elaborates: "What you get, especially from newlyweds, people with one or two young children, is – what is the hope of peace, will there be a ceasefire? But people are not directing anger at Sinn Féin as being the bad guys. They are just, especially the young people, looking for hope." Thus the McGuinness doorstep presentation is designed to reflect nationalist voters' concerns back to them: the toppling of McCrea and a new ceasefire. In Bellaghy the two have become jumbled up.

McCrea may or may not survive. But the most important thing is that on many doorsteps Sinn Féin candidates are receiving the message that the grassroots are hoping and indeed expecting another IRA cessation after the election. This in itself is enough to keep alive the hope that peace remains a possibility, and that hope and history may yet come to rhyme.

In the cockpit seat of West Belfast supporters of John Hume's SDLP are today distributing leaflets bearing a more prosaic message: "Make sure your vote – and not a stolen vote – elects your MP." The message is plain. The SDLP is accusing Sinn Féin, who are trying to win the seat back for Gerry Adams, of resorting to personation and electoral malpractices. If the party is correct, the ancient and dishonourable art of personation and vote-stealing still has its practitioners.

The electoral authorities privately acknowledge that there are wrong-doings and irregularities but their extent is in dispute. The official line is that while it is pretty much endemic, its scale is probably limited. Others disagree, alleging it is widespread.

The persistence of irregularity is perhaps hardly surprising, given that for centuries it has been a recognised part of the Irish political scene. While much rhetorical lip service is paid to the democratic processes, electoral practices have not been held in reverence by either unionists or nationalists. My mother recalled the late Terence O'Neill, while prime minister of Northern Ireland, shaking her hand and urging her to "vote early and vote often". My grandmother's parlour, one election day in the 1960s, was filled with hats and coats to give personators a change of clothing. It is, in other words, part of the culture and regarded as a feature of politics, at most a venial sin and certainly not a mortal one. It ranks on a par with offences such as tax-dodging and distilling poteen in illicit stills.

In Northern Ireland it is one of the survivors of a one-time battery of highly questionable techniques which included gerrymandering, the drawing of boundaries designed to maximise the value of unionist votes. Most of these old ways have gone but the tradition of vote-rigging lingers on. Though the practice is publicly condemned, Northern Ireland politicians – including some MPs and even members of the Lords – cheerfully recall how they operated in the old days. It even had its own vocabulary: "plugging" meant to cast someone else's vote, while an "open box" was a polling station devoid of personation agents. An open box was "riddled", meaning numerous fake votes were cast.

The old 1960s civil rights slogan of "one man one vote" takes on an ironic aspect when the folklore is recounted of individuals voting dozens of times. Even though all this was illegal, both unionists and nationalists observed certain conventions and customs. It was considered bad form for a unionist personator to plug a nationalist vote; what he did was to vote on behalf of those unionist electors too apathetic to vote themselves.

It was the entry of Sinn Féin into the political arena in the early 1980s which shattered all the old protocols and swept away the traditional niceties. The republicans, according to all other parties, simply plugged every vote they could get their hands on. One telling indicator of this was in the soaring numbers of tendered ballot papers, signifying people who arrived at polling stations to find their vote had already been cast. In a 1982 poll there were more than 700 of these; the following year there were almost 1,000, together with 149 arrests of alleged personators. This was the hey-day of vote-stealing. The situation was described by the late Unionist MP Harold McCusker, who told the Commons: "In the comparatively recent past there occurred benign personation, practised by both sides, operated by both sides and with unwritten rules. But that has now changed because Sinn Féin have broken the rules – they have engaged in vote-stealing on a massive scale."

The government claimed then that perhaps 20 per cent of Sinn Féin's 102,000 votes in 1983 were obtained by electoral abuse, and the laws were considerably tightened, with voters required to produce medical cards or other identification. At that point the issue seemed to die down, though the occasional sign emerged to suggest that abuses had not been eradicated. At the last general election, for example, another journalist and myself stopped at a Sinn Féin caravan parked outside a major polling station in west Belfast. Propped up on a shelf in the caravan was what looked like a batch of new medical cards. The first in the sheaf was certainly a medical card, and the edges of what appeared to be others could be seen behind it. Gerry Adams later suggested to us that a medical card might have been left in for somebody coming in later, but stressed that was entirely speculation on his part. Any suggestion that false cards were being used was completely untrue, he said: "The allegations are not true. The electoral office has asked the SDLP on numerous occasions to produce evidence and they have not been able to do so. It's the worst sort of negative campaigning."

People in authority say privately that vote-stealing does go on, but argue that it is on a much smaller scale than the SDLP maintains. They also say it is by no means confined to Sinn Féin: "Everybody abuses," according to one senior figure, "it's just that the Provos are probably more organised than anybody else." The extent of abuse is, it seems, impossible to pin down. But it does seem the case that there are still political apparatchiks working away in the political undergrowth to maximise their votes through the black art of vote-stealing.

The possibility of a change of government raised the question of whether a new Labour government would act like previous Labour administrations, whose record over the years had been somewhat erratic.

Labour's Irish question mark

Hard-headed political operators in both the unionist and nationalist camps say privately that the most vital point about the next British general election is not who wins it, but the strength of their majority. Unionists want a weak government, whether Tory or Labour, with a slender majority which will induce reliance on unionist votes in the Commons. Nationalists want a stronger government with no need of unionist assistance.

But the fact that a Labour government is a possibility means that in Belfast and Dublin politicians are already flicking back through Labour's past record for indications on how a Blair-led government might perform. Their legendary compendious political memory banks still hold every detail of how, at various stages, Harold Wilson offended the unionists, how Jim Callaghan alienated the nationalists, and so on.

Judged on its record in office, Labour policy on Ireland has seesawed wildly over the years, going through nationalist periods but also decidedly unionist phases. In many ways it is a tale of radical instincts curbed by the exigencies of office. Although there has been much change since Labour was last in power, the fact is that many of the same factors and forces, and indeed some of the personalities, will be faced by Tony Blair and Marjorie "Mo" Mowlam, whom everyone assumes will be his Northern Ireland Secretary. New Labour will have to face the old Irish questions.

Mowlam has held the Northern Ireland brief for many years, but Blair has shown only the most perfunctory interest in Ireland. Their party has, though, gone through the same painful learning curve as everyone else, and in that at least will have an advantage over past Labour ministers. The record shows that they considered Irish matters only when they absolutely had to, and approached them in a state of almost complete ignorance.

The first occasion a Labour government ever really came to grips with Ireland was almost half a century ago, in an episode which, though now part of history, offers a telling glimpse into the party's perspectives. In 1948 the Dublin government unexpectedly announced that Ireland, though effectively independent for many years, would formally declare a republic and leave the Commonwealth. This huge constitutional change meant the Attlee government needed new legislation to regularise Northern Ireland's position.

Up to that point the Labour government had exhibited what one of its junior ministers, the pro-nationalist Lord Longford, described as "a rather hazy benevolence" towards southern Ireland. This was very much a traditional Labour approach, for expatriate Irishmen and their descendants had played a significant role in the movement since its early days.

When it came to brass tacks, however, such sentiment went by the board. The government inserted a clause in the new bill laying down that Northern Ireland would remain in the UK so long as there was a majority for this in the Stormont parliament in Belfast. Since Stormont had an inbuilt unionist majority, nationalists protested that the clause copper-fastened partition. But the prevailing sentiment in the cabinet was in favour of the unionists, largely because Attlee's deputy, Herbert Morrison, was much impressed by the Stormont prime minister, Lord Brookeborough, and by Northern Ireland's role in the Second World War.

There also emerged a certain resentment against the south, partly because of the undiplomatic way in which its plan for a republic was announced without notice, and partly because of its neutrality during the war. However, the issue was decided not on sentiment but on hard political judgements. The first of these concerned the reality of Protestant power, and a desire to avoid stirring up Protestant anger. The cabinet talked about the 1912 period, when Unionists had armed themselves with German guns and formed the Ulster Volunteers, declaring themselves ready to use force to resist home rule. The 1949 cabinet minutes record the conclusion of Labour ministers: "Unless the people of Northern Ireland felt reasonably assured of the support of the people of this country, there might be a revival of the Ulster Volunteers and of other bodies intending to meet any threat of force by force; and this would bring nearer the danger of an outbreak of violence in Ireland."

The second issue was closer to home: that of the UK's wider strategic defence considerations. These were spelled out by the cabinet secretary, Lord Normanbrook, who wrote that the south's severance of its links meant that keeping Northern Ireland within the UK was now "a matter of first-class strategic importance to this country". Normanbrook went on to argue that Northern Ireland was so important defensively that it was unlikely any British government would let it leave the UK, even if the people of Northern Ireland wanted a united Ireland. The new bill had in effect formulated a principle which is still a matter of everyday political argument: that Irish unity can only come about with the consent of a majority in Northern Ireland.

What went by the board in 1948 was the issue which came back to haunt these islands in 1969: the question of the fairness of the Stormont system. Some pro-nationalist Labour MPs argued that vesting Northern Ireland's future in a Stormont vote meant relying on a vote in a controversial institution whose voting system had, they alleged, been gerrymandered and rigged to maximise the unionist vote. But when Longford protested to the cabinet that Catholics were being discriminated against he was heard out, he recalls, with "chilly indifference". The young Michael Foot supported the bill but went on to call for a commission of inquiry into Stormont's "monstrously undemocratic methods". The cabinet discussed this proposition but, the minutes show, decided London should keep its distance: "It was the general view of ministers that the UK government would be ill-advised to appear to be interesting themselves in this matter." Exactly two decades later, another Labour administration was in power when the civil rights issue spilled over into the streets and into violence.

In the 1960s and 1970s governments headed by Harold Wilson twice considered, among other options, the idea of a united Ireland. The decisions not to follow this course seem to have been taken to Wilson's personal regret. And, demonstrating the continuity of the Irish issue, they were taken at least in part on similar grounds to those which influenced the Attlee administration. But Wilson, unlike Attlee, took a much closer interest in the issue of civil rights for Catholics. His election as prime minister in 1964 coincided with the arrival of a new Ulster Unionist prime minister, Terence O'Neill, pursuing reformist policies. Wilson welcomed this approach, supporting O'Neill while expressing open hostility towards anti-reformist unionists such as the Reverend Ian Paisley and William Craig, an early mentor of David Trimble.

Wilson himself came under pressure to intervene more directly from a large number of Labour MPs, many of whom, such as Kevin McNamara, had Irish backgrounds and sympathies. Wilson was conscious of the large Irish presence in his own Liverpool constituency, remarking often that he had more Irish voters in his constituency than had many Dublin politicians. His own instincts were radical, and the idea of pulling out of Northern Ireland was secretly considered, though rejected, before the August 1969 eruption of violence made the deployment of British troops necessary. Wilson was fully prepared to scrap Stormont if the unionists did not hand over many of their security powers, but they agreed and their institution survived.

While the issue of civil rights assumed a new importance in 1969, some points were practically unaltered by the passage of time. Like the Attlee cabinet, Wilson's ministers worried about a revival of the Ulster Volunteers. According to Tony Benn's diaries, defence secretary Denis Healey warned the cabinet that "although he had sympathy with the Catholics, he had to point out that if we had the majority of the population against us, we should be once again in the 1911–14 situation".

Britain's strategic military interests also remained a consideration, one of Wilson's aides noting later: "There were and still are arguments for Britain not pulling out of Ireland. However, the only positive reason for staying in which really mattered in Whitehall was defence."

From then on Wilson was increasingly unpopular with unionists as he insisted on a far-reaching reform programme. But it was during his period in opposition, from 1970 to 1974, that he really appalled unionists, for two reasons. First, he openly espoused the aim of Irish unity, recommending a gradual British disengagement. Second, he secretly met the IRA on at least two occasions, infuriating not only unionists but also the Irish government. Dublin felt he was not only encouraging terrorists but also undermining democratic politicians, Garret FitzGerald, later Taoiseach, describing his approach as "an act of treachery".

Unionists were therefore apprehensive when Wilson returned to power in 1974. They were right to worry, since in strictest secrecy he established a cabinet office committee to review options which included British withdrawal and independence. But within months unionists inflicted a decisive defeat on his government's authority by staging a general strike which brought down the powersharing executive of the time. When Wilson referred to loyalists as "spongers" they responded by defiantly sporting pieces of sponge on their lapels.

Many, including Wilson, took the success of the strike as the clearest possible indication of the unionists' strength of numbers. It was, in effect, a stark demonstration of the Protestant power to which Attlee and Healey had accorded such wary respect. His sights lowered from the aspirational to the managerial, Wilson and his hapless Northern Ireland Secretary, Merlyn Rees, afterwards presided over a policy still remembered for its confusion and lack of direction. Local politicians were assembled in a constitutional convention but could not reach agreement. Government talks with republicans produced a short-lived ceasefire but this petered out, to be followed by an upsurge in violence.

Amid the confusion Garret FitzGerald, worried that Wilson might opt for British withdrawal, lobbied US Secretary of State Henry Kissinger. He told Kissinger that Dublin might seek American assistance "in persuading Britain not to embark on a course of action that could be so fraught with dangers". FitzGerald's fears, as he later acknowledged, were groundless. The great irony in Labour's Northern Ireland record is that during the Callaghan era of 1976–79 the party executed a dramatic change, transforming itself from the one-time champion of Catholic rights into, at least temporarily, the sponsor of unionist interests.

Roy Mason, as Northern Ireland Secretary, revelled in the pro-consular trappings of the office, eschewing political initiatives in favour of a hardline security policy which included extensive use of the SAS. This was coupled with police interrogation methods which earned condemnation from Amnesty International and others. This approach was so popular with unionists that years later the mention of Mason's name could still draw applause from an Ulster Unionist party audience.

The tough security policy was accompanied by concessions to unionism at Westminster, where Callaghan's minority government needed Ulster Unionist support in the lobbies. This switch from Labour's traditional green coloration to an approach of an orange hue led to several junior resignations from the government, but Callaghan clearly put the survival of his government over all other considerations. He paid the price, however, when his policies led the then leader of the SDLP, Gerry Fitt, to vote with the Conservatives in a no-confidence motion. "Labour policy since 1974 has been disastrous," Fitt said in an emotional, still-remembered Commons speech. "The government has disregarded the minority and appeased the blackmailers of the unionist majority." Fitt's vote – the first he cast against Labour in 14 years – helped bring down the last Labour government.

Out of office, Labour at first reverted to a more pro-nationalist line, in the early 1980s adopting a policy of pursuing Irish unity with unionist consent. In the last few years, however, Blair has significantly softened this approach. He first removed Kevin McNamara, the shadow Northern Ireland spokesman who was both identified with "old Labour" and had over the decades rendered such sterling service to the Irish nationalist cause. His replacement, Mo Mowlam, and Blair himself have since made it clear that while the party is still technically committed to unity by consent it will not push unionists in that direction.

But although their agenda does not include any Wilsonian notions about withdrawal, they will nonetheless go into the election with a greenish policy, though the shade of green is much paler than Wilson, or McNamara, would have wished for. It places a high priority on an Anglo-Irish approach, involving the south in the administration of the north and increasing London–Dublin co-operation. The Irish vote may no longer be a factor of note in British politics but it has been replaced with the much stronger influence wielded today by Dublin.

This mild greenery is derived not so much from Labour's own instincts as from the general consensus (with the significant exception of the unionists) that the political facts of life are Anglo-Irish. But many of the issues faced by Blair's Labour predecessors will still be there. The defence issue may have dimmed, but the issue of the integrity of the UK will be on the Conservative agenda and therefore on Labour's too. And while the south's influence has grown, the reality of unionism's strength of numbers is still evident. This year's Drumcree episode, which amounted to a minor key rerun of the 1974 loyalist strike, provided a salutary reminder of the realpolitik of potential Protestant power.

Of Blair's predecessors as prime minister, Wilson had radical instincts which in power were stifled by a combination of establishment caution and Protestant muscle. Callaghan was propelled by the parliamentary circumstances of the 1970s into a deal with unionists. Blair would bring to the post no strong instincts on Ireland, though his general approach suggests he would opt for continuity and avoid Wilson-style adventurism. His policies may be further circumscribed by the Tories, who in opposition might well opt for a stronger pro-union line.

But the most important determinant of Labour's approach, as it threads its way through the Irish minefield, may well be the size of its majority. A strong Blair government will have a tricky enough task in working towards peace and agreement; but a weak administration, dependent on unionist support in the lobbies, would be something close to a nightmare for nationalists, and indeed for Blair himself.

The Labour landslide in the May general election and Northern Ireland's own results unsettled unionists and encouraged nationalists. Gerry Adams and Martin McGuinness were both elected and the SDLP vote also held up.

The new prime minister moved quickly to break the log jam, visiting Belfast's Balmoral Show to announce the reopening of direct contacts with Sinn Féin. While this pleased republicans, unionists drew comfort from Blair's statement that "none of us in this hall today, even the youngest, is likely to see Northern Ireland as anything but a part of the United Kingdom".

Blair milks good will in Belfast

Tony Blair, meeting the crowds at an agricultural show in Belfast yesterday, came into direct personal contact with Ulster's horny-handed sons of toil. "I'm getting really firm handshakes here," he said over his shoulder. Kyle Lucas, 18, from the splendidly named Nutts Corner, made the reverse observation after shaking hands with the prime minister: "He hasn't milked many cows, that boy. He has nice soft hands," he remarked to the *Independent*.

There were cows aplenty at Balmoral, but Blair milked none of them. He worked the crowd to perfection, however, delighting the normally taciturn farmers and farmers' wives who flocked to shake his hand. "I got his autograph," beamed one matron. "I'm all pleased."

Her companion enthused: "He's very nice, very friendly, I was very taken with him. Lovely soft hands, he doesn't do much work. We've hard hands, we're farmers." And her hands were indeed tough, firm, hardened: when Tony pressed her flesh, she had clearly forcefully pressed back.

Mo Mowlam, his new Northern Ireland Secretary, followed in his wake. She is another crowd-pleaser, the first touchy-feely cabinet minister ever to be based in Belfast, as cordial and friendly as her predecessor, Sir Patrick Mayhew, was patrician and remote. The PM had just snatched a quick lunch in a function room with 12 sides, a construction which gives it the nickname of the Thrupenny Bit. There he delivered a speech intended to give new impetus to the Northern Ireland political processes, which by common consent has recently lacked direction. Just over two years ago John Major stood in the same hall to launch the Framework Document, a joint London–Dublin paper sketching out a future in which Northern Ireland would remain within the union but take on an increasingly Anglo-Irish aspect.

As the months passed and the authority of the Major government ebbed away the Framework Document was barely mentioned, but yesterday Blair reinstated it as one of the central columns of his policy. Sinn Féin, the IRA and loyalists were invited to arrange themselves around that proposition: the IRA was told to stop the violence and loyalists were warned to avoid trouble in the summer's parades.

Most Protestants want to avoid another bad marching season, but some elements are apparently intent on putting their right to march above almost all other considerations. Many republican supporters now want another IRA ceasefire: Blair's move will put to the test their ability to deliver the whole republican movement. Certainly, all sides appreciate that it will need an audacious group to be the first to pitch itself in direct confrontation with a government of such authority.

His political messages delivered, it was outside into the sunshine to meet the farming community, which exuded sunny good will but also anxiety about its livelihood. "I asked him to do something about BSE," said James Newell from Ballymoney, County Antrim, holding one of the prize Hereford bulls in the judging ring. "I said that all these cattle were destined for the burner, to be destroyed and incinerated, unless something was done. He said he had inherited a very difficult situation and would do his best."

A woman from Meath was delighted when Tony Blair told her his mother's family came from Donegal and were farmers. And a blond woman with a matching prize-winning bull, a blond D'Aquitaine, chuckled: "We introduced our bull to him. He's called Major, we told him he was the only Major to win anything this year. He just laughed."

The outcome of the Westminster election, taken together with the local government results, revealed hugely important demographic changes.

Northern Ireland changes colour

The political map of Northern Ireland has just changed dramatically, with profound implications for its politics, its future and how its people live together. The balance of power between nationalist and unionist has fundamentally shifted.

Northern Irish nationalism is unmistakably on the move, making dramatic advances politically, socially, economically and numerically. Even a preliminary bout of number-crunching in the wake of recent elections shows that something big is happening.

Those numbers, and much else, are changing fast; and since Northern Ireland's history and politics are based on the numbers game, its very fabric is being transformed. The ratio of two-thirds Protestant to one-third Catholic which was the consistent backdrop to politics for so many decades has gone, to be replaced by a new mathematical and political model.

And not only are there more nationalists than ever before: they are more confident, younger, and better off than ever. They have, in John Hume and Gerry Adams, formidable political leaders with a flair for publicity and, abroad, a talent for winning friends and influencing people which is the envy of their unionist opponents.

Unionists will find a great deal to worry about in last week's results which show up both falling numbers and falling morale. They will worry in particular about Sinn Féin, whose popularity is soaring at a rate never before seen in Northern Ireland politics. Catholics have increased from one-third to at least 43 per cent of the population, and probably more. The political effect of this, masked for many years because much of the Catholic population was under voting age, is now impacting on politics.

In 1983 nationalists held 2 of the 17 Westminster seats; today 5 of the 18 MPs are nationalist. In the general election the nationalist share of the vote touched 40 per cent for the first time ever. In the 1985 local government elections Sinn Féin and the SDLP together won 189,000 votes; in last week's council elections they polled 237,000. The unionists lost control of four councils, the western territories of Cookstown, Fermanagh, Strabane, and, carrying a huge symbolic change, Belfast itself. Before last week 16 of the 26 councils were controlled by unionists, 6 by nationalists and 4 had no overall majority. Now unionists control only 13, nationalists have 8 and 5 have no clear majority. Citadels are crumbling.

The fall of Fermanagh, the western-most and one of the geographically largest councils, means none of the west is under unionist control. Overall there is still a clear Protestant majority but increasingly it is concentrated in the east, particularly in the Greater Belfast area.

The Ulster Unionists and Sinn Féin, with 13 councillors each, are the largest parties in the city, which now resembles a political doughnut, with an ever-more nationalist core surrounded by Protestant satellite towns. Both middle-class and working-class Protestants are resorting to a local version of white flight, moving out to leave the city to the Catholics. This phenomenon, mischievously described by a nationalist councillor as Orange flight, may well be accelerated by the fall of city hall.

This exodus is one unionist response to the new demographic realities. Another section of the Protestant electorate has simply switched off and stayed home on polling day. "There's apathy and confusion among the unionist people," one defeated Belfast councillor complained. "They've nobody to blame but themselves because they didn't come out to vote."

One key question is how the traditional unionist parties will react to the shifts in population and hence in power. The septuagenarian Ian Paisley is too old a dog to learn new tricks. His deputy, Peter Robinson, might some day do business but not until his Ayatollah departs the scene. In the meantime Paisley, having spent three decades in the last ditch, is not about to leave it now.

The focus of attention is therefore on David Trimble and his Ulster Unionists, who are still the largest party. If Paisley will not do a deal – either with Sinn Féin or without it – then in logic the Ulster Unionists are the only remaining candidates. The party's performance has been mixed, with a poor forum election last year, then a good Westminster result, but the local government outcome was cheerless for them. The theory goes that Trimble, now that he has reached an election-free zone, will have more room to manoeuvre. It is not a particularly comfortable position for him, for the Paisleyite fundamentalists have not gone away. But on the other hand Tony Blair and Mo Mowlam – the woman who put the Mo in momentum – will be pushing him hard to show new flexibility and early movement.

The changing demographics and other elements argue for a historic new deal, which means a historic new compromise, but Trimble will be well aware that previous unionist leaders who struck out in that direction quickly perished. One set of voices within unionism argues – quietly, for the charge of heresy is still a potent accusation – that it is time to make a deal, on the grounds that the demographic and other factors mean unionism's position weakens with each passing year.

A key defining moment will come, perhaps quite soon, if and when the IRA declares a second ceasefire. If they do, it will be because of a government assurance of speedy entry into round-table talks, and Paisley has made it clear that if republicans walk through the front door, he will be storming out the nearest exit. At that point the Ulster Unionists must decide whether to go with him, or stay and negotiate.

While a Paisley walkout would exert a powerful pull, Trimble could receive a fair amount of cloud cover, should he decide to stay, from the fringe loyalists. Several of their members are still slightly hungover from celebrating their conspicuous electoral success. These groups, the PUP and UDP, are known as the public voice of the illegal loyalist paramilitary groups, but after winning a number of council seats they can now claim to have their own mandate. While their associates have guns and bombs, most of those who voted for them did so because the PUP and UDP project a willingness to compromise. The fact that they have established an appreciable foothold in electoral politics is a serious nuisance for the established unionist parties, since it means the Protestant vote is fragmented. But the loyalists will probably stay in talks if Sinn Féin come in, and London and Dublin hope that that would encourage Trimble to stay too.

Just as thousands of Protestants believe the loyalists when they say they want to be less paramilitary and more political, so do most nationalists accept that Sinn Féin wants a new peace process. As one seasoned observer put it: "The nationalist community has accepted that Sinn Féin and the IRA want to pack it in, move away from the violence and get some sort of overall settlement. The nationalist community believes them."

This may well be the principal explanation for the extraordinary rise in Sinn Féin's vote, which leapt from 12.4 per cent four years ago to 16.9 per cent last week. The fact is that nearly all of the fast-growing nationalist vote is going to Sinn Féin, while support for the SDLP remains static. In the 1980s Sinn Féin built a solid but limited electoral base of around 11 per cent of the vote, but since the early 1990s, when republicans adopted the language of peace and later staged their 17-month ceasefire, this has skyrocketed to almost 17 per cent.

There are other explanations too. If the allegations are correct and republicans have indeed been stealing votes, this clearly augmented their total, though hardly by more than a few thousand of their 107,000-vote total. But whether or not Sinn Féin has been stealing SDLP votes, they have certainly been stealing the SDLP's clothes in terms of policies, concepts and language. Language like peace, peace process, the need for the two governments to work together and so on, all originated with the SDLP and have been appropriated by the republicans. "The Shinners have been copying Hume's eckers," complained an SDLP teacher.

Sinn Féin have also been reaping the rich harvest of new nationalist voters, in particular those who were jolted into voting for the first time by last year's Drumcree disturbances. The sense of nationalist indignation at that episode has scarcely dimmed since last July. They are also mobilising a younger and more dedicated, if only because more unemployed, constituency.

It is impossible to say which of these ingredients has contributed most to the new republican voting surge, though it is likely the peace aspect has provided the greatest boost. But the bad news for unionists is that there are more nationalists than ever and they are more ambitious and energetic than ever. This new assertiveness, coupled with the relative decline of the Protestant population, is the key to explaining why so many controversies arise over loyalist marches. In most cases the problems arise when loyalists attempt to continue to parade through districts which were once largely Protestant but are now Catholic. Firstly the districts have changed their religion; secondly their denizens no longer accept without demur what are viewed as triumphalist exercises.

The day when nationalists might one day actually have a majority is still far off in the remote future. But the rise in the Catholic population, taken together with this new nationalist confidence and a lack of unionist direction, means that the whole system is changing.

Nationalists in general, and the republican movement in particular, have clearly become empowered politically: the hope is that this will lead the IRA to conclude that a real and ready-made alternative to violence exists. The chances of a new ceasefire have been strengthened by the new sense that nationalism is on the move and that a new political landscape is fast taking shape.

Reprinted in the Belfast *Irish News*

The talks at Stormont reconvened at the beginning of June, overshadowed by uncertainties on the state of play within the IRA and Sinn Féin and the fear of a violent marching season. The funeral of an RUC officer kicked to death by a

loyalist mob in Ballymoney, County Antrim, cast a pall over proceedings, as did the discovery of a 1,000-lb bomb in west Belfast.

When a leading loyalist ex-prisoner was shot dead on the Shankill Road there was panic at first, for it looked like a deliberately provocative republican attack. The killing, however, turned out to have its roots in the 1970s.

12 JUNE 1997   THE INDEPENDENT

From killer to victim: Basher's death sums up the futility

Robert "Basher" Bates, who was gunned down in Belfast yesterday, was an icon. To some he represented the very worst that the troubles has produced: to others he was testimony that even the most brutal terrorist might not be beyond redemption. Two decades ago the 10 murders he was involved in were among the most barbaric ever seen. He shot some of his victims but others he killed in the most cruel fashion, he and his associates wielding butcher's knives, axes and cleavers on random Catholic victims. The Shankill Butchers slaughtered human beings like animals.

The horror of those 10 mid-1970s killings took Belfast to a new low. Yesterday his death conjured up the most appalling vista of all: that the IRA was intent on regenerating the troubles. The relief was palpable when it emerged that he had been killed not by the IRA but by a loyalist in what is thought to have been personal revenge for the murder by Bates of a close relative in a bar-room brawl 20 years ago.

While loyalist groups have accounted for close on 1,000 of the 3,500 victims of the troubles, the ferocity and awfulness of the Shankill Butchers killings have remained in the public memory for two full decades. A book dwelling on the graphic details has been a local bestseller for 10 years and can still be picked up in many of the garage shops of Belfast. It was, for example, the favourite reading of Thomas Begley, the young IRA man who four years ago carried a bomb into a Shankill Road fish shop, killing himself and nine Protestants.

Bates was not the prime mover in the Shankill Butchers gang: that was UVF man Lennie Murphy, who was shot dead by the IRA in 1982. But he was one of the leading lights during their two-year reign of terror, and one photograph of him, looking like an unshaven, unkempt dullard, has remained lodged in the communal memory as a vision of a psychopathic killer.

The judge who gave him 16 life sentences for his killings told him, correctly, that his actions "will remain forever a lasting monument to blind sectarian bigotry". When he told him he should remain behind bars for the rest of his natural life society shuddered and hoped it had heard the last of Basher Bates. But Northern Ireland has a scheme, not found in the rest of the UK, for the release of even the most notorious killers, and more than 300 loyalists and republicans have been quietly freed over the last decade. Many of these former lifers engross themselves, as Bates seemed to be doing, in community or welfare work.

As the years passed in jail Bates was at first a difficult prisoner, then a troubled soul and finally a remorseful born-again Christian, praying fervently for forgiveness. One who knew him in prison said of him: "He's now a shell of a man, very quiet and inoffensive in a bland kind of way. The hair has gone, he's prematurely bald. He has found the Lord and he's no threat to anyone."

Basher Bates was one of hundreds of convicted killers released after serving an average of a decade and a half behind bars. There are hundreds of unsettled personal grudges in Northern Ireland: quite a few people know, or think they know, who killed their fathers or other loved ones, yet this seems to have been the first-ever personal revenge killing of a released prisoner.

Basher Bates made a long and painful journey from merciless assassin to man of God. His personal odyssey seemed to be over: neither he nor anyone else could have foreseen the fateful circularity which in the end transformed him from killer to victim.

On 16 June IRA gunmen shot dead two
policemen on foot patrol in Lurgan,
County Armagh, only a few miles from
Drumcree. The killings seemed to deal a
grievous blow to hopes of averting
serious marching season trouble, and
for the reinstatement of the IRA ceasefire.

But far from abandoning the peace
process, the new government pushed
on, London and Dublin together telling
local parties that it would not insist on
IRA de-commissioning as a condition for
Sinn Féin entry to talks. This was seen
as a calculated gamble by Tony Blair
and Mo Mowlam.

27 JUNE 1997   THE INDEPENDENT

Blair sets Ulster its biggest test

At this moment hope and dread co-exist in Northern Ireland. Tony Blair's energy and attack this week instilled unfamiliar urgency into the search for progress as he set timetables for both the paramilitaries and the politicians. But at the same time the dreary steeple of Drumcree parish church casts a long and ominous shadow over not just politics but all of life in Northern Ireland, for fears are high that another confrontation is on the cards when the Orange brethren gather there on 6 July.

The large number of sashes sold to new Orange members shows that many in the Protestant grassroots are gearing up for another determined assertion of what they see as their heritage. Since last year's clashes the Orange ranks have been swelled by hundreds of recruits, many of whom have what might be described as a militant tendency.

While many Orange greybeards would prefer to avoid confrontation, power in the marching season passes from the stately Grand Orange Lodge of Ireland to the men and youths on the streets. As one senior Orangeman said this week: "There's an air of excitement among the younger ones in the [Orange] institution. The overriding thing is that at this time of the year they're easy worked up.

"There's large numbers of them unemployed, the economy doesn't make any difference to them. A lot of them don't start out to wreck the town but they come out and somebody says 'Right boys' and they get going and then there's no stopping them."

Many non-members of the Order, Protestants and Catholics both, are voting with their feet in a rather different way, by simply getting out. Travel agents report a huge increase in the numbers heading for Britain, the Irish Republic and further afield to escape Drumcree, variously describing the exodus as overwhelming, amazing and astounding. In other words Northern Ireland has just invented refugee tourism. It is another example of how the reality of things here can be so different from their appearance: those people in the airport departure lounge are going to look like holiday-makers but actually they'll be evacuees.

It is obvious that these are far from ideal conditions for the launching of the type of political initiative which Blair unveiled this week. A bad Drumcree would be a major setback for it and so too would be more IRA violence, but the Blair message was that he would be deflected by neither. Either side, or both, may well flex their muscles and in their different ways cause trouble, but if they do there will be a political price to pay. The Blair approach means taking risks, but it has also captured the moral high ground in a way which John Major never quite managed to do.

The government has laid down that political talks will start in earnest in mid-September. Sinn Féin will be allowed in six weeks after an IRA ceasefire, with no requirement that republicans should pay an admission fee of handing in guns up front. For David Trimble and the Ulster Unionists the bad news was that the previous government's de-commissioning demand has been dropped.

The period between now and mid-September may well provide a real test of the government's nerve. It will certainly test, and may provide a final answer to, crucial questions over the sincerity of those Sinn Féin leaders who say they want, and can deliver, peace and negotiations in place of war.

On one reading these new arrangements can be portrayed as a victory for the republicans, who, ever since the ceasefire of August 1994, have been demanding entry to talks without the de-commissioning of IRA weaponry.

Even after the ceasefire broke down in February of last year the central republican proposition has been that of a new cessation in exchange for real talks. Tony Blair's approach has been to examine the stated republican requirements for talks and in effect to agree to each one of them. They wanted guaranteed entry, a brisk timetable and the removal of the de-commissioning proviso: they got them. Some fine-tuning of detail may be necessary, but in its essentials the full republican shopping-list has been granted.

Yet the initial republican response has been one not of jubilation but of uncertainty. Sinn Féin may in fact be experiencing a sense of loss as its familiar and long-successful arguments have been removed by Blair with almost surgical precision. His operation was described by one observer yesterday as something of a controlled experiment. As he tests whether the republicans are serious about peace he does so in a transparent manner, eschewing secret meetings with the republicans in favour of openly announced contacts, and publishing his correspondence to them.

The methodology is almost as important as the substance, for with his open manner Blair has generated new funds of trust with important elements such as the Irish government, John Hume and the Clinton administration. Where John Major was always dogged by the charge that he was in hock to unionist MPs, Tony Blair is already establishing a reputation for proceeding in good faith. This is doing the republicans no good at all, since they are much more at home with a confrontational, hectoring prime minister than with a reasonable and obliging one. The republican publicity and propaganda machine may now need re-programming. The real test for republicans may come in the second half of next month, assuming that Drumcree passes without developing into major catastrophe.

Although Blair refrained from spelling out a deadline in a challenging fashion, entry into talks in mid-September requires a ceasefire by the end of July. The IRA and Sinn Féin could opt to play it long but there is no evident advantage in delaying a ceasefire until, say, next year rather than calling one next month. It is unlikely that the terms of entry would be any more favourable to republicans then.

The real test for unionism will come possibly at Drumcree but certainly by mid-September, when it should start to become obvious whether David Trimble is to shape up as an unyielding tribal warrior or a leader capable of working out a historic new accommodation with Irish nationalists. If there is no IRA ceasefire, the talks will begin without Sinn Féin, with Trimble and Hume under pressure to do real business together. That will be difficult enough, but talks with Sinn Féin present will represent a huge challenge to unionism. Ian Paisley and his allies will immediately exit, leaving Trimble to decide whether to stay on as the republicans walk in or to join the Paisleyite exodus.

Remaining would represent a huge step for a party which has traditionally regarded Sinn Féin as irreformable cheerleaders for IRA violence; but going means consigning the Protestant community to the wilderness, with potentially dangerous consequences. The decision would truly be a defining moment.

Thus the coming months may substantiate or demolish some of the most fundamental theories underlying the Northern Ireland question, including whether republicans are capable of delivering peace and whether unionists can reach accommodation with nationalists. But although May of next year has now been set as a deadline for political progress, most observers – and participants – will be amazed if any deal has been hammered out by then, whether or not Sinn Féin is part of the negotiations.

In the meantime most attention will focus on whether or not the IRA will cease fire again. Most immediately the republicans will want cast-iron guarantees that the de-commissioning card cannot be pulled from the pack by unionists during negotiations in a way which could see Sinn Féin ejected from the talks. If that assurance is given, then the last of Sinn Féin's technicalities will have disappeared.

What will remain, however, is the miasma of mistrust which has for so long enveloped politics, the peace process and indeed everyday life in Northern Ireland. This comes not just from the dread of Drumcree but also from the IRA's mistrust of all things and all politicians British, and from the poisonous state of community relations. Two huge forces are at work here, pulling in opposite directions, both stemming mainly from the troubles. One is the desire for peace, based in large part on the shared experience of a quarter-century of conflict with the lesson, learned the hard way, that there will be no absolute victory for any side. But another is that quarter-century's baleful legacy of mistrust and ill-will, which has left the two communities poles apart. The next few months will help answer the nagging question of which of these forces will prevail, and whether the people of Northern Ireland can ever learn to live together, if not in harmony then at least in peace.

July brought intensive activity. Though the IRA response was still unreadable, republican demands had been met, and meanwhile Drumcree 3 arrived.

Preparations by the Orange Order for the highlight of the marching season included the blocking of key roads and a wave of marches intended to swamp the police. A senior Orangeman privately admitted: "The idea is to try to stretch the security forces to such an extent that they can't control things."

Attempts by Mo Mowlam to avert another Drumcree clash ended in failure. On 1 July a threat was made in the name of the Loyalist Volunteer Force, which was headed by Billy Wright, who had led a breakaway from the UVF. Civilians in the Irish Republic would be killed if the Orangemen were not allowed through Garvaghy Road, they said.

This year the RUC did not attempt to stop the Orangemen, simply pushing the march through. Beginning at 3.30 am on the morning of 6 July, up to 2,000 troops and police with more than 100 armoured vehicles sealed off Garvaghy Road. In the early afternoon they escorted 1,200 marchers past angry protesters.

Rioting broke out in Catholic districts throughout Northern Ireland but was clearly restrained to some degree by republican pressure. There was more tension, however, with the prospect of major disturbances during the Orange

Twelfth of July marches. But then the Orange Order made an unexpected move.

Ulster rides a rollercoaster of relief and fear

In Northern Ireland these days one emotion has hardly time to take root before it is rudely shouldered out of the way by another. The dread before Drumcree was afterwards replaced by depression; yesterday it was suddenly superseded by an exultant euphoria. The hope is that the huge sense of relief generated by the Orange Order's dramatic decision not to press ahead with four contentious marches will endure, and will not be abruptly supplanted by some less pleasant feeling.

That decision transformed the atmosphere – "Do you know," said one woman wonderingly, "people are walking up and down the Lisburn Road smiling." Protestants seemed as pleased as Catholics, though there is a political shadow for them in the fear that another piece of their Protestant heritage has been chipped away. The Orange decision was breathtaking in that it came out of the blue, and in that it had so few precedents in the Order's two-century history, a history characterised much more by the single-minded determination to march than by any pragmatic flexibility.

Instead of assembling in Londonderry where thousands of Bogsiders were prepared to stage protests, up to 20,000 Orangemen will instead gather at nearby Limavady, where there is no chance of confrontation. In Belfast the march scheduled for the bitterly contested Lower Ormeau has simply been called off, together with two other more minor parades elsewhere.

While the decision was taken by many of the Order's senior figures, yesterday brought signs of serious dissension in the ranks. In particular, the important County Grand Lodge of Belfast deplored the move, calling on David

81

Trimble to lead the Ulster Unionist party out of political talks in protest. He is unlikely to do so on this issue.

Joel Patton of the militant Spirit of Drumcree ginger group issued a direct challenge to the Orange leadership, which he accused of showing "complete incompetency and cowardice". His call for Orangemen to "make their views known at the demonstrations" may lead to heckling at today's parades and will provide a test of the strength of feeling in the grassroots. The Reverend Ian Paisley, who is not himself an Orangeman but has influence in the ranks, was furious: it was a complete and total sell-out, a decision of surrender; it was Munich 1938 all over again.

The decision appears to have been taken primarily on security grounds rather than political considerations. When RUC Chief Constable Ronnie Flanagan was invited on Thursday to the House of Orange, the Order's Belfast headquarters, he delivered a sobering and highly convincing security assessment. It may have gone something like this: that with up to 75,000 Orangemen on the move right across Northern Ireland, there simply are not enough police and troops to guarantee their safety and the maintenance of public order. With Orangemen mustering at 18 major centres, there will be scores of "feeder" marches before the main demonstrations and scores more afterwards as they parade homewards. There was the possibility of clashes with various nationalist residents' groups; the possibility of the small but ruthless Irish National Liberation Army shooting at Orangemen; the possibility that disorder which began at one spot could spread all over. With the security forces at full stretch, the nightmare scenario was that of unpoliced sectarian clashes.

Noel Ligget, who as district master of Ballynafeigh was a key figure in deciding to abandon the Lower Ormeau parade, spelled out some of this when he said: "In the past I have been very sceptical of Mr Flanagan, but he clearly indicated to us that there were elements within the republican community who were looking to create the maximum amount of civil disorder. The final bottom line was that there was a significant opportunity of a loss of life, and at the end of the day we felt under those circumstances it would not be right to proceed with the parade."

The decision leaves many issues unresolved: a pessimist might point out that the Order preferred to make a unilateral decision, even one that went right against all its cherished traditions, rather than enter into dialogue with nationalists. But last night most in Belfast were simply overjoyed that the decision went a long way to ensuring that the Twelfth could pass off without major disorder.

That was certainly the overwhelming sentiment yesterday at St Malachy's Catholic church, close to the Lower Ormeau, where a congregation gathered for a mass of thanksgiving for the unexpected Orange decision. Father

Anthony Curran said it was "a wonderful decision, a great move and everybody in this community will be delighted". It is not often that a Catholic priest acclaims a decision of the Orange Order as a miracle, but that was exactly the word Father Curran used: a miracle.

Then, a bare week after the Twelfth, came a broad hint from Gerry Adams that a new ceasefire was imminent, a move which for most observers came out of the blue. The decisive factor for the IRA had evidently been Tony Blair's decision to abandon John Major's stress on de-commissioning before negotiation began. When the ceasefire came reactions were muted.

21 JULY 1997   THE INDEPENDENT

Mistrust mars Ulster hopes

Nobody in Northern Ireland was indifferent to the IRA cessation of violence which came into effect at noon yesterday; but nearly everyone pretended to be. Most people simply stayed home, lounged in the garden or visited the pub or the supermarket: no cheers went up, no champagne popped, no church bells rang. It was a most understated ceasefire.

If few emotions were expressed it was not because they did not exist: rather it was that there were too many of them, and that they went too deep. There is hope for the future, relief and a deep desire for peace; but there is also bitterness, suspicion, fear and even rejection.

There was the saintly father of a murdered Catholic girl who, in the depths of his grief, found the courage to say he would be elated if she were the last victim of the troubles. Born as she was in 1978, the previous ceasefire was the nearest thing to peace she ever knew.

But the experience of that last cessation in 1994 was that a ceasefire is only a beginning. It might be consolidated into lasting peace but it might not: the last one lasted 17 months, and no one is betting on how long this one might endure. The effect of the last one was to drastically decrease the killing rate, to bring new hope where there was none, to give a glimpse of a new and brighter future. But the rate of deaths was only reduced, not ended.

It did not end the so-called punishment beatings; it did not lead to the dismantling of the paramilitary organisations, republican or loyalist; it did not remove the poisons that pollute community relations; it did not bring a political settlement into being. Many unionists will say in fact that it was bogus; though most nationalists will retort that an imperfect ceasefire still had great worth. The arguments over those points, familiar from 1994, have already resurfaced.

There was no euphoria yesterday, but then people have forgotten that there was none in 1994 either. The *Independent* recorded at the time: "People did not dance in the streets. They said, 'I'll believe it when I see it.' They said, 'I wonder what the murdering bastards will get out of it.' They said, 'It's a con.'"

The IRA is putting the same deal on the table again: soldiers and police and town centres and Canary Wharf are no longer at risk, but the organisation will not disband or hand over guns and will never say that the cessation is permanent. London and Dublin have accepted these terms; the Protestant and unionist community is wondering whether it should too.

In the meantime there will be a sharp rise in political discord as unionist politicians decide whether to sit at the table with Sinn Féin or whether to risk walking into the wilderness: each course carries huge risks. Yesterday seemed, however, to be mostly a day for quiet contemplation rather than heated controversy or excitement.

Up the Falls Road just after midday Tom Hartley of Sinn Féin told a crowd of less than a hundred outside a heavily fortified RUC base: "We choose to mark the first minutes of the ceasefire here because the ceasefire will bring our freedom, will bring the realisation of our hopes and our aspirations, will bring equality, will bring the release of prisoners. When you look around the crowd here today you see in so many of our faces the hopes for the future."

The faces did indeed reflect some hope but there no euphoria in sight. He did not promise them that this promised land would be achieved quickly; if he had, they would not have believed him. Instead, they, like everyone else, hoped that a start had been made and that this cessation would be longer and more productive than the last. But they also conveyed that the road, wherever it led, would be a long and arduous one, with no one knowing exactly where it would lead.

Furthermore, that success will entail from every side compromise on fundamental positions of a type which Northern Ireland has never yet seen: there is no other way. This sobering knowledge helps explain why it was such a subdued ceasefire.

The spotlight now fell on David Trimble, leader of the Ulster Unionists, the largest of the Protestant parties.

22 JULY 1997 THE INDEPENDENT

Will he stick his neck out for peace?

Twenty-two years ago a much younger and clearly more naïve David Trimble stuck his neck out in a bold move aimed at making a historic deal with Northern Ireland nationalists. He promptly had his head chopped off by the Reverend Ian Paisley. He and a small number of unionist politicians – most of whom had, oddly enough, previously been known as hardliners – broke ranks with the unionist mainstream to suggest a system of "voluntary coalition". Under this modest proposal a unionist prime minister would invite nationalists into his cabinet and thus in effect set up a powersharing administration.

The idea of having Catholics and nationalists in government was too much

David Trimble, late convert to the peace process

for the leadership of unionism, and when the plan was revealed the wrath of Paisley and other loyalist leaders was terrible to behold. Trimble and his associates were denounced, anathematised and pilloried.

Although then only a minor figure, Trimble incurred Paisley's particular anger when, speaking at the final session of the Northern Ireland constitutional convention, he closed his speech with the words: "We should look for our brave men in prisons and for the fools among politicians." White and trembling, Paisley got to his feet to deliver the most extraordinary personal attack on Trimble. When Paisley refused to give way uproar ensued, Trimble and his colleagues walking out.

They walked out to oblivion: their party, the Vanguard Unionists, split in two and fell apart. Although Trimble quietly joined the Ulster Unionist party a few years later, his record told against him. Even though he was obviously one of the party's most articulate, energetic and best-educated members, it was not until 1990 that he found a Westminster seat. That done, it took only five years for him to become leader and two more to come to his present dilemma. Once again, he is at the point of choosing between far-reaching negotiation or of aligning his party with the nay-sayers led still by Ian Paisley.

His years in the wilderness must prey on his mind, together with the recognition that Paisley still retains the power to savage unionists who step outside the laager. But he also knows that unionism is in need of modernisation, that Tony Blair's peace train is just about to pull out of the station, and that the outside world will not easily forgive a refusal to take part in this determined bid to end the troubles.

Trimble is almost a child of those troubles. Born in Belfast in 1944, he was studying law at Queen's University in the late 1960s when some of his fellow students took to the streets as part of the civil rights movement. He took no prominent part in events and, having taken a first-class law degree, stayed on at Queen's as a lecturer. His first foray into politics came in the early 1970s when he joined Vanguard, an unusual entity which was part political party and part attempt to draw some of the splintered shards of loyalism under one umbrella. The irony is that Vanguard's *raison d'être* was its belief that the Ulster Unionist party (which Trimble now leads) was too soft.

Vanguard's leader was Bill Craig, a controversial figure who in 1968 had been sacked from his Stormont cabinet post by the reforming Ulster Unionist prime minister Terence O'Neill. He seemed to stand for unyielding opposition to the civil rights movement and for a readiness to challenge the British government's authority over Northern Ireland. Freed from the responsibilities of office, Craig flirted with some loyalist paramilitary organisations including the Ulster Defence Association, which was declared illegal in 1992. Advocating a semi-independent Northern Ireland, he alarmed the authorities in 1972 by staging a series of Oswald Mosley-style "monster rallies", arriving complete with motorcycle outriders to inspect thousands of men drawn up in military-style formation.

What Craig said at the rallies and elsewhere was even more alarming. In a series of what became known as the "shoot-to-kill" speeches he openly threatened the use of force, declaring: "We must build up dossiers on those men and women in this country who are a menace to this country because one of these days, if and when the politicians fail us, it may be our job to liquidate the enemy." Addressing a meeting of the Monday Club, he added: "When we say force we mean force. We will only assassinate our enemies as a last desperate resort when we are denied our democratic rights." Asked if he meant the killing of all Catholics, he replied: "It might not go so far as that but it could go as far as killing."

There were calls for Craig's prosecution: some argued he was giving voice to legitimate Protestant anger, while others complained he was fanning the flames of violence. Whether the shoot-to-kill speeches were cause or effect, almost 500 people died that year, the worst death toll of the troubles, as loyalist violence augmented that of the IRA.

While some grainy black-and-white television footage survives showing Trimble perched on the corner of Vanguard platforms, he was in those days a figure too minor to attract attention. And while his leader was making such hair-raising remarks, the newspapers of the time carry no trace of Trimble personally endorsing such sentiments. His own contributions of the time tend more to the pedantic than the inflammatory.

Two years later he supported the 1974 loyalist strike, during which Protestants, including paramilitaries, took over the streets of Northern Ireland in a direct and successful challenge to the powersharing experiment of the time and indeed to the overall authority of London.

Emerging from such a background, it was all the more surprising that Craig, with Trimble and others in support, should propose a scheme such as voluntary coalition, which amounted to powersharing under another name. One of the mysterious little paradoxes of the history of the troubles, it was the beginning of the end of Craig's career and a severe setback for that of Trimble.

Entering the Ulster Unionist party, his career was comparatively quiet until the Anglo-Irish agreement of 1985. All unionists hated the London–Dublin accord but Trimble, apparently feeling that his party's opposition did not go far enough, became involved in a new organisation, the Ulster Clubs. The Clubs organised street protests and rallies during the tense period of 1985–86, and produced some nice historical ironies. The Clubs picketed the office of unionist MP John Taylor, who is now Trimble's deputy; they were also scathingly denounced by Ken Maginnis MP, now one of his leadership team.

The Ulster Clubs leader, Alan Wright, employed Craig-like rhetoric: "Faced with treachery as we are today, I cannot see anything other than the Ulster people on the streets prepared to use legitimate force." Trimble said at this time that he had no objection in principle to "mobilisation and citizens' army calls", adding: "I would personally draw the line at terrorism and serious violence. But if we are talking about a campaign that involves demonstrations and so on, then a certain element of violence may be inescapable."

While some may regard this as evidence of irresponsibility, it clearly falls far short of any advocacy of violence. The point must also be made that a trawl through the utterances of a great many unionist politicians would produce a great many more examples of statements which verge on the dubious which they made at times of crisis and high tension. But the Irish, north and south, have elephantine political recall and the Trimble record is there. One veteran observer explained: "People have long memories – they remember Vanguard and the Ulster Clubs and all that, and then they hear him going on about IRA de-commissioning and relying on democratic methods alone."

When Harold McCusker died of cancer in 1990 Trimble was not first choice for the safe seat, but following his election, his energy and articulacy made him stand out in a party with notorious communication deficiencies and a high level of geriatric representatives. Even so, he was very much an outsider in the 1995 leadership contest caused by the resignation of James Molyneaux.

Most believe it was the Drumcree factor which won him the prize, the party opting for the man whose uncompromising stand had helped get the 1995 Orange march through in the teeth of police and governmental opposition. Since then his party's identification with Orangeism has deepened as the marching issue has remained highly significant.

The hectic political scene has meant spending less time with Daphne, his second wife, and their three young children in their modest suburban home not far from Belfast. A former student of his, she describes herself as "the domestic backup". For recreation he listens to Wagner, Verdi and Strauss.

But the grand sweeps of opera have yet to provide him with the inspiration for the new vision which, unionists admit, their cause so desperately lacks. Trimble proved effective enough at dealing on a tactical day-to-day basis with a weak Conservative government, but is now being put to the test by a strong Labour administration.

While his career illustrates that he comes from the far-right of unionism, the voluntary coalition episode shows that on at least one occasion he was prepared to contemplate a radical new departure. Last time he did that he was vanquished by Paisley: this time his choice is between taking on Paisley or taking on Tony Blair. It may be the most critical decision of his entire career, past and future.

The atmosphere lightened greatly. Drumcree 1997 had been less disruptive than Drumcree 1996, and now there was a new IRA ceasefire. Suddenly the popular will to see peace established seemed to be winning out over cynicism and near-despair.

A happy ending for Ulster?

Much of the Northern Ireland body politic might presently best be described as bemused, as both players and observers struggle to come to terms with the extraordinary events of recent months. They are also grappling with the biggest question of all: can there be peace? The question is a huge one, dependent on so many permutations, personalities, forces and future events.

The path ahead is strewn with potential crises. There will be many fraught moments. But when all factors have been weighed, and all bets hedged, the answer to the question is: yes, there can be peace in our time. It seems too much to hope that there will be harmony, integration and trust for many years, but, yes, there can be peace.

But equally there are no guarantees, and it is as well to acknowledge the negatives and obstacles in the way. This is, after all, Northern Ireland, which for more than a quarter of a century has stood as an international metaphor for violence, religious bigotry and political intractability.

The IRA ceasefire came as a surprise to most, and no one can predict with complete confidence that it will last. Even if it does, fringe republican groups such as the INLA and Continuity Army Council wait in the wings, ready to pounce on anything that can be presented as a betrayal of traditional republican ideals.

On the extreme Protestant side the loyalist ceasefire may have lasted almost three years, but its stated terms are highly conditional, much more so than those of the IRA. It has also proved an imperfect ceasefire, since the major loyalist groups have broken it to carry out seven killings in the last seven months. The loyalist paramilitary underworld also has its own equivalent of the INLA and CAC, the Loyalist Volunteer Force. This small but dangerous breakaway group, which has already killed two people and staged prison protests, could provide a focus for disgruntled dissident loyalists who may conclude in the months and years ahead that too many concessions are being made to republicans.

On both sides, in other words, the traditional terrorist groups remain out there, their arms un-decommissioned, and with smaller and more militant rivals hovering in the background. The sheer longevity of the conflict has produced a society all too familiar with the gun. The number of men who are or have been in prison for murder approaches 1,000; 10,000 or more have served time for other terrorist-related offences. Thousands more have simply never been caught.

On the legal side of the violence equation, the number of local men who are or have been members of the heavily armed security forces probably exceeds 50,000. Such official resort to the gun may have been necessary, but it is clearly not healthy for a society to have so many imbued with the notion that resolving conflicts is achieved with firearms rather than politics. To that feeling can be added all the other negative sentiments stockpiled in this damaged community: bitterness, bereavement, segregation, the anger and hatred generated by the troubles which have augmented the existing repositories of historical recrimination.

Given all that, where is the hope for peace? The answer lies essentially in the proposition that the troubles have provided not just misery but an education. The argument is that lessons have been learned the hard way, and that such lessons are often the most valuable of all.

It has been established that both sides have developed self-replicating para-military structures with a flow of recruits ready to replace those imprisoned or killed. Neither the IRA nor the loyalists were actually compelled to go on ceasefire: both could have fought on. Yet both seem to have been affected by the widespread feeling that, while more years of terrorism were possible, they were unlikely to advance the cause of either. Both sides proved their ability to kill and to suffer losses; but along the way the feeling took root that neither would achieve eventual victory. The air became permeated with a sense of mutual unbeatability. And the stalemate and stand-off gradually gave way to an understanding, in many quarters, that if victory was not in prospect then the logic pointed to some sort of negotiated settlement. To this was added a palpable sense of relief that while the war could go on for ever it might not have to, and that a retreat from terrorism, if it could be effected without loss of face, was highly desirable.

As with so much else of the political agenda since the late 1960s, the peace process developed from the Irish nationalist side. It was therefore hardly sur-prising that it was regarded with much suspicion and scepticism by unionists. It still is, though it has had a deep effect on the thinking of many Protestants. Those most opposed were senior unionist politicians, some of whom were clearly more comfortable dealing with IRA terrorism than with Sinn Féin's political gambits. But unionist political denunciation of the peace process does not tell the whole story of the present Protestant state of mind. Most senior loyalist paramilitaries, for example, now approve of that process: this does not mean they are about to buy rounds of drinks for Gerry Adams and Martin McGuinness, but the years of imprisonment and loss of colleagues has produced an empathy with the republicans. This has translated into a willingness to talk to Sinn Féin.

Most of the Protestant population seem to favour engagement in talks together with Sinn Féin. Although many believe the republicans should continue to be held at one remove, this is in itself a remarkable state of affairs, since in the last five years no major unionist political figure has advocated negotiations with Sinn Féin. Thus Protestants at large have become more flexible than their political leaders, and willing to contemplate steps which are without precedent in their history. It also seems to show that something of the philosophy behind the peace process is taking root, principally the sense that a settlement which excludes a significant section of society is unlikely to work.

The trick in the negotiations ahead may be to amplify this still controversial premise into one of the central foundations of a new political disposition. Sinn Féin is not about to get a united Ireland; unionism is not about to get a strengthened union with Britain. The only logical common ground would therefore seem to lie in an equality agenda in which the rights of all were protected.

But there is a long way to go before it comes to that. The political talks are due to reconvene in Belfast on 15 September. Assuming the IRA ceasefire holds, Sinn Féin will be there, leaving David Trimble to decide whether or not to take the Ulster Unionists into the same conference room as Sinn Féin. At present the betting is that he will not lead his party into the same room, but the betting is also that he will not walk away from the process. The immediate outcome could therefore be proximity talks, a form of dialogue at a distance. But the talks will go ahead, in whatever format, Tony Blair having laid down that he wants agreement by May 1998. Few believe that he will get it, but by May it should be apparent whether real engagement is taking place.

If, however, the talks remain bogged down in the all-too-familiar procedural trench warfare, the government may resort to the option of thrashing out a new agreement with Dublin, to be presented to the parties at a later date. Nobody wants to talk up the idea that the talks are doomed to failure, but it has to be pointed out that so many previous rounds of inter-party talks did not succeed. (The sole exception, in 1974, produced an agreement which lasted less than six months.)

But the optimists contend that this time it could be different. For one thing, the strength of Labour's majority and the fact that it is likely to be in power for at least two terms gives Tony Blair an authority that John Major lacked. For another, all the previous negotiations took place against an atmosphere of continuing violence: the expectations of the two communities were low, and those parties who exhibited intransigence suffered no electoral penalty for doing so.

This time, the theory goes, there could be a new magic ingredient: peace. If the ceasefires hold, there will be progressively more confidence in them and steadily increasing hope that they can be maintained. In these circumstances the parties might experience more and more communal compulsion to stay at the table and do real business. The public mood would be against walk outs and obstructiveness, since these could endanger the peace.

Conflicts of nationality are notoriously difficult to settle and there is still no precise answer in sight to the question of how to reconcile a tradition which wants to be Irish with another which is determined to stay British. Huge questions remain on how far unionism and nationalism might be prepared to compromise.

But five years ago few dreamt that it could get as far as this, with ceasefires in place and talks in prospect. There will undoubtedly be much turbulence ahead, but there could also be a powerful new sentiment from the grassroots. This is the feeling that while their unionism and their nationalism are important, so too is the necessity of hammering out the type of deal necessary to ensure that the war does not break out all over again.

After months of uncertainty David Trimble finally took the plunge, leading his troops into the same talks building as Sinn Féin.

Unionist standard-bearers square up to Sinn Féin

The Ulster Unionist at the gate, wearing a pin-stripe suit and holding an incongruous can of Coke, got the message to his party colleagues that Gerry Adams and Sinn Féin had safely entered the talks building. The coast was clear. The cheerful Stormont gatekeeper swung open the big gate and in they flowed, a tight slow-moving phalanx of 30 men and a couple of women, the standard-bearers of Ulster unionism on their way to confront Sinn Féin.

David Trimble led the way, flanked by MPs John Taylor and Ken Maginnis, walking determinedly towards the massed ranks of the media. He had, as they say up the Shankill, brought backings with him, for he led in not just his own party but also the two small but important loyalist groupings, the PUP and UDP. They made their way towards the second gate at a suitably dignified pace, then Trimble paused to tell the cameras: "We are not here to negotiate with Sinn Féin but to confront them – to expose their fascist character. Unionism will not be marginalised."

Unknown to Trimble a Sinn Féin representative leaned in from the edge of the media scrum to hear his words, with what looked suspiciously like the trace of a smile playing about his lips. He seemed pleased at the UUP leader's words, signifying as they did that a face-to-face encounter was not far off.

David Ervine of the PUP said a few words and then so did the UDP's Gary McMichael, whose father John, a loyalist paramilitary leader, was killed 10 years ago by the IRA. Then without further ceremony they flowed through the doors that would lead them into talks.

Close up, it seemed less like a bold radical initiative than a reluctant bowing to the inevitable. With John Major in power, the UUP spent many months successfully fending off contact with the republicans; the change came when Tony Blair took over. Yesterday the party was caught in a pincer movement, one part of which was the unrelenting pressure from the government to get into talks. The other part came from underneath – from, astonishingly, the once legendary intractable loyalist grassroots.

First, an opinion poll showed 93 per cent of the party's supporters wanted talks, and then, at Saturday's meeting of the party executive, more than 30 of the 36 speakers urged dialogue. Together these forces made entry into the talks an imperative which even the bombing two days ago in Markethill, County Armagh, could not deflect.

The Reverend Ian Paisley's party remains aloof from the process, accusing Trimble of caving in and being "terrorised to the talks table". But the loyalist paramilitary hardliners, who are in a position to attack the talks with much more than mere rhetoric, were there with Trimble, ready to talk.

The three-party arrangement represented a display of unionist and loyalist solidarity, though it did so at some cost to the arguments Trimble will use in the talks when he insists on arms de-commissioning. In the ranks of his phalanx were four men who committed seven murders and served long sentences for them. Though known now as politicos, the illegal groups which their parties represent are as adamant as the IRA that no guns will be de-commissioned this side of a settlement.

Ken Maginnis seemed his usual affable self during the long walk, but the day must have been difficult for him, since the IRA tried to kill him on five separate occasions. He has been an IRA target for more than a quarter of a century, first as a member of the Ulster Defence Regiment and then as an MP. He lost many friends and colleagues to IRA bombs, but yesterday he walked into Stormont to sit down at the table and see whether he could do business with republicans, wondering along with everyone else whether through talks the hurt might some day be replaced with hope.

For many of the participants, the talks meant unaccustomed and unwelcome proximity, and potentially painful confrontation.

Behind every seat at the peace table stands a ghost

Cormac McCabe was a County Tyrone headmaster and friend of unionist MP Ken Maginnis: both men also served as part-time members of the Ulster Defence Regiment. One day in 1974, as McCabe was dining in a hotel with his wife and physically handicapped daughter, IRA gunmen took him away and shot him dead.

Now at Stormont in Belfast, Maginnis is at the negotiating table along with Sinn Féin, whom he bluntly describes as "unreconstructed terrorists", in talks aimed at working out a better future for Northern Ireland. Quite a few of those at the table can recall the names of friends, colleagues and relatives killed in the troubles; they can also glance round the room and see people whom they hold responsible for deaths. Dealing with this proximity can be difficult.

Ken Maginnis recalled: "I have a deep, deep bitterness about the IRA. I think I have lost almost all my closest friends in the UDR. I lost my company sergeant-major; I lost Cormac, who used to come round to the house quite a lot; George Shaw, who took me to my first scout camp; Eric Shiels, who I was very friendly with in the rugby club – all decent, dependable fellows. There are lots more who come to mind. I don't see my presence at Stormont as staying in the talks with Sinn Féin, but rather as refusing to give up political ground. It's not a question of spite, it's a question of disgust. I could never give cognisance to them, not as long as I live."

Gary McMichael, leader of the UDP, suffered even more directly at the hands of the IRA: almost exactly 10 years ago his father, John McMichael, was killed by the republicans. Gary, who was 18 at the time, said yesterday: "It's very, very difficult for me, because they not only killed my father but also my best friend, and three years ago they tried to kill me.

"That obviously makes it more difficult to even be in the room with representatives of those people, never mind engage in any form of negotiation with them. But it's actually that suffering that makes us take the line that we do, and makes us go that extra mile to try and remove the threat against the community for ever. That means that we have to tackle republicanism, because we know that if we walk away from this process, there's going to be another stage of conflict, that others will have to go through what we've gone through."

One of the features of the Northern Ireland conflict, however, is that victims often have their own victims. John McMichael was one of the leaders of the paramilitary UDA, which itself killed more than 400 people. Today Gary's party represents the UDA at the table. One of those killed by the UDA was Paddy Wilson, an SDLP politician who died in 1973, the victim of a frenzied knife attack in which he was stabbed 32 times. The man who killed him was caught and jailed for life. But he has now been released and today, as one of the UDA's political representatives, he sits in the talks right next to the SDLP, almost literally rubbing shoulders with the party he attacked so violently a quarter of a century ago. Among the loyalists present, in fact, are four men who have served life sentences for murder, for killing a total of seven people.

Meanwhile Sinn Féin, which sits on the other side of the SDLP, bears the brunt of loyalist and unionist condemnation of republican violence. Yet the party has itself been on the receiving end of violence, at least 18 members or relatives of members being killed during the early 1990s. One of its talks delegates, Alex Maskey, was a favourite target for loyalists. In 1986 the UDA shot him: "I got a sawn-off shotgun blast in the stomach. I lost half a kidney, half my bowel, half my stomach and I still have shrapnel inside me," he said yesterday. "I also had my house petrol-bombed by loyalists – I had to drag my kids out of bed and down a burning hallway. That was very traumatic for them." In 1993 he and a friend, Alan Lundy, a father of five children, were building a new security porch on his home when the loyalists arrived again. UDA gunmen pursued Lundy through the house before shooting him dead in front of Maskey's two teenage sons, another traumatic experience.

According to Maskey: "All too often people talk as if only one side has a monopoly on suffering. I'm here trying to reach out to people associated with organisations who spent a considerable amount of time and energy trying to assassinate me. I'm trying to get on with people who tried to murder me, and that's because I want to make sure others don't have to endure the suffering that we have. We now have an opportunity to break the log jam."

Many of those in Stormont have thus brought a good deal of personal as well as political grievances with them into the negotiating room. If the talks are to be successful, the hope is they will not only make political progress but also make a start on laying so many troubled spirits to rest.

The talks moved slowly. On 13 October Tony Blair arrived at Stormont for formal meetings with the party leaders, trying to provide fresh impetus. His handshake with Gerry Adams was the first between a British prime minister and a republican leader since the 1920s. The same period had also seen the last meeting between republicans and unionists, an altogether more colourful business than Stormont in the autumn of 1997.

24 SEPTEMBER & 14 OCTOBER 1997   THE INDEPENDENT

A bunch of toughs, a bottle of Guinness, aristocratic sex, and the odd de Valera lecture on Irish history

The tale of the last time Ulster Unionists formally met republicans, three-quarters of a century ago, involves political drama, a great deal of violence, several bottles of Guinness and a certain amount of sex. In 1921, with killings going on in both parts of Ireland, James Craig, prime minister of the fledgling Northern Ireland state, courageously placed himself in the hands of the IRA to meet Eamon de Valera in Dublin.

Escorted by what he described as "three of the worst looking toughs I have ever seen", Craig was brought to de Valera in Dublin. It was an awkward encounter, not least because of the fact that a duplicitous British official had told each man that the other had requested the meeting.

De Valera recalled: "I said after the first few moments' silence, 'Well?' I then said, 'I'm too old at this political business to have nonsense of this kind, each waiting for the other to begin', and I started putting our case to him." De Valera launched into one of his legendary protracted reviews of Irish history, Craig later recounting that after half an hour he "had reached the end of the era of Brian Boru". The meeting came to nothing, Craig judging de Valera "impossible".

A series of more promising meetings took place the following year between Craig and Michael Collins. Winston Churchill, as colonial secretary, brought them together, later recording: "They met in my room at the Colonial Office which, despite its enormous size, seemed overcharged with electricity. They both glowered magnificently but after a short, commonplace talk I slipped away upon some excuse and left them together. What these two Irishmen, separated by such gulfs of religion, sentiment, and conduct, said to each other I cannot tell."

Churchill sent them in for lunch not only mutton chops but also several bottles of Guinness, apparently ignorant of the fact that Collins did not like porter. Even without its lubricating qualities, however, Craig and Collins unexpectedly succeeded in reaching agreement on a number of issues. According to Craig's account, he asked Collins "straight out whether it was his intention to have peace in Ireland or whether we were to go on with murder and strife, rivalry and boycott and unrest in Northern Ireland". Collins, he reported, "made it clear that he wanted a real peace, but hoping to coax her [Northern Ireland] into a union later".

Within days, however, the accord was swamped by escalating violence. Two further meetings were held, the second producing a detailed agreement headed by the striking statement: "Peace is today declared." Once again, however, the tide of violence swept the agreement aside as the south degenerated into civil war.

The element of sex in the tale came from the exotic Anglo-Irish Londonderry family. Craig was accompanied at the final meeting by Lord Londonderry, a member of his cabinet, who also met Collins privately and later enthused: "I can say at once that I spent three of the most delightful hours that I ever spent in my life."

Londonderry may not have known that his wife had formed a close and apparently sexual attachment to Collins. In a passionate letter Collins wrote to her of her husband: "I contrast myself with him, my uncouthness with his distinction, my rough speech with his unconscious breeding and the worst of it is I like and admire him and feel that he is brave and honest." The 1920s meetings contain many echoes of modern politics but seem to offer few historical lessons, apart, perhaps, from the general point that busy politicians should keep an eye on their spouses.

The last occasion when a British prime minister formally met leaders of Sinn Féin was in 1921, Lloyd George seeing first Eamon de Valera and later Michael Collins, on each occasion in London. At four one-on-one meetings de Valera treated Lloyd George to extensive displays of his legendary gifts for verbosity and ambiguity, his lengthy account of England's historic wrongs against Ireland leaving the prime minister, by one account, "white and exhausted".

Nonetheless the PM was quite taken by Dev, summing him up to a confidant as "a nice man, honest, astonishingly little vocabulary, wants to settle but afraid of his followers". The PM had made special preparations for the meeting, his secretary (and lover) recording in her diary: "I have never seen him so excited as he was before de Valera arrived. I could see he was working out the best way of dealing with de Valera – as I told him afterwards, he was bringing up all his guns."

Lloyd George, in a move which could hardly be described as subtle, had the cabinet room decked out with a huge map of the world emphasising the large areas which then belonged to the British empire. De Valera, however, resolutely refused to be impressed. In their talks Lloyd George could get few straight answers from him, remarking with exasperation that negotiating with him was "like trying to pick up mercury with a fork".

Their discussions ended without agreement but later in the year a full republican negotiating team arrived in London, this time dominated by Michael Collins. Collins arrived armed with a study of Lloyd George provided by a senior British legal figure who knew the PM well. This assessed Lloyd George as follows: "He sees in a flash the essentials of a situation for immediate political purposes. He is adroit, tireless, energetic and daring, with uncanny intuition. He would like to go down in history under big names, possibly as the man who made peace between England and Ireland."

The two men did not get on, Collins finding Lloyd George "particularly obnoxious". The PM originally judged the republican to be "undoubtedly a considerable person", but he later changed this opinion, dismissing him as "an uneducated, rather stupid man".

A problem arose when some British ministers did not wish to shake hands with the Sinn Féin delegation, regarding them as murderers. To deal with this Lloyd George alone shook hands with the republicans. He then introduced them to his ministers across the cabinet table, the broad expanse of which made handshakes impossible.

Lloyd George never managed to establish working relationships with republicans, though Collins went on to develop useful relations with ministers such as Winston Churchill and Lord Birkenhead. But the talks exercise was in republican terms disastrous, leading as it did to the signing of the Anglo-Irish treaty, the split within republicanism, the death of Collins and the cementing of the partition of Ireland.

It took some months for John Hume to decide he would not put himself forward as a candidate for president of the Irish Republic in succession to Mary Robinson, who had moved on to an important United Nations post in Geneva. Another northerner, however, was to dominate the contest.

8 OCTOBER 1997   THE INDEPENDENT

Does Ireland's destiny lie with a woman from the north?

With Mary Robinson now in Geneva as UN commissioner for human rights, the clear favourite to succeed her as president of the Irish Republic is a woman whose Belfast home was once machine-gunned by loyalists. The Republic may be on the point of choosing, for the first time ever, a woman from the north to be its president. The election of Mary McAleese would signify that the south is in the process of losing some of its aversion towards the violent north. Her election would not be popular with northern unionists, for it would represent the most visible sign yet of the northern Catholic minority's power, abilities and potential. But it would be a landmark, both north and south, in symbolising both how much unionism has lost and how far nationalists have advanced.

Northerner who made good in the south: Mary McAleese, whose journey took her from Ardoyne to the Irish presidency

Mary McAleese is a highly complex woman. Once highly supportive of the Catholic church, she has more recently been a trenchant critic. A child of the troubles who comes from the once politically impotent Belfast ghetto Catholicism, she has risen to become one of the city's most influential women.

The shooting attack came when she was a teenager in Ardoyne, one of Belfast's most violent districts. She once recalled: "My brother, who is deaf, was very badly beaten by a bunch of thugs at our front door. Then they shot dead our neighbour, Gerry Kelly, in his shop. We thought we might get petrol-bombed but in fact they emptied the contents of two machine guns through the windows. It was just God's mercy none of us was killed."

The family fled the district. Professor McAleese, now 47 and married with three children, studied law at Queen's University Belfast, then at a young age became Reid professor of law at Trinity College Dublin, succeeding Mary Robinson in the post. She went on to become a familiar face as a broadcaster with RTÉ in Dublin.

Some who had casually assumed her to be a liberal feminist were startled when, in the Republic's bitterly fought battles over abortion and divorce in the 1980s, she took on the role of loyal supporter of the Catholic hierarchy. One hostile newspaper called her a "seductive siren of the status quo", its cartoon depicting her brandishing a flag emblazoned "Guardian of Irish morality".

Her evident ability and articulacy held out the promise of a southern political career, but when she stood for Fianna Fáil in 1987 she was defeated and later that year returned to academic life in the north. The job she took up, as director of the Institute of Legal Studies at Queen's University, was important for a number of reasons. The first was that Catholics, and Catholic women, were not normally appointed to such key posts; the second was that the candidate she defeated, the only other person on the short-list, was David Trimble, then a law lecturer.

The fact that the job went to a nationalist woman rather than a unionist man did not spark off huge publicity, but it sent shock waves through the Protestant establishment. A senior professor at Queen's later described the university's background: "Historically, Queen's has been perceived as a Protestant university and some people believe that Queen's should remain a bastion of unionism." There were, literally, questions in the House, with four MPs from Trimble's party questioning McAleese's suitability for the post in the Commons. Some years later Trimble returned to the attack, alleging that two further promotions she won were perceived as "a response to political nationalism and to some extent to pressure from Dublin and elsewhere".

The McAleese response was brisk: "The distillation of those questions was really – why was this Roman Catholic getting this job? There is a type of unionist who simply cannot bear the thought of any Catholic getting anywhere on their own merits. It is a frightening prospect for them."

When the university ran into deep trouble over religious imbalances in its workforce it turned to Mary McAleese, among others, to supervise a wide-ranging affirmative action programme. Some of the inequities, and much of the old ethos, have now gone: "We've brought about seismic cultural change here," she later said.

Judging from her public utterances, seismic change was also the order of the day in her views on religious matters. The person who in the mid-1980s seemed the bishops' favourite woman was, like so many Irish Catholics, outraged by the wave of scandals which swept through the church. While her personal attachment to her religion is as strong as ever, she has in recent years been merciless in her criticism of her church's handling of child abuse cases. She denounced "a shabby bleak procession of Pontius Pilate look-alikes, abusing priests, disinterested abbots, impotent cardinals and unempowered parents".

In an interview with the *Independent* she said of the Irish hierarchy: "They have very old, rather seigneurial, magisterial ways of dealing with problems. But the world now is infinitely more democratic, infinitely more intelligent, more questioning and challenging than the world they're equipped for."

Yet another seismic change may be indicated by the fact that she is clear favourite, and is standing with the support of both parties in the south's governing coalition, Fianna Fáil and the Progressive Democrats. Until now the southern electorate has been decidedly leery of northerners, with the conspicuous exception of John Hume. When Austin Currie, another northern nationalist, unsuccessfully ran for the presidency in 1990 his party's research identified his northern background as the strongest negative element being held against him. Currie recently wrote that he understood why this should be: "The Provo murder campaign, unionist intransigence, the 1974 Dublin–Monaghan bombings and the sense of continuing vulnerability, the cost in financial terms, the threat to jobs and tourism, northerners taking southern jobs, the fact that not all northerners are likable people – is it surprising that some say to me they would like to see Northern Ireland towed to mid-Atlantic and sunk?"

So far at least Professor McAleese's northern background is not being held against her, a sign perhaps that the ceasefires and the peace process have softened attitudes and made the south more welcoming towards northerners. Some observers predict that anti-northern feeling may yet well up, however, to deny her victory.

A victory for Mary McAleese will have no bearing on the fact that many unionists are unable to cope with the new breed of confident, articulate middle-class northern nationalists which she typifies. But southerners may finally be ready for a northerner, and one whose life has reflected so much of Ireland's recent eventful and often traumatic history.

Reprinted in the Belfast News Letter

The election of Mary McAleese pointed to a new southern openness towards northerners.

One woman shows southerners they have new friends in the north

Although the president of the Irish Republic is supposed to have few powers beyond the strictly ceremonial, the election of Mary McAleese contains great significance for north–south and Anglo-Irish relations. It comes as representatives of the British and Irish governments and most of Northern Ireland's political parties are ensconced in Stormont working on a new dispensation which could be as far-reaching as the 1920s arrangement which created Northern Ireland.

The south's choice of Professor McAleese, by the biggest winning margin in the Republic's history, says much about what it wants to see emerging from the Stormont talks. The extraordinary campaign gave telling insights into southern opinion and in particular the state of Irish nationalism.

She is the first British citizen to be elected president of the Republic. Her predecessor, Mary Robinson, has gone down in history as the first woman to hold the post: Professor McAleese will go down as the first northerner. This is in itself hugely significant, since being from the north has traditionally been a drawback in southern politics. Even before the troubles many in the south found many northerners rather too blunt, too hard, too harsh for comfort. Decades of violence and political deadlock sharpened that original distaste into real aversion. Yet the belief is now widespread in the south that the troubles are almost certainly over, and this rapidly growing feeling seems to have brought with it a new fellow-feeling for northern nationalists. The presidential campaign provided firm evidence of this.

The dominant issue in the campaign was that of the nature of Mary McAleese's nationalism, which assumed centre stage when leaked documents were produced which were used to allege that she was secretly sympathetic to Sinn Féin. Up to that point the campaign, with its five well-mannered candidates, had been gracious and genteel, but the leaks issue ignited it.

Someone had gone through sensitive Irish foreign ministry documents, copied anything which looked damaging to Professor McAleese, and posted them to newspapers. Questioned about these, her explanation was that she had been part of a behind-the-scenes peace initiative under the auspices of the Redemptorist Order. Redemptorist priest Father Alex Reid, who helped bring about the first IRA cessation of violence, was trying to bring about a second ceasefire and she was helping him. Around this time she also received what looked like the endorsement from hell, when Gerry Adams announced that if he had a vote, he would cast it for her. John Bruton, leader of the largest opposition party, Fine Gael, seized on this and attacked the Adams endorsement.

At that point Professor McAleese was slightly ahead in the polls. Whoever leaked the documents clearly hoped to wreck her campaign, while her political opponents hoped to tap into what they assumed was a latent vein of anti-northern sentiment. The opinion polls which followed, however, told an astonishing story: both the leaks and the criticisms had backfired and been counter-productive. She sailed even further ahead in the polls while the approval rating for John Bruton dropped like a stone from 60 to 43 per cent. After that Professor McAleese never looked back as waves of sympathy brought more and more support from those who believed she was a victim of dirty tricks.

The psychiatrist Professor Anthony Clare, for example, wrote of "a smear of McCarthy-ite proportions hatched, fanned and daubed all over the McAleese campaign – the classic smear of guilt by association, used with a gusto reminiscent of J. Edgar Hoover at his most malign".

The episode cast light on the overall peace process. There is a strain of opinion in the south, particularly well represented in the media, which has deep concerns and reservations about the course of the process which has led to the IRA's present ceasefire and Sinn Féin's subsequent entry into talks. This worry, presented in its most aggressive form, has been used to argue that those attempting to bring Sinn Féin into mainstream politics are naïve and foolish or, alternatively, crypto-republicans. They believe that Sinn Féin will not be tamed by the political system but will instead pollute and poison it.

The McAleese leaks provided the most acute test of support for this proposition. The result appears to have been an emphatic endorsement of the McAleese approach and the peace process as a whole, as the allegation that she was a "sneaking regarder" of republicanism was briskly rejected.

The election may also have shown that southern voters, in this contest at least, were not overly concerned with the effect of the result on those other important northerners, the unionists. This point is, however, highly arguable, since unionists themselves sent very mixed messages during the campaign. Some contradicted Professor McAleese's assertion that she had the private good will and support of many unionists, though later a number of Protestant clergy spoke publicly of her as both a peacemaker and a committed ecumenist. The clincher, for those southerners worried about unionist opinion, probably came when Ulster Unionist deputy leader John Taylor said that while she was "an out-and-out nationalist" she was by no means a republican sympathiser and was "a most able person, quite easy to work with".

Nonetheless, the McAleese success will give many Protestants cause to reflect on the steady rise in northern nationalist power and what they view as its unfortunate corollary, the steady decline in unionist influence. The new Irish president has emerged from the trauma of the troubles a remarkably self-confident and assertive person; and there are plenty more where she came from. Quite a few of them are present inside the Stormont talks, while many more today play a leading part in Northern Ireland's public life. Unionists will be all too aware that these are people who regard themselves as being on the way up. They clearly will not endorse any settlement emerging from Stormont which does not give full recognition to their Irishness, as the south's electorate has just endorsed the Irishness of the first northern president, Mary McAleese.

Two days after Christmas the Loyalist Volunteer Force leader Billy Wright was shot dead inside the Maze prison by members of the Irish National Liberation Army, ending the career of one of the best-known loyalist assassins.

"King Rat"
foresaw his death

Billy Wright: child of the Troubles, icon of loyalist violence

Some years ago Billy Wright, after surviving a number of IRA attempts on his life, mused about his prospects: "People are writing stories about me, Catholics, nationalists, left-wingers. I know what they are trying to do," he said. "Personally, I'm a dead man. It would be morally wrong to back off. I have to give my life now. I am married, I have kids, but morally I have to lay down my life now. If I was shot dead in the morning, I would laugh in my grave."

By that stage he had become the latest in a long line of paramilitaries to become larger-than-life public figures of great notoriety, attracting publicity, fascination, fear and hatred in great measure. Such people often end up dead or in prison, for they become marked men.

Johnny "Mad Dog" Adair of the UDA has been jailed for 17 years; Jim Craig of the same organisation was killed by his own men; Dessie O'Hare of the INLA has been put behind bars for 40 years; his former colleague Dominic McGlinchey was gunned down by his own side; loyalist John McKeague was killed by republicans.

Wright had so many enemies that it was initially unclear whether he had been killed by republicans or by fellow loyalists on 27 December, for he has spent more than a year under a death threat from the UVF. There are many extreme loyalists who will regard his passing as occasion for celebration rather than regret.

Many in authority will privately feel much the same, for he and his small but dangerous band of associates represented a significant threat to the peace process. His breakaway Loyalist Volunteer Force killed three Catholic civilians during the year and was plainly intent on doing all it could to return Northern Ireland to full-scale conflict.

Wright was a child of the troubles. Born in 1960, he had already had a disturbed childhood and was living in a welfare home following the break-up of his parents' marriage when the IRA killed 10 Protestants not far from where he lived in south Armagh.

On a January night in 1976 a gang of IRA gunmen stopped a busload of workmen at Kingsmills, lined them up on the roadside, weeded out the Catholics and opened fire on the Protestants. Ten men were killed. Republicans attempting to excuse the carnage argued that the incident was an attempt to shock loyalists into ending a wave of attacks on Catholics in the county. If so, it could hardly have been more counter-productive, for it galvanised the 15-year-old Wright into paramilitarism. The Catholic community has paid heavily for that ever since.

Wright joined the UVF, committing his first killing at the age of 21. He was charged with murder for this, the death of a Catholic in a drive-by shooting, but was acquitted. His militancy increased when three of his relatives – his father-in-law, brother-in-law and an uncle – were killed by the IRA.

He spent much of his life in the sectarian cockpit of Portadown, base of the UVF's mid-Ulster brigade which was responsible for the killings of more than 40 people, most of them Catholic civilians. He is thought to have been involved in planning or carrying out over a dozen of these. Over the years he was in and out of jail, though in paramilitary terms he was lucky in that his longest stretch was only three years. He was also, unusually for a UVF gunman and commander, a religious man with a leaning towards Paisleyism. For a time he was a lay preacher.

As his reputation grew the authorities tried harder and harder to lock him up for good, while republicans tried harder and harder to kill him. Following a string of assassination attempts, he turned his home into a fortress, varying his movements and his sleeping arrangements. The police arrested him regularly, but he gave nothing away under interrogation: detectives regarded him as one of the cleverest loyalist paramilitaries.

His profile became even higher when he and his associates featured prominently at Drumcree in 1996, then later figured again in the news when it emerged that he had met Trimble during the stand-off. Trimble has said he asked Wright to use his influence to keep things calm in the Drumcree churchyard. The unionist leader has explained: "I noted that persons involved with the paramilitaries had arrived. That is why I felt it necessary to remonstrate with them and their apparent leader. He was there with a group of men who had a digger which they intended for use as a sort of tank. We had to urge them that on no account were they to use it."

It was reported that a close associate of Wright's was ready to drive the digger at the Drumcree obstacles and into the RUC lines. This did not happen, but some miles away a Catholic man was shot dead. Wright and some of his associates were questioned about the killing by police but released without charge.

The murder was regarded by the UVF leadership as a flagrant breach of the loyalist ceasefire and led to the announcement that its mid-Ulster unit was being disbanded. When it became evident that the unit would not meekly accept this, the death threat was issued against Wright, making it clear that his celebrity would not prevent the organisation from using violence against him.

Defiance was his keynote. At the time of the loyalist death threat he attended a rally dressed in a shirt emblazoned with the words "Mid-Ulster UVF – for God and Ulster – simply the best". He claimed he had widespread support in his dispute with the leadership of the UVF and the other loyalist paramilitary organisations.

Wright was cheered by more than 200 people who had gathered at a club in Portadown for a function to raise funds for the family of a UVF prisoner. He declared: "I believe that the huge crowd vindicates my belief that what I am saying is correct and my assessment of the situation is correct." He pledged to "defend the loyalist cause as long as I live". He now joins those whom he himself helped add to Northern Ireland's toll of death.

The killing of Billy Wright came just
two weeks after Liam Averill, an IRA man
serving a life sentence, walked out of
the same prison dressed as a woman
after a Christmas party attended by
prisoners' relatives and children. The
question was asked: what sort of
prison is this?

29 DECEMBER 1997   THE INDEPENDENT

Guns get into the Maze
because it's an extraordinary
kind of a jail

How, everyone asks, could it have happened: how on earth, in what is
supposedly the UK's most secure penal institution, could one set of
desperados smuggle in two guns and assassinate another inmate? The answer is
actually quite simple, for there are both precedents and explanations for what
happened on 27 December.

The key to the authorities' perpetual problems with the Maze lies in the fact
that so many of its inmates think and act not just as individuals but as members
of organised, resourceful and ruthless paramilitary groups. In England
prisoners without benefit of paramilitary backup can manage to have large
amounts of drugs brought into the jails. In Northern Ireland prisoners have a
comprehensive support system capable of providing large amounts of money,
material and other services. In a contest between a system and an individual the
system will normally win. But in the Maze, groups such as the IRA and INLA
maintain command structures which wield great influence and which are
closely linked to the organisations on the outside.

Thus the Maze works on a balance of power. The authorities run the jail but
there are limitations to what they can do, limitations whose boundaries have

111

been drawn up in blood. The central event in the jail's history was the hunger strike of 1981, when 10 republicans starved themselves to death rather than conform to prison rules which equated them with non-paramilitary prisoners.

Those 10 deaths, and the many others which took place on the streets during that traumatic period, plunged Northern Ireland into perhaps the worst convulsions it has ever seen. The communities reached new levels of polarisation and division, creating new depths of bitterness. The IRA and Sinn Féin were revitalised, laying the basis for a new cycle of violence. It was a terrible time.

The fact that 10 men went to their deaths made the point, in the starkest possible way, that imprisoned paramilitaries have an extraordinarily strong sense of community. The 10 individuals gave their lives for what they saw as the collective good. Since that awesome display of sacrifice and resistance no one has really believed that republican and loyalist prisoners are the same as non-terrorist inmates: they may be regarded as better, or as worse, but they cannot be viewed as indistinguishable.

Furthermore, those in authority have since then acknowledged that the Maze can be no ordinary prison, and that the paramilitary groups will always exercise considerable power. The authorities have sought to minimise that power as much as possible, but they have never managed to eradicate it completely.

The prisoners and the paramilitary groups use various weapons against the system. Over the years almost 30 prison officers have been shot dead by the IRA on the outside. There are regular escape attempts, some of them on the most ambitious scale. In 1983, for example, IRA prisoners assembled an armoury of 5 guns, 5 hammers, 10 chisels and 3 screwdrivers. In the mass escape that followed 38 IRA members got through the gates, though many were quickly recaptured. Such materials are just a part of the contraband which has turned up over the years: highly realistic facsimiles of rifles, together with mobile phones, video cameras and poteen stills have also been found.

The inquiry into the 1983 breakout ranged over some of the ways contraband could have been smuggled in. Apart from the obvious possibilities of visits, organisations have been able to infiltrate or intimidate private firms and tamper with supplies for delivery to the prison. The inquiry also concluded that the possibility that a member of staff had carried the guns in could not be discounted.

Staff can be pressurised in a number of ways, including bribery and threats. A decade ago a senior officer, who some nights was duty officer for the whole prison, with access to every key, was discovered to be the victim of an IRA "honey-trap", having being lured into a relationship with a woman who was both an actress and an IRA intelligence officer. The plan was to free 25 or more

IRA prisoners in an operation involving arms and explosives smuggled in by prison officers and using a helicopter. Such plans are possible when a large organisation is involved.

The Wright killing came as something of a surprise in that organisations do not for the most part authorise attacks on each other's members in the jails. There have been exceptions to this, most notably when an IRA bomb killed two loyalist prisoners in Belfast's Crumlin Road jail in 1991, but groups generally direct their attention to the authorities rather than towards each other.

But Billy Wright, in the words of one republican, "broke the barrier". By virtue of his penchant for self-publicity he achieved ogre status among republicans, while by making it clear that he wanted no part of any peace process, he made himself an obvious target for attack. The INLA machine on the outside somehow supplied the guns and Wright was shot dead. The familiar attempts will now be made to tighten security, but within a year or two paramilitary power will reassert itself and the prison will again be run on an uneasy form of joint authority.

Viewed in this light, the Maze can be seen as a symbol of implacable paramilitarism, yet there is something of a silver lining to its sorry history. The tabloids used to call it "the academy of terror", but behind its walls and barbed-wire fences valuable changes of mind have taken place. In the IRA H-Blocks the idea of a peace process took root at an early stage as long-term prisoners contemplated both their own futures and the prospects for the republican movement in general. Most of those who have emerged from the Maze in the 1990s have lent support to the peace process, giving an influential form of endorsement of the IRA ceasefire. Something similar was happening in the UVF and UDA H-Blocks, where the first generation of imprisoned loyalists had time to ponder on whether a better alternative to violence was possible. The new fringe loyalist parties which emerged from this experience, arguing that dialogue was better than the gun, now play an important part in the talks.

Most of the republican and loyalist negotiators at the multi-party talks have spent time in the cells of the Maze. They, like everyone else, will be hoping that the killing of Wright and the retaliation which followed it will not worsen their chances of arriving at an agreed political settlement.

The shooting of Billy Wright created a wave of political and paramilitary turbulence. More killings followed, particularly in Belfast, as loyalists took revenge by shooting Catholic civilians.

When UDA prisoners in the Maze voted to withhold their support from the peace process the Northern Ireland Secretary, Mo Mowlam, did something remarkable: she went into their H-Block to meet them. But first she allowed the media inside for a glimpse of life in the jail.

7 JANUARY 1998   THE INDEPENDENT

Inside the Maze

The last time I saw Michael Stone, in 1988, he was throwing fragmentation grenades and firing a Browning automatic pistol at a crowd of us at a republican funeral in Belfast's Milltown cemetery. Yesterday he stood in the corridor of H-Block number 8 in the Maze prison, evidently a more thoughtful man, and reflected: "It's all about dialogue and that's what we've been pushing. If we can get through this current situation with loyalists, anything's possible."

Today Stone will be one of four UDA prisoners sitting across the table from Dr Mo Mowlam to tell her of their concerns about the peace process. The unprecedented meeting could be vital in helping persuade loyalists to maintain their three-year ceasefire. Yesterday the signs were unexpectedly good. The four UDA leaders due to meet Dr Mowlam sat in one of their recreation rooms in the wing which they describe as home and, far from being warlike, sounded relaxed, open-minded and keen to talk.

"Home" is a gaily painted wing festooned with UDA and loyalist signs, flags and mottos. Men in casual clothes, some in shorts, strolled along a central corridor, while others lounged in a kitchen and recreation room. From the

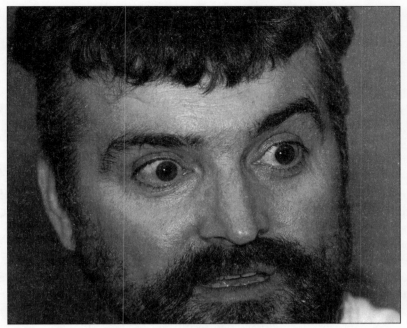

Michael Stone: jailed for six murders, he talked to Mo Mowlam of peace

background came the pounding of disco music. The cells are homely: prisoners can buy and bring in televisions and hi-fis, and many have wallpapered their cells. "This is where these blokes live," the governor, Martin Mogg, commented.

There is clearly a balance of power in operation here, for no prison officers were on the wing, staying on the other side of a set of bars. But there were security cameras trained along the corridor, and when the governor ushered reporters into the wing his presence was affably accepted. The authorities offered to bring in the media because they, the loyalists and IRA prisoners, all feel aggrieved at newspaper stories suggesting that prisoners serving sentences for terrorist-type offences live a life of Riley in the Maze.

It is indeed a most peculiar prison, but the governor, the UDA and the IRA all wanted to set the record straight. Asked if prisoners control the wings, Mogg answered: "Yes". They ran their wings, he explained, while staff had control of everywhere else in the prison. Regular searches would be held, he said, and head counts were carried out twice a day.

He and the prisoners took exception to reports that drink and drugs are freely available, that sex takes place on visits, that prisoners have mobile

115

phones, and that they can have cases of wine brought into the jail. UDA commander Sam McCrory declared: "There's no booze, there's no drugs, there's no sex on the visits and we don't have guns. Drugs are totally out of the question. Anybody caught with drugs in any of the UDA wings will be expelled from the organisation and put out of these blocks.

"It's embarrassing and humiliating for our families when they read about sex on the visits, they're taking drugs, they're running about drunk. The majority of people in here are health and fitness fanatics, so they're not going to take drugs. Half of them are on fat-free diets or they're vegans," he said.

"Sex on the visits?" said Michael Stone: "I wish. What is it? – a kiss and a cuddle with your wife or fiancée, that's all."

Over in an IRA H-Block, some 12 sets of gates away, IRA OC (officer commanding) Paudraig Wilson said the same thing: "Most of what has been said is untrue and sheer fantasy. We are political prisoners and, yes, this is a different prison from probably any other prison in the English system. Our families are grossly offended and stigmatised by these stories."

Martin Mogg said that while he could not guarantee that contraband such as drink and drugs were not smuggled in, the Maze had much less of a problem in these areas than many other prisons.

Sammy McCrory, heavily tattooed on his neck, arms and cheek, explained life in the jail: "This prison works on a day-to-day system of co-operation with the management of the prison. We can ask for something and a PO [prison officer] will tell you no. So we ask to see a governor, and we'll sit down and we'll negotiate and we'll come to some sort of arrangement. You mightn't get what you want but you might get a piece of it.

"But you'll not do it without co-operation, you don't bully these people into it. We've been reading that staff feel under threat from us. Well, we've had three football matches with the prison staff. And afterwards we went into the gym and we had crisps and Coke and sandwiches and we all had a good laugh with each other."

The approach is different in the IRA H-Block, which is more soberly decorated. On the walls are silhouettes of Che Guevara and some armed men, a notice about International Women's Year, a pro-Palestinian poster and Irish language material. Wilson said that people complained about prisoners having access to computers, but said the two in the wing were needed for educational purposes: 50 republicans were doing Open University degrees, 5 working for master's degrees and 2 studying for Ph.D.s, he said. "We live in the real world – there have to be head counts, there have to be searches," he added. Another IRA leader, Harry Maguire, chipped in: "What we have here is a degree of progressivism, pragmatism and realism." A third, Jim McVeigh, added: "Unpalatable as it may seem, we are prisoners of war. We act as an army, as a disciplined group of men, we act in a very disciplined and determined manner." They felt they now had the conditions which Bobby Sands died for in his 1981 hunger strike.

Wilson was very open on the question of IRA escapes, explaining: "Unfortunately, from our point of view, since the big escape of 1983 we have only managed to get out one other prisoner, Liam Averill. We very much regret that we have not been able to secure the successful escape of larger numbers of republican prisoners. We see it as our duty."

Back in the UDA block, McCrory was clearly looking forward to meeting Dr Mowlam. "We've our own thoughts, she'll have her own thoughts, we'll get round a table," he said. "It's not a negotiation thing, it's a talk, a conversation and a listening exercise. From Sunday to now we have not stopped – meeting after meeting after meeting. We know the way forward is dialogue. We want a level playing field."

Within hours of the Mowlam meeting, UDA prisoners renewed their support for the peace process. But on the outside the loyalist killings continued.

25 JANUARY 1998   THE INDEPENDENT ON SUNDAY

Extreme loyalists who have chosen to let their guns do the talking

Inside the Maze prison earlier this month Johnny "Mad Dog" Adair, one of the leading lights of the UDA, posed for the cameras in front of one of the UDA wing's many warlike decorations. This one, a flag featuring a fierce knife and grinning skull, was emblazoned with the slogan "Kill 'em all – let God sort 'em out!" There could be no better summary of the essence of loyalist violence, as practised by the UDA and others such as the Loyalist Volunteer Force.

Two of the Catholic men killed and injured by the UDA and LVF since Christmas have been distant relatives of Sinn Féin figures, but in both cases the connections appear to be purely coincidental. All seven of those who died were killed not because of their associations or their political beliefs: they died simply because of the long-established and truly primitive loyalist principle that "any Catholic will do".

Seamus Dillon and Terry Enright were doormen standing outside discos; Edmund Treanor was having a new year's eve drink in a bar; Fergal McCusker was walking home after a night out; Larry Brennan was waiting in his taxi for a fare; Ben Hughes was on his way home to his children and grandchildren from the shop in a Protestant district where he had worked for almost 30 years. Each one fell into the category of being Catholics who had the misfortune of being within easy reach of the loyalist gunmen. Each one was easily identified as Catholic by Northern Ireland's sectarian geography. At one time in the 1970s some loyalists would deny they were motivated by straight tribalism but today, as Adair's pose illustrates, the long years of killing have removed any embarrassment.

In truth, it was obvious from the very start. Matilda Gould, a Protestant woman attacked in the first fatal incident of the troubles in 1966, had the words THIS HOUSE IS OWNED BY A TAIG (Catholic) daubed on the wall of her home. The RUC's files are littered with confessions from Protestant assassins illustrating their sectarian motivation. "We decided to pick up a Taig and do him in," more than one confessed. Another said he had killed a Protestant woman "because she was a Taig-lover". One shot dead a Catholic man after telling a friend: "I'm going to kill a Taig and the best place to find one is in the Cliftonville Road." This last was an illustration of how history can repeat itself with grim precision in Belfast, for that was in 1976, and it was in a Cliftonville Road bar that Edmund Treanor died.

The statistics tell the story. Of the almost 1,000 people that loyalists have killed in the troubles, more than 600 were Catholic civilians gunned down, blown up, stabbed or beaten to death in an expression of religious hatred.

Because both loyalists and the IRA have killed so many people, casual observers sometimes make the mistake of assuming that the extreme Protestant groups and the republicans are essentially mirror images of each other. This is not the case. Security sources and those working with prisoners readily confirm that the loyalists are less disciplined, less organised, less educated, less political and much worse at PR than the IRA. More have been in trouble with the law for non-terrorist offences. They are more hot-blooded and more eager to seek speedy vengeance, as has happened in recent weeks.

Loyalists themselves sometimes characterise their violence as "counter-terrorism", arguing that their attacks are essentially retaliation against republican violence from the IRA and INLA. This is partly true but it is highly misleading to suggest it is the whole story.

While the seven killings of recent weeks have indeed represented savage vengeance for the INLA's killings of two loyalist figures, the fact is that violence from extreme Protestants is almost commonplace. It comes from organisations which are supposed to be on ceasefire, others which are not, and sometimes it comes from mobs belonging to neither category. Last year, for example, loyalists were involved in up to 15 killings, compared with 4 carried out by republicans. Some were the work of the LVF, while some were "internal" or "disciplinary" shootings.

A Catholic man was beaten to death in the bitterly divided town of Portadown, while in County Antrim a policeman was kicked to death by a mob which resented his part in halting loyalist marches. In Belfast a former Protestant minister of religion, wrongly suspected of being a paedophile, sustained two broken legs, a suspected fractured skull and puncture wounds in a beating incident, and later died. Such is the stuff of loyalist paramilitarism.

While the IRA has always had its political wing, these have only emerged recently in groups such as the UDA and UVF. Within the multi-party talks the UDP, headed by Gary McMichael, speaks for the UDA. Most of the politicians involved in the talks privately accept the bona fides of the leaders of these political adjuncts. It is obvious from the recent killing spree, however, that the parent paramilitary groups remain ready to resort to violence at any moment.

This highlights the dilemma for the authorities and the others involved. Kicking the UDP out of the talks might well send the UDA back to full-scale violence, thus triggering an IRA response and thus wrecking the entire peace process.

But allowing the UDP to stay means that the two governments and the conventional political parties will be sitting at the table with those associated with an unapologetically active terrorist organisation. All involved will be making their judgements on whether the true face of the UDA is that of Gary McMichael, or of Johnny Adair, and whether the former might ever displace the latter.

Hope remained alive, but it took a
fresh pounding as news of each new
violent incident came through.

Back to the butchery in Ulster. Can Mo Mowlam save the day?

People in Belfast now fall silent at television and radio news bulletins, waiting in dread to hear whether and where the gunmen have struck again, wondering how long the slaughter will go on at this appallingly metronomic rate. Hope remains alive for the peace process, but it takes a fresh pounding as news of each incident comes through. Police report there's been a shooting; later bulletins say a man's been rushed to hospital; his condition is critical; he is dead.

Next come the pathetic details: a newly created widow, a shattered family, the sorrow of yet another funeral. Sometimes the victims are quiet family men, sometimes outgoing community activists. The man killed on 23 January helped care for his two blind brothers. The awful thought persists that even if the peace process ultimately succeeds, these families will never again know peace.

There have been 10 dead since Christmas, 2 of them loyalist activists and the other 8 Catholic civilians. The latest, killed on 24 January, was murdered by loyalists who flagged down his taxi, forced him to drive to a quiet spot, shot him and left him like a bundle of rags at the side of the road. In Catholic areas in particular there is now an atmosphere of subdued terror. Women are asking their husbands to take some time off work, and not to go into potentially dangerous areas. Mothers are begging their sons not to leave the house. This has gone beyond retaliation for republican violence. These gunmen are operating on sectarian hatred, beyond politics, beyond reason, beyond reach:

Mo Mowlam, the most unorthodox Northern Ireland Secretary ever

far from seeking entry into the peace process, they hope to wreck it. Raised in the troubles, violence became for them first a way of life and then the only way of life.

The Catholic community is overwhelmingly in favour of an inclusive peace process but now faces a terrible dilemma. The process goes on, with attempts to achieve the lift-off which has so far eluded the politicians. Yet one of the next items of business will be the question of the expulsion of the UDP from the talks because of its close association with the UDA. The UDA has just admitted it killed three of those Catholic victims but says its violence is at an end. Ejection would constitute a powerful affirmation of anti-violence: then again, it might

121

spark off yet more shootings. The dilemma was summed up at the weekend in a thoughtful intervention from John Major, who declared: "It's a very fine call. If the UDP are removed, there is a danger it would precipitate the collapse of the talks. It being Northern Ireland, it is equally true that if they are not removed, it could precipitate a collapse in the talks."

The feeling among most of the parties involved is that the UDP should be allowed to remain. This is not least because while the UDA as a whole is plainly not committed to non-violent means alone, its chief political representatives, Gary McMichael and David Adams, are generally accepted as genuine men.

The talks will seek to make political progress both for its own sake and in the hope of providing a new focus and leaving no vacuum for the gunmen to fill. Mo Mowlam said of the dilemma yesterday: "It's competing moralities. We have the competing morality of the integrity of the talks, the three murders and the Mitchell principles on non-violence on one side, versus trying to hold the talks together and making sure more lives are not lost.

"If we want to try to stop this thing from escalating to the bad old days, we have to make what progress we can to make sure this is a totally inclusive process. If we keep the talks going, it's our only possible route to saving other lives. That's the decision I've got to make, not an easy one."

Belfast city council opened a "Book of Peace" for people to sign. Those who trudged into the city hall to do so looked sombre and drawn in the wintry light, not only because of the January cold but because of the demoralising violence. Most of them seemed to come not out of hope so much as from sympathy for the bereaved, and to register their distress and opposition to the recent killings in and around the city. A man from Hillsborough, County Down, wrote: "No piece of land is worth such pain." Another who signed wrote: "Those who committed most of the recent murders claimed to do so on my behalf. I repudiate this as strongly as possible." Another asked: "Why should thugs decide my life for me or my family?"

Later a woman told the *Independent*: "I signed the book because I came through 27 years of this. My grandchildren are four and five, and I don't want them growing up with this. I'm coming through a bereavement myself for a natural death, but what must these people feel whose loved ones have been shot down in the street like a dog?" And an old lady, who has lived through not just this bout of troubles but others in Belfast's sad and recurrently violent history, shook her head and said: "It's so sad. It's the one God who judges us all, isn't it? He doesn't ask you what side you're on, if you're a Protestant or a Catholic. God help those poor people, their families, they must be destroyed."

Outside on the streets there was much support for the talks process. But while the UDA said its killings have stopped, no such assurances have been given by loyalist splinters like the LVF or republican splinters such as the INLA. While death continues to prowl the streets, many people are for the moment concentrating on simply staying alive.

POSTSCRIPT

In the event first the UDP and later Sinn Féin were temporarily excluded from the talks as political penalties for killings carried out by the UDA and IRA. Both parties later returned to the negotiations.

As the violence continued the echoes of previous deaths continued to have an effect. Tony Blair agreed to the establishment of a public inquiry into the events of Bloody Sunday in 1972, when 14 unarmed demonstrators were shot dead by paratroopers in Londonderry's Bogside. That controversial incident had many lethal sequels.

2 FEBRUARY 1998   THE INDEPENDENT

Ripples still spreading from Bloody Sunday

In a small house in a small Catholic estate in the killing fields of north Belfast, far from Londonderry and yesterday's Bloody Sunday commemoration, a father and mother sat and talked about what that event did to their family.

They wanted to explain but they did not wish to be identified.

Although it was 26 years ago, its effects reverberate to this day, frightening them still. Just two weeks ago the life of their 11-year-old newspaper delivery boy was threatened, an act which they think can be traced back to that grim day more than a quarter of a century ago. Their son Brendan was 17 when the paratroopers opened fire that day. Three days later, according to his father Jack, Brendan and two close friends, also teenagers, travelled into a republican stronghold and joined the IRA.

This act went against decades of family tradition. In the Second World War Jack's father had served with the RAF in the African desert, fighting through Sicily and into Italy. One of Jack's uncles served with the Royal Artillery, while another, a company sergeant-major, was killed in Italy in the closing stages of the war. Jack himself served first in the Territorial Army and then the Ulster Defence Regiment. "This was a non-political family," he said. "We never talked politics; Irish history never meant anything to us. We watched Bloody Sunday on the television but we never discussed it."

But three days later his son was in the IRA. According to Jack: "The three boys were as thick as thieves – whatever one did, the others would do too." Some 10 weeks later there was an explosion at a lock-up garage at the edge of the little estate. Since there was little or no IRA activity in the district, many at first assumed it was a loyalist bombing.

Jack recalled: "I didn't know anybody was killed until I was told there was flesh over the road and on the roofs. It was a cold April day, there were pieces of flesh and bone all over the place, and the steam was rising off it all. When Brendan didn't appear for his evening meal that's when we started to worry, and then it was confirmed. The police and a priest came down, and they had a piece of shirt with them. It was Brendan's favourite shirt: he died in it."

The next morning Jack was taken by police to the Belfast mortuary. More than 25 years on there was still shock in his voice as he relived the experience. As he spoke his wife gazed abstractedly out of the window towards the scene of their son's death, less than a hundred yards away. Jack said: "Under the first sheet was the top half of one of the lads, just the upper torso, all covered in cement dust. Under the next sheet there was nothing recognisable at all, nothing, just a heap of flesh and an evil smell. The next one was the same, a big tray, a big steel tray. The only identifiable piece of a human being was a human tongue sitting on the top of it all. That memory hasn't left me. The smell sticks in your mind."

Jack and his wife were insistent that the three teenagers were not working on a bomb in transit. By making discreet enquiries, he said, he had discovered that the three had been ordered by the IRA to remove gelignite which was in a dangerous condition.

124

They refused to allow any paramilitary trappings at their son's funeral. A senior republican appeared at their home to pay his respects. Jack recalled: "He was commiserating with us. I told him to fuck off. He had all this patter about the three volunteers and all. I said, 'Fuck off, they're three dead volunteers now, they're no use to anybody.'" The families of the other teenagers also had no republican connections, the father and brothers of one of them also being ex-servicemen. But the explosion branded the little estate as a centre of IRA activity, and loyalists went for it. The father of one of the teenagers, who worked as a cleaner at the High Court in Belfast, realised he was being stalked as he went to work. He gave up his job, and died soon afterwards. Later in 1972 a brother of the other teenage IRA member was walking home after work when loyalists shot him dead.

In 1974, two years after Bloody Sunday, five young people from the estate were in a car driving to their work in a nearby factory when loyalist gunmen, one armed with a machine gun, stepped in front of it and opened fire. Jack related: "It was a two-door Ford Anglia. The two lads in the front were able to scramble out and run but the three in the back were just stuck there, and they kept firing and firing." A 16-year-old youth from the estate, who was in the back seat, was killed.

Also in the back seat was Jack's daughter Margaret, who had just turned 18 and was engaged to be married. She died of her injuries a week later. The third person in the back seat was another teenage girl whose brother had died in the garage explosion. Although she was hit by 12 bullets she miraculously survived. She married, but in 1983 her husband was shot dead by loyalists while cleaning the windows of a local shop where he worked. It was their 11-year-old son whose life was threatened two weeks ago.

Jack summed up as his wife looked out the window: "That's why I say Bloody Sunday is still an ongoing thing. We are three families, and each of us had another death resulting from the deaths of the lads in that explosion. How many other sons like mine joined the IRA after Bloody Sunday? I'm sure and certain there were many like them.

"When Bloody Sunday comes on the TV I walk out, I can't bear to watch it. It was the beginning of the end for my son, and then for my daughter. It's like the pebble in the pool. Bloody Sunday was the pebble in the pool and the ripples went out. And they're still going out."

Belfast was all too accustomed to violent death, but in many parts of Northern Ireland there were little pockets of comparative peace which had remained largely untouched by the troubles. One of these was the small County Down village of Poyntzpass.

5 & 7 MARCH 1998   THE INDEPENDENT

Fatal ill-luck of friends across Ulster's divide

Philip Allen and Damien Trainor first lived together and then died together, the blood from their bodies mingling as they breathed their last on the floor of a little pub in Poyntzpass. A Protestant and a Catholic, they had the good fortune to live in a little oasis of community harmony amid the rolling drumlins of Armagh and Down. But they had fatal ill-luck to live within striking distance of other places which have been poisoned by deep wells of sectarianism.

The two friends were having a quiet drink when loyalist gunmen burst in, shouted "Get down you bastards" and fired repeatedly into their bodies and those of two other people. The fact of their different religions, and thus their different politics, did not interfere with the close friendship between the two men. Philip, who was 34, had just asked 25-year-old Damien to be best man at his wedding.

Damien's uncle said: "All Damien lived for was cars and a few drinks along with his mate who was murdered. They've grown up together as pals the way both their fathers did. The families have a long, long history – never any animosity among them, just the best of pals, the best of friends."

They were both drinking orange juice in the little bar when the gunmen arrived. The bar owner's son described the scene: "It was quite simple. There was two men came in through the front door of the bar and they shouted in very rude terms for everybody in the bar to lie down, and everybody just lay down. They did not ask for denominations or anything, they just opened fire on the fellas that were on the ground."

When Father Desmond Corrigan was summoned to the bar he found the two fatally injured men. "I saw Damien and Philip lying on the ground just behind the door," he said. "I administered the last rites to Damien and prayed with Philip. They were still conscious at that stage and I tried to console them. I tried to talk to them, to encourage them, give them some hope. They responded for a short time but then we were losing them. There was no pandemonium. Everyone was just trying to do whatever they could for the boys."

Poyntzpass is named after Lieutenant Poyntzpass, an English officer given 500 acres of land by Elizabeth I in reward for defeating soldiers of the Earl of Tyrone. Until nine o'clock on Tuesday night it was just one of the many obscure backwaters, tucked away throughout Northern Ireland, which had made it through the troubles unscathed.

The village is majority Catholic, its surroundings are majority Protestant. It is free of the flags, graffiti, bunting and slogans which both decorate and deface so many towns and villages: lying between loyalist Portadown and nationalist Newry, it has chosen not to display its colours. The village's three pubs are all Catholic-owned but all have mixed clientele, a fact which bolstered the general assumption that they would not be targeted by loyalists.

The gunmen are today probably celebrating their achievement of adding two more names to the list of the dead, and thus sending another palpitation of dismay and doubt through the peace process. They will congratulate themselves on having killed Damien, because he was a Catholic. They will be less happy about killing Philip, because he was a Protestant, but will console themselves with the thought that he brought it on himself by drinking in a Catholic-owned bar with a Catholic friend. "He shouldn't have been there," a loyalist source once explained about a similar shooting in the past. "He shouldn't have been mixing like that."

The two friends were buried in different cemeteries. They lived not far away from each other, socialised together and this week they died together, shot when the balaclavaed gunmen burst into their local bar. Buried in cemeteries just around the corner from each other, they will never again be far apart.

Damien's service came first, at the Catholic church in Chapel Street at noon. Philip had his service in the Presbyterian church in Meeting Street, just round the corner, at 2.30 pm. It rained and rained all day, starting before Damien was buried and going on until after Philip was laid to rest. It was a grey, drizzly, cheerless day, the rain as relentless and pitiless as Northern Ireland's stream of killings.

In Chapel Street the village stood in a throng as Damien's coffin was brought slowly into the church. Only the rain broke the silence as Philip's three brothers, drenched, carried the dripping coffin of his friend on its last journey. The little church was so packed that most of the village stood outside. Some mourners sheltered under umbrellas, while others stood bareheaded for over an hour as the service took its course.

In the church parish priest Father Brian Hackett attempted to address the killers, suggesting that peace might be on its way and that they might be afraid of peace and of living together. "If you want to terrorise us, yes we are terrorised, if that's what terrorism is all about. And if you ask us were we scared, Yes, you have scared us. But perhaps I could say to the men of violence – 'Were you scared by Damien and Philip? Were you scared when you realised there were other Damiens and Philips around Poyntzpass and, as it has come home to us, all over Northern Ireland?'" Perhaps, he suggested, the writing was on the wall for the men of violence: "Maybe I am a dreamer, maybe we're all dreamers around Poyntzpass, but I can ask the question – is it all over bar the shouting? Maybe the men of violence realise that, as we give our support to the peace negotiators."

A little while later the village lined Railway Street as Philip's body was carried along it, his grieving family oblivious to the falling rain, clinging to each other for support and solace. His fiancée was among them, going not to a wedding, as she had hoped, but to a burial. The men of the village fell in behind the cortège as it passed, nodding sombrely to one another. The coffin paused for a moment at the Railway Bar where the gunmen had carried out their murderous work, and which is now marked by a little pile of bouquets.

In the Presbyterian church the Reverend Joseph Nixon spoke of the two victims: "Philip was one of the lads around the village and was like a brother to Damien. Philip was a young man of good character and a steady worker. Damien was always obliging, a bright and cheery person. He was well liked and admired. There is no difference between Catholic and Protestant. We are all God's creation. We are all flesh and blood. The terrorist's bullet has the same effect on us all. It robs us of life and plunges our families into grief and despair."

Back at the Railway Bar two policemen stooped to read the inscriptions on the flowers, which had been placed around a small red candle, which, despite the rain, somehow stayed alight. One card said "Unreal but true – our hearts are numb and ache with pain at this unbearable loss of Philip and Damien." And another described how Poyntzpass will always remember them: "Great friends in life, now greater in death."

The talks were difficult but they were not deflected by the violence. And although many differences remained, a moment arrived when success began to seem a real possibility.

6 APRIL 1998   THE INDEPENDENT

Ulster moves towards its Mandela moment

In South Africa they speak of "the click" that happened sometime in the negotiations which made Mandela president. It marked the sudden arrival of a common sense of purpose and a feeling that a deal was on the cards. A Northern Ireland version of that might, just might, have happened in Belfast last week. Somewhere along the line in the course of the week came a moment when its people began to think that success in the talks was more likely than not.

This must seem a pretty audacious observation, given that the week ended in setback when chairman George Mitchell was unable to produce a vital working paper; given that so many key points remain unresolved; and given that the prevailing mood can fluctuate dramatically, sometimes on an hourly basis. Success is by no means assured, yet there is a sense in the air that some sort of corner was turned back there. This is not to assert that some new bonds of friendship and fellowship have been forged: it's not like that. This is Northern Ireland, and there remain vicious personal antagonisms, both between unionism and nationalism and indeed within those two camps. If there was a change in the chemistry it is a political phenomenon and not a personal one.

Yet there are underlying relationships which, though often obscured, are among the important factors working towards agreement, and which will strongly underpin any new deal. The most fundamental of these is probably the London–Dublin relationship, as established in the Anglo-Irish agreement of 1985. While this has had many ups and downs, its strength is that the two governments have come to see their interests as being almost identical, in that both of them prize the goal of stability over everything else, including any territorial ambitions.

The next relationship is what used to be known as Hume–Adams, which began as a dialogue between the leaders of the SDLP and Sinn Féin and has since matured into the concept of political inclusivity. Just about every Irish nationalist now subscribes to this theory, which in practical terms means they believe there can be no omission of Sinn Féin from any deal.

Back when Albert Reynolds was Taoiseach the relationship between Dublin, the SDLP and the republicans used to be characterised as a "pan-nationalist front". Any resemblance to such a front pretty much fell apart when John Bruton replaced Reynolds. But with Bertie Ahern as Taoiseach a new understanding appears to have been reached among the three nationalist elements, and in negotiating terms they all seem to be in the same neck of the woods. Although this fact is not being trumpeted abroad, it will greatly strengthen Gerry Adams's hand in dealing with dissent in the republican ranks.

The first IRA ceasefire was sold to republican hardliners on the argument that they could achieve more politically, in co-operation with Hume, Reynolds and indeed Clinton, than they could through violence. The creation of a renewed sense of nationalist unity would greatly increase the chances of the present ceasefire holding.

If there is a deal, Adams and company will sell it as an interim arrangement, a staging post on the road to eventual Irish unity. Although there are some republican dissidents who are doubtless at this moment pondering how to get bombs into England, the chances are that the vast majority of republican activists and voters will not approve of this. Adams has shown himself to be an astute assessor of the republican grassroots, as is illustrated in the achievement of pushing the Sinn Féin vote up over the years from 11 to 17 per cent. He has been a moderniser but also a highly cautious one: if and when he does go for a deal, he will be confident he can sell it.

In one sense he can afford to move further than David Trimble, for most of the republican grassroots are, like the Sinn Féin leadership itself, highly pragmatic. The unionist grassroots are much less so, being more worried and more divided and thus more problematical for everyone. Because of this the position within unionism is much less certain. Unionist leaders who have shown pragmatism and flexibility have very often wound up as scalps swinging on Ian Paisley's belt, and Trimble has no desire to join them.

The next key relationship in this series is therefore that between Trimble and Tony Blair. The prime minister has given the unionist leader unprecedented access in recent months, and has been supportive towards him in very many ways. Tony Blair privately acknowledges the constant threat to Trimble from

Paisley and other critics within his own party. "Giving comfort to the Ulster Unionists is vital," the PM told a private gathering of Irish-American politicians two months ago. The trick, in the final four days of negotiation ahead, will be to continue with that comfort, while nudging Trimble towards the nationalist position.

This will not be easy since some unionist negotiators, including possibly Trimble himself, have clung to the idea of finding an agreement without Sinn Féin. Some of them thought, and indeed actually hoped, that the IRA ceasefire would have broken down by now; they believed in the mirage of Dublin and the SDLP splitting off from Sinn Féin. Because of this the psychology of deal-making has not permeated the Ulster Unionist party as thoroughly as it has most of the other parties involved. It is this which now makes the Trimble–Blair relationship so vital and so delicate: the PM must judge just how much pressure the unionist market in general, and Trimble in particular, will bear.

The things that might still go wrong are legion. There could be violence on the outside, or splits on the inside; there will certainly be a great deal of brinkmanship before Thursday's deadline. But as against that there is the feeling that last week a little click was faintly but distinctly heard: that the sense of momentum which was missing for so long has now arrived, and may carry this phase of the enterprise to success.

As the Easter deadline neared, more people came to believe that a historic breakthrough could be at hand.

The long road to peace:
how blood enemies
learned to talk

PACEMAKER

Bertie Ahern and Tony Blair in Anglo-Irish agreement

Everyone came to the Stormont talks with the hope of finding a new Ireland, a new agreement for the new millennium, but everyone arrived carrying decades if not centuries of political baggage with them. This was embodied in the person of the Irish Taoiseach, Bertie Ahern, who left the talks for a time on Wednesday to bury his 87-year-old mother Julia. Born in 1911, she often told the family about growing up in west Cork during the south's troubled passage towards independence. Bertie's father was a member of the 3rd Cork brigade of the IRA. In later life Mrs Ahern would tell tales of how the Black and Tans shot all the turkeys on the family farm and how, during the civil war, Free State forces would come to their home and "turn it upside down" because it was regarded as a republican household.

Bertie Ahern has always been a constitutional nationalist politician, vehemently denying that the IRA of today are the legitimate heirs of the republican forces of the 1920s. Nonetheless, folk memories and family recollections have played an important part in moulding even his generation of southern politicians.

This week the Irish prime minister found himself negotiating with northerners whose lives have been more deeply and more recently touched by violence. The purpose of the enterprise was to find a new political dispensation to supersede the imperfect arrangements of the 1920s.

There has never been such a wide-ranging negotiation, involving so many points of the political compass, and rarely has such a sense of a historic new beginning been generated. Ahern found himself coming to grips politically with, for example, Jeffrey Donaldson, one of the Ulster Unionist party's chief negotiators. Donaldson still remembers learning in 1970, when he was seven, that a cousin had been killed by the IRA. An RUC constable, he was one of the first policemen killed in the troubles.

Also in the talks was Gerry Adams, who is used to accusations that he has been a supporter of violence. But his family too have suffered: a nephew was savagely killed by extreme Protestants in the mid-1970s, while his niece's son died, also at the hands of loyalists, in January of this year. Others in the Sinn Féin delegation, perhaps a majority of them, have been to jail.

Across the table from them were delegations associated with loyalist paramilitary groups. These also contained people who have lost loved ones, and who have taken life: four of the loyalists there yesterday have killed seven people, and spent much time behind bars as a consequence. In one sense it was time well spent, for most of them emerged from the Maze prison changed people, disenchanted with violence and hungry for politics. One of them killed two men and once threatened my life, actions which in the 1970s were the stuff of paramilitary politics: today he has a deep and genuine longing to have done with war. It is the sight of conversions such as these, in which hard men learn the hard way about the facts of civilised political life, that give most hope for the future.

It was John Hume, leader of one of the few parties which have never been overtly or covertly involved with violence, who years ago set out the conceptual framework for the talks. He maintained that they should deal with three key sets of relationships: those between unionists and nationalists in Northern Ireland; those between north and south; and the east–west relationship between Britain and the island of Ireland. Its strength was that it was an agenda designed to cope with the facts of history and geography.

The purely political parties, excluding Sinn Féin and the loyalists, had been talking together on and off since 1991, when Peter Brooke as Northern Ireland Secretary first brought them together. Those early efforts seemed to come to nothing, though it can now be seen that valuable groundwork was laid for later advances. John Major and Sir Patrick brought the parties together again in mid-1996, but they became bogged down in procedural trench warfare and made little headway.

Then came Sinn Féin. Ian Paisley walked out but crucially David Trimble stayed, though at no point have his party members negotiated with or even spoken to Sinn Féin members. The talks moved slowly, and not as the government would have wished, but despite difficult moments they did not fall apart. Until this week they tended to take the form of speechifying rather than productive negotiation, with parties almost endlessly rehearsing their cherished beliefs rather than suggesting compromises. It is a fair bet that without the government's insistence on a deadline they would continue to rehearse them for many more months.

A particularly bad period came at the turn of the year when, despite strenuous efforts, the parties adjourned for their Christmas break after failing to reach agreement even on an agenda. There were also ominous signs outside the talks, with some important republican figures breaking away from the IRA and some of David Trimble's MPs pressing him to quit the negotiations.

When republicans shot Billy Wright in the Maze, triggering loyalist retaliation, politics seemed for a moment to have lost its primacy. But the talks resumed on schedule, though the progress of negotiations was halted by the temporary expulsions first of the UDP and then of Sinn Féin. There continued, however, to be violent noises off, with occasional killings and the ominous emergence of a new and unnamed republican group – its nucleus, those who had left the IRA in December.

By this time the outline of an eventual settlement had become clear. A new devolved assembly would be set up in Belfast, while a north–south council would link the two parts of Ireland. A new concept, that of a British–Irish council, would connect devolved institutions in Belfast, Edinburgh and Cardiff. The new deal would include measures to protect civil and political rights, promote equality, and go on to consider the issues of policing, prisoners, the justice system and arms de-commissioning. In total this amounted to a new political geography of these islands which would address Hume's three-cornered concept.

But while the outline was clear enough, its vital details remained stubbornly unresolved. Arguments continued over arrangements for the assembly and its relationship with the north–south council. Unionists advocated a modest assembly and an even more modest north–south body: the assembly, in their view, should have no legislative powers and no cabinet to run it, while the north–south institution should be merely consultative.

Over the months Sinn Féin delegates played their cards close to their chest, favouring a strong north–south body but refusing to admit publicly that an assembly should be part of any deal. This seemed illogical, in that any cross-border institution would have to be anchored in a Belfast assembly, but it made sense politically, in that it meant the republicans gave no hostages to fortune and made no concessions.

The SDLP and Irish government pursued agreement much more actively. They advocated a strong assembly with legislative as well as administrative powers, to be run by a new cabinet-style administration including both unionists and nationalists. They argued for a powerful north–south body with wide powers and enough independence to thwart any moves by a unionist-dominated assembly to neuter it.

Behind the arguments lay two very different philosophies. A strong consensus had developed within Irish nationalism that any settlement which excluded Sinn Féin would, in the words of a former Irish government adviser, not be worth a penny candle. For nationalists, therefore, the talks were a phase not just in a talks process but a peace process, their analysis being that the best way to underpin the IRA's ceasefire was to involve Sinn Féin ever more deeply in politics. On the unionist side, however, a number of the negotiators readily contemplated co-operation with constitutional nationalists such as the SDLP but baulked at the idea of ever working with Sinn Féin. A few months ago unionist negotiator Ken Maginnis, for example, described Sinn Féin as "unreconstructed terrorists", declaring: "I could never give cognisance to them, not as long as I live."

This philosophical gap, and many of the practical details, remained unresolved all along the way. But by late March more and more business was being done in the talks, although this fact was often masked by the aggressive soundbites some participants felt obliged to deliver to the waiting cameras. The useful thing was that all the parties became familiar with the details of each other's positions. The problem was that the talks remained stuck on the point of each party's preferred options, with no one sure how far others were prepared to move.

The talks building itself has been no help to negotiation. A modified civil

135

service office block within the sprawling Stormont estate in east Belfast, it was described by one who knows it well as "the original sick building". Character-less, cheerless and boxy, delegates complained that its stark sixties design offered no intimate hidey-holes for private politicking. In the canteen most politicians tended not to mix, while the bar was found unappealing. Com-paring it to an RUC interrogation centre, Gerry Adams called it "Castlereagh with coffee".

But not all the business was done at Stormont, with over the months both Tony Blair and Bertie Ahern receiving a flow of visitors to London and Dublin. Adams went to Downing Street several times, but a much more frequent visitor was David Trimble. The prime minister knew that no deal could be arrived at without the approval of the Ulster Unionist leader, and set out to win his trust. He appears to have succeeded in this – which was no mean feat, since Trimble's precise thought processes all along remained a mystery even to some of his closest associates in his own party.

One of the few moments of levity came earlier this month when Mo Mowlam announced that so much progress had been made that the deadline had been advanced. This turned out to be an April fool jape; in fact the story of this month has been one of hold-ups and apparent setbacks.

In the final days Tony Blair and Bertie Ahern arrived, bringing with them the political muscle to dislodge the parties from their treasured positions. They have been days and nights of hard pounding, but they have ended in success. The spectre of all that unresolved history lay heavily on everyone, but in the end it proved not strong enough to overcome the spirit of peace and the desire to put an end to war.

The outcome, following a marathon session, was something which will go down in history: the Good Friday agreement. A complex document full of checks, balances and trade-offs, it set out a blueprint for a new constitutional settlement. There would be a new assembly in Belfast, headed by an executive formed by the largest parties; there would be new north–south institutions and new arrangements linking Belfast with the new devolved bodies in Scotland and Wales.

All parties promised to work towards arms de-commissioning, while new commissions would review future policing requirements and emergency legislation. New bodies would safeguard human rights and equality, while, most controversially, prisoners from subscribing paramilitary groups could expect release within two years.

The republican community did not take long to give its general endorsement. Within the Ulster Unionist party, however, the agreement produced deep divisions, some major figures opposing it. The dilemma of party activists was summed up by one pro-agreement councillor who said: "The past is gone, the present is full of confusion and the future scares the hell out of me."

There were a great many loose ends but the deal was breathtaking both in its scope and in the fact that so many of the major political parties signed up for it. It felt like the stuff of history.

A rare moment to celebrate as Ulster's old absolutes crumble

There is a long way to go in this peace process, with many difficulties and probably violence ahead. But the events of this weekend justify those who support it luxuriating in a moment of celebration. It is impossible to find in either mainstream unionism or mainstream republicanism anyone who loves the Good Friday agreement, for it contains much to dismay members of each tradition. Yet over the weekend almost three-quarters of the Ulster Unionist Council voted in favour of it, while at the Sinn Féin *ard-fheis* republican leaders carefully laid the groundwork for its qualified acceptance in time for the referendums of 22 May.

These are both momentous developments, for the UUC and the *ard-fheis* are no ordinary gatherings. They are repositories of the theologies of unionism and republicanism, keepers of the faith of their fathers. And since those fathers have cordially detested each other for a couple of centuries, it is truly amazing to watch their offspring moving towards acceptance of the same document.

They are doing so in very different styles. Gerry Adams and his associates are as cautious as ever, gently massaging their supporters towards a Yes vote in the referendums, but giving them time to come to terms with a deal so different from the republican goal of Irish unity. Many in the unionist grassroots have been thinking in terms of a deal such as this for several years now, ever since the first IRA ceasefire in 1994. The Protestant business community has been ready for it, as have the loyalist paramilitary groups and most church leaders. But the Protestant political classes were the last to catch on, clinging as they did first to their parliamentary arrangement with John Major and latterly to the expectation – which for some of them, sadly, became an actual hope – that the IRA would break its ceasefire and have Sinn Féin expelled from the process.

It was the UUC which chose David Trimble as party leader in 1995. It is a fair bet that many and probably most of those who voted for him thought they were choosing not a deal-maker but a champion of the hardline. Many of these were consequently shell-shocked when he emerged from the Stormont negotiations with a document which proposed letting out nearly all the prisoners, overhauling the RUC and possibly having Sinn Féin members as part of a new administration. Perilously little groundwork had been done to prepare them for such radical moves.

In opting for the agreement they went against the advice of the Orange Order and resisted the clamour of Ian Paisley. They declined the counsel of 6 of their party's 10 MPs, ranging from the most experienced to the most ambitious. These were the people who used to reject powersharing with John Hume: now they have not ruled out powersharing with Gerry Adams. A body famous for just saying No, just said Yes.

This is not, of course, the end of the matter: in Northern Ireland it never is. With more than a month to go to the referendums there is the possibility that anti-agreement elements within the party, Orangeism and Paisleyism can together mount an effective campaign for a No vote. A weekend opinion poll indicated that there is still much to play for, showing that 34 per cent of Protestants presently intend to vote Yes, while 22 per cent mean to vote No. There remains a huge number of Undecideds who might go either way.

Since Catholics are markedly in favour of the agreement, it would only take a minority of Protestant Yes votes for the referendums to succeed. To give it real moral authority, however, it needs a majority of Protestants to vote in its favour. It is realistic for the pro-agreement elements to hope that David Trimble's signal success on Saturday will create a bandwagon effect which will bring on board most of the Undecideds. There is plenty of uncertainty and anxiety around for the Paisley camp to prey on, but so far the pro-agreement people seem to be winning. Their most potent arguments are that no more favourable deal is on offer now or in the future, that rejection would condemn unionism to isolation, and that no realistic alternative is being put forward.

Underpinning all of this is the sense that acceptance could lead to peace and stability, while rejection would certainly mean stalemate and, almost certainly, more war. This last argument is also the strongest card in Gerry Adams's hand as he coaxes the doubters among his grassroots to accept the accord.

The logic of almost a decade of peace process is for Sinn Féin to recommend a Yes vote in the referendums and go on to take seats in both the new assembly and the new administration of Northern Ireland. That last sentence contains three concepts which even a couple of years ago would have been regarded as simply inconceivable for republicans. Like the UUC's ground-breaking decision, they demonstrate how old rules and habits are being shattered and how the basic grammar of Northern Ireland politics is changing.

That republican Yes recommendation will be a Yes But, since there is just too much in the agreement for republicans to swallow in one go. Despite the reservations, however, it will open the way to actively working the accord.

That is how it is all heading at the moment, though there are scores of hurdles ahead which will require the most meticulous micro-management. Yet it is a marvel to see David Trimble and Gerry Adams working in the same direction, and to think that the hostile parallel lines of unionism and republicanism might this weekend have begun to converge.

The moment of celebration for all this may be brief, before the next battery of difficulties and complications arrives. But it is a genuine moment for those who support the agreement to take heart, as they witness the old absolutes of unionism and republicanism settling for the imperfect, and preparing to make sacrifices in the cause of peace.

The elation was followed by doubts as it became clear unionist opinion was split down the middle.

18 MAY 1998   THE INDEPENDENT

Unionists march towards bitter future battles

The IRA's Balcombe Street gang did a great deal of deliberate damage to life, limb and property, killing 16 people in and around London in the mid-1970s. Last weekend they did another huge amount of damage, this time unwittingly, when they were fêted almost ecstatically at the Sinn Féin *ard-fheis* in Dublin.

Their intention was to signal support for the peace process but ironically it appears they instead dealt a grievous blow to its chances of success. Over the years that process has often looked doomed: one 1996 book by a Belfast academic has a whole chapter entitled "The end of the peace process", explaining how it died out that year.

Yet still it moves, though the referendums to be held on 22 May look set to represent a setback rather than the momentum they were supposed to deliver. This is because a majority, or near-majority, of unionists look poised to back the Reverend Ian Paisley's No campaign.

The Good Friday agreement already represents an extraordinary achievement, winning as it has the endorsement of 95 per cent of nationalist Ireland, of every British political party and of every involved international player, including Bill Clinton. Nobody likes all of it but all of them regard it as a fair and workable compromise.

The exception is unionism where the agreement has exposed a fracture in its ranks so fundamental that it may result in new party alignments. The main grouping, David Trimble's Ulster Unionist party, is clearly split from top to bottom, and so too is the Protestant community in general. One gloomy scenario compares Trimble to Captain Terence O'Neill, the reformist unionist leader of the 1960s who concluded that change was necessary but lacked the political skills and support to bring his followers along with him.

Irish nationalists were amazed, to the point of shock, when Trimble signed up for the Good Friday accord, given his record of rejecting almost all such compromises in the past. Initial amazement turned to delight as he robustly stood by his decision, but now it is turning to dismay as his capacity to deliver is cast in doubt.

If the opinion polls are correct, and if no reversal of present trends takes place before Friday, it seems that more than half of unionists will vote against the agreement. This stance is an informed one: the grassroots are attentively reading the papers and, especially, watching television programmes on the issues. And the majority unionist view, put with classic simplicity by a leader of the Orange Order, is: "We've looked at this agreement and we don't like it." In vain, it seems, have David Trimble, Tony Blair and Bill Clinton asked them to vote Yes; in vain has Gordon Brown visited Belfast distributing money. They just don't like it. In vain do the Yes campaigners argue publicly that voting No means opting for the past rather than the possibility of a brighter future, and that No campaigners have advanced no feasible alternative. In vain do they argue, more privately, that a No vote would mean the world writing off Northern Ireland as an intractable problem unworthy of further attention.

The government itself has opted for offering plenty of carrots but hiding the stick. The agreement's virtues are lauded, but Tony Blair has carefully avoided issuing even implicit threats about what a big No vote would mean. If the prisoners question were the only sticking point, it is possible that something could be done to make the arrangements more palatable. But although it is the issue most highlighted by the unionist critics, it is obvious that the opposition to the agreement goes much deeper. A senior Protestant cleric said yesterday: "I haven't found one Presbyterian minister who's voting No, they'll all be voting Yes. But a number of people in the congregations who were waverers saw the Balcombe Street gang on TV and said, 'That's it, we're voting No.' "

There is an awful lot of bigotry about in Northern Ireland, and a good proportion of the No voters are not just anti-republican but frankly anti-Catholic. Then there are others who agonised about the decision but were swayed not by the Balcombe Street gang event itself but by what it symbolised: a whole new political dispensation, part of which is to be the entry of Gerry Adams into a new government. More than half the Protestants are, it seems at this moment, not prepared to go out and vote for that, whatever political and financial resources the government deploy to entice them. Most of them want peace, but not at this price; and some sound suspiciously more at ease with the old paradigm of conflict than with the prospect of change.

Voting No will automatically put them into the Paisley camp, and it is here that a possible melt-down scenario heaves into view. A vote of say 60–40 in favour of the agreement will technically provide the necessary endorsement for it, but would also make clear that a substantial majority of unionists are opposed. The battleground will then immediately switch to the elections to the assembly which are to be held on 25 June. Trimble is trying to ensure that his party selects pro-agreement candidates but a strong No vote in the referendum will make him look like a loser and portray Paisley as a winner. At that point the more nervous in the unionist Yes camp may give up the battle, for this has certainly been the pattern in the past. Absolute disaster for the government will come if a coalition of Paisley members and anti-Trimble unionists make up more than 60 per cent of unionists in the assembly, for under the rules they could block every vote and paralyse the agreement.

While that is the government's nightmare, the chances are it will not be so bad. It seems inevitable, however, that a civil war is beginning within unionism between those who want a deal and those who don't. The new assembly could be the scene for many bitter battles.

It may take years to resolve this internal strife, with no guarantee that the Trimble camp will ever triumph over their Paisleyite opponents. One unionist Yes campaigner said mournfully yesterday: "From the Nos you get a focused, clear, direct, simple message – just say No. It's not like that for us, we have to make complicated arguments."

One astute nationalist commented: "The unionist case for the agreement is hard to make because it's actually negative. It's hard for them to say to their people – 'Look, this is the best we could get, if we don't accept this, it'll only get worse for us.' " The campaign thus goes into its final week with the Paisley No camp in the ascendant and their opponents fervently hoping for a dramatic reversal of fortune. Once again the peace process is in need of last-minute deliverance from those who wish it dead.

Tony Blair made intensive efforts to secure a Yes vote, repeatedly visiting Northern Ireland. The No campaigners opened strongly, but in the air was a sense of a whole new beginning.

22 MAY 1998   THE INDEPENDENT

Nothing will ever be the same again

The tectonic plates are shifting in Northern Ireland, bringing a new order into being. David Trimble and John Hume have beamed and shaken hands together, Bono of U2 between them, establishing a new template with that single powerful image.

Northern Ireland has never been any sort of agreed society. Nationalists felt disaffected and unwelcome, and there were always plenty of people like Ian Paisley to reinforce that feeling of alienation. With today's vote it may take a step in the direction of becoming a civil society rather than a tribal entity.

There is much sectarianism and tribalism and fierce mistrust. More than a few people feel unable to relinquish the old model in which incompatible ideologies remain locked in interminable conflict. You can see it in their eyes: that excited gleam when their side scores, the glumness when the other side scores a goal. This is politics as a soccer match, with added violence.

As of today, however, new models are on offer. The tribal model will still be there, a unionist majority pitched against a Catholic minority. But there is also going to be a new civil majority consisting of the people who will put this

Three key players in deciding Northern Ireland's future: David Trimble, Tony Blair, John Hume

referendum through. They include almost all Catholics and a substantial number of Protestants.

There will also be an all-Ireland model, for the fact is that the south is voting too, and will overwhelmingly vote Yes, thus providing an island-wide endorsement of the agreement. To that can be added the important international dimension, Bill Clinton taking a personal interest in urging a fresh start.

Then there is the Blair dimension. Margaret Thatcher was passionate about Northern Ireland but only sporadically; John Major had a deep interest, but lacked the political strength to act with real boldness. Tony Blair has sustained determination, an extraordinary attention to detail and an eye for the big picture. His campaigning zeal has undoubtedly added many points to the Yes vote.

The changes which are on the way are being eagerly embraced by the Catholic community, whose communal experience in the old Northern Ireland has left it hyper-politicised, with a great appetite for innovation and a great relish for politics.

Gerry Adams sits in West Belfast, preparing for government, having led a republican movement, profoundly steeped in militarism, to the point of participation in a new Northern Ireland administration. That transition to the purely political will take years to complete. But a historic start has been made, and in this seismic shift he has brought almost all his people with him, shedding along the way only a few splinters rather than splits. More than 90 per cent of his people, and those of John Hume, will today be voting for the Good Friday agreement.

The importance of this change in nationalist attitudes has been obscured by the recent concentration on the divisions within unionism, as that community faces a painful defining moment. The pace of the coming change will be influenced but not controlled by the outcome of that internal strife and the size of the No vote. The referendum is going to pass in Northern Ireland; with virtually all the Catholics and nationalists on board, the main point of uncertainty is how many Protestants are going to vote Yes. Whatever the figures the internal civil war is set to continue, since the Reverend Ian Paisley, whatever else he is, is not a quitter.

The assembly is going to witness bitter scenes, since such institutions provide great opportunities for Paisleyite histrionics. His DUP glories in conflict and accepts apartheid as the natural and indeed preferable order of things, opposing both social and political reconciliation. Most of its activists, and certainly its leader, believe this is primarily a religious and not a political problem. Under this definition the search for compromise is not just futile but dangerous.

The No voters will not all be Paisleyites. Some are indeed just bigots who dislike not only Adams, not only Hume, but Catholics and Catholicism in general. Others live in a world of intense mistrust – of Catholics and nationalists, of British governments, of any unionist leaders who argue that partnership and co-existence is the way ahead.

One telling feature of the intense debate within unionism is that the No campaign has signally failed to attract the public support of the Protestant intelligentsia. This is not to say that No voters are not intelligent – a number of the politicians around Ian Paisley are among Northern Ireland's brightest. But the intellectuals, the senior businessmen, churchmen, academics and so on seem overwhelmingly to be for a Yes vote.

The point is, though, that much of the Protestant working class and the small farmers have over the years stuck with Paisley through thick and thin. Every opinion poll suggests his core support is unmoved by all the talk of reconciliation, fresh starts and new horizons.

One of the features of the referendum mechanism is that it requires doubting Protestants to actually go out and vote. Much of the change that has already taken place in Northern Ireland has involved only their passive acceptance, but this time they are being asked to perform an act of positive affirmation for radical reforms. On one reading this is a drawback for the Yes campaigners but on another it may prove an asset, since it will increase the sense of personal and communal commitment to the new deal.

But whatever the result, Paisley is not going to go away, you know, for after today's vote it will be straight back into the political trenches for the assembly elections of 25 June. One appalling vista for the authorities has him, in concert with the No faction within the Trimble camp, harrying and harassing the weaker links until the whole deal becomes completely bogged down.

But another theory, which is not at all fanciful, sees a decent Yes vote, following which many unionist doubters accept that a cross-community majority has spoken, that the movement of those tectonic plates is irresistible and inevitable, and that the agreement should be given a fair wind. If that is the case then perhaps the sky's the limit. Intense political controversies will go on for years but perhaps the dead weight of all that awful history, all that stifling sectarianism, all that culture of confrontation will gradually begin to lift. A good Yes vote could open the floodgates to a new surge of reasonableness.

Some will continue to revel in division but a clear majority in the populace as a whole is simply fed up with the whole thing, wants it over and wants to stop fighting and get down to constructive business. Today they will speak in the referendum, signifying that they believe in their bones that there can be a better life for all.

The referendums passed, north and south, with strong votes. Some 1,175,000 people were entitled to vote, by putting an X in Yes or No boxes beside the question: "Do you support the agreement reached at the multi-party talks on Northern Ireland and set out in Command Paper 3883?" The Northern Ireland vote in favour was 71 per cent, while in the Republic it was over 90 per cent. It was another pivotal moment.

The people choose
a different future

The result of this referendum will be in every history book to be written on Ireland in the next century, the authors explaining that the people of the north finally found something to agree on. Just after 3 pm yesterday the Good Friday agreement became the people's agreement, the first time in history that unionists and nationalists settled on a common agenda. It offers the chance to settle disagreements by argument instead of by force.

It is not perfect; it will not simply dissolve away the ancient problems; it will face many hurdles and stiff challenges. But it has allowed all the main paramilitary groups, and nearly all the politicians, to subscribe to an agreement which is nobody's ideal but almost everyone's acceptable second choice.

Peace is difficult to define. This result does not mean we have seen the last dead body or heard the last bomb: but from now the people are entitled to expect that acts of violence will be an increasingly sporadic and declining phenomenon. It doesn't mean the big paramilitary groupings disbanding and handing in their weaponry, for paramilitarism is a symptom of mistrust and that still abounds. But it does mean that the people of Ireland have spoken, and they have spoken of an end to violence. This is an enormous advance, for not too long ago the widely held assumption was that Northern Ireland was fated to be locked for ever in endless war. That cheerless belief has now been replaced by the sense that the agreement amounts to the terms for an honourable peace.

The obstacles ahead are formidable. The parties have to learn to work together in a new assembly, co-operating in an executive which has been designed to house both David Trimble and Gerry Adams, two men who have yet to speak to each other. Ahead still lie the thorny questions such as arms decommissioning, release of prisoners, reform of policing, the management of the marching season – all huge problems. Yet a glance back over what has already happened makes them seem much less intractable. The British and Irish governments are pretty much at one on Northern Ireland. The IRA and the loyalist groups have maintained imperfect but worthwhile ceasefires; they still have their guns but the communal tolerance for their use has dropped dramatically.

Almost all the parties have co-operated in hammering out this agreement and went on to campaign for its endorsement. They will now move on to the new assembly with almost everyone, the Paisley camp excepted, seeking to make the new structures work. There are already encouraging little signs of personal and political bonding.

Practically every nationalist in both parts of Ireland voted for the agreement. The pattern was different among unionists, where a substantial section of Protestants was unconvinced about the new deal and voted No. The hard core of Paisleyite fundamentalists voted against but a very large majority of the Ulster Unionist party, the largest Protestant grouping, followed David Trimble's call to take a leap of faith and support this radical departure from the old ways. In doing so they endorsed the creation of a new unionism, a phenomenon as momentous in its way as Tony Blair's new Labour or the new nationalism brought into being by John Hume and Gerry Adams. Northern Ireland will continue to be divided into two political cultures, unionism and nationalism, but now another template has been superimposed on that old division. From now on people will also be categorised into the Yes and the No camps.

The voters did not banish the past yesterday, but they did opt solidly for a fresh start. They sent an instruction to their paramilitary groups to keep the guns silent, while to the politicians they said that the time had come to work together to create stability, and to put an end to war. In doing so they wrote themselves into the history books.

One of the key components of the agreement was a new commission on policing, to be headed by Chris Patten, the senior Conservative minister who had gone on to act as Hong Kong's last British governor. It was clear to all that he had taken on a formidable task.

The new front line

There are two RUCs. The first is the force which describes itself as "quite simply the bulwark between anarchy and order", which has for nearly three decades been in the front line of the battle against the IRA. With its officers daily risking their lives, it has paid a heavy price in the war against terrorism: 300 of its men and women have died violently, with no fewer than 8,000 injured. Many, horribly, have been killed while off-duty in the presence of their families.

Other forces such as the FBI regard the RUC as one of the most professional police operations in the world, but it also faces a charge sheet drawn up by republicans, nationalists and human rights groups. Efficiency, say the critics, is no substitute for community acceptability, a police force's most valuable asset; and the force's undoubted sacrifices, they argue, do not exonerate it from blame for its own alleged wrong-doings. The longevity of Irish memory banks means that the critics can reel off a list of alleged offences: the "shoot-to-kill" era, the Stalker affair, the Castlereagh interrogation controversy, the use of plastic bullets, the perception that officialdom conspires to cover up its misdeeds: the list is almost endless.

Critics and defenders can, and do, argue the toss about these ad infinitum, but one unarguable reality is the make-up of the force: it is 92 per cent Protestant, and some of those other 8 per cent are Catholics from England. The reasons for the imbalance are hotly debated, but its existence is unquestionable. Its internal ethos is also problematical.

It is beyond question that the RUC has a credibility problem with the nationalist population. For some years its image gradually improved, but then came Drumcree 1996 with its television images of RUC officers in Robocop-style outfits forcing aside local Catholics to allow Orange marchers down Portadown's Garvaghy Road. It looked like a repeat and an update, in vivid colour, of the grainy old 1969 pictures of burly RUC men bashing Catholic civil rights marchers in Londonderry. Those original images helped ignite the troubles; the new ones meant that the hard-won levels of nationalist acceptability vanished overnight and nationalist confidence plummeted.

The man who has been chosen to usher in a new era of policing in Northern Ireland is former Hong Kong governor Chris Patten. As head of a commission set up under the Good Friday agreement, his task is to provide Northern Ireland with what it has always lacked, a police service supported by all sides. The one-nation Tory is being asked to reconcile Ireland's two nations.

The old Chinese curse – may you live in interesting times – seems to have fallen on Patten sometime during the 1970s, and is still very much in force. Back then he was spoken of as a future leader of the Conservative party but the fates were not kind, conjuring up as they did Margaret Thatcher. His moisture content being far too high for her, he was consigned to the same desert as other wets and for a long stretch confined to minor office. The end of the Thatcher years seemed to promise a new era for Patten, but his part in the 1992 Major election victory was accompanied by the personally catastrophic loss of his own seat, and it was off to Hong Kong.

If the new task lacks the sweep and grandeur of his oriental exploits, it is certain to provide just as many pitfalls and difficult moments. Getting it right will help make a historic new start in Ireland: getting it wrong could sow seeds which might condemn future generations to renewed conflict.

Policing reform is embedded in the Good Friday agreement. So too are reviews of security arrangements, emergency legislation and the overall criminal justice system, including the prosecution process and the appointment of judges; and so are the questions of prisoner release and arms decommissioning. Add to this new administrative arrangements which will probably put Sinn Féin into government as well as creating new north–south links, and the scope of the envisaged change becomes clear. This is nothing less than the creation of a whole new political order.

This is presumably why the government believes Patten's political background and far eastern experience fits the bill. He has brainpower, experience of adversity and, perhaps most of all, he comes from the now slightly old-fashioned tradition of classic Tory gradual reformers. He is in the Macmillan–Prior–Whitelaw tradition which believes in the careful but determined management of change, in effecting movement while working with the grain.

Patten's time at the Northern Ireland Office means he comes back to Belfast with a certain amount of baggage. Last time round some unionists took exception to his Catholicism, while some of them were enraged when he allowed the second-largest city council to change its name from Londonderry to Derry. The fact that a unionist politician threw a tricolour at him in protest against the name change will serve as a reminder of the potency of symbol. While most in the RUC accept it is destined to become smaller, the force is deeply devoted to its symbols, treasuring the Union flag and other emblems and most of all cherishing the "Royal" in its title. Any attempt to change that name will meet fierce opposition.

Size is important, but the issue of how big the police force should be immediately reopens political questions. The RUC has 8,500 regular officers, 4,300 reservists and 2,700 civilian support staff. It seems obvious enough that the numbers can be reduced by running down the reserve and relying on natural wastage. But finding the optimum level will be a matter for fine judgement. Everyone hopes for peace, but there is no absolute assurance that the IRA and loyalist ceasefires will be permanent; and even if they are, there are maverick minor groupings out there on both sides.

Then there is the question of public order. A new Northern Ireland may be in the making but a resolution of the old marching disputes has yet to be found, and everyone has seen how Drumcree confrontations can bring things to the precipice. That is a sobering reminder that Northern Ireland is not a totally stable society, with paramilitarism still strong in both communities. Those communities are only at the beginning of the process of working out how to co-exist without open conflict. There will have to be enough police in reserve to deal with sudden eruptions of violence or disorder.

Once the question of the size of the police force has been resolved the question of its composition comes into focus. The trick here will be to reduce its overall strength while bringing a sizeable number of nationalists into the ranks to make it a more representative force.

But getting Catholics in appears inevitably to mean getting Protestants out. For a new force of say 6,000 officers to be representative, 2,000 or so of its members should be nationalists. Achieving this would mean displacing thousands of regulars, all the reservists and all the civilian support staff. The mechanics and dangers of this are enough to give the most ardent reformer pause, for the last thing anybody wants is large numbers of disgruntled RUC men thrown on the streets, exuding dissent.

Then there is RUC ethos. One expert has described its canteen culture as "stubbornly male, Protestant, British, unionist and laddish". Thirty per cent of Catholics in its ranks say they have experienced religious discrimination or harassment, while half its female members say they have suffered sexual harassment. It sounds as though the new force will need a new ethos.

The government, in choosing Patten to examine all of this and in giving him very wide terms of reference, appears to be signalling that it believes widespread change is essential. A police force which is heavily Protestant, heavily armoured, highly technological and largely geared to fighting an anti-terrorist war is going to be out of place in a more peaceful Northern Ireland.

In turning to Patten the government seems to want a blueprint for gradual but far-reaching reform, for a process where nothing will happen suddenly, for a plan which will be innovative and imaginative without being disruptive and unsettling. Not for the first time, New Labour is finding merit in Old Tory values.

24 JUNE 1998   THE INDEPENDENT

At last, Trimble has a big idea to sell to Ulster

Malone House, where on Monday David Trimble depicted a new unionism based on partnership and mutual respect, commands a view over many County Down drumlins, the little hills which give the countryside its basket-of-eggs appearance. Estyn Evans, an academic with a rare gift for blending geography and history, once related those fertile hills to the politics of the Protestants who farmed them. "I suspect that people living in such closed-in lowlands with restricted horizons tend to have a limited vision and imagination," he wrote. "I always like to contrast that kind of hidden landscape – Protestant landscape, shall I say? – with the open, naked bogs and hills which are naturally areas of vision and imagination, which are poetic and visionary and which represent the other tradition in Ulster."

David Trimble has long been aware that the cause of Ulster unionism has traditionally suffered from the criticisms that it is negative, defensive and backward-looking; that it needs to climb out of the trenches. Nationalists have always had the better tunes, the better poets, the grander dreams.

Four years ago Trimble told loyalists on the Shankill Road that what unionism desperately needed was a Big Idea to allow it to become pro-active rather than perpetually reactive. On that occasion he admitted he did not know what this new concept might be. Back then the Ulster Unionist party was led by James Molyneaux who took active pride in the siege mentality. He once compared his role to that of "a general with an army that isn't making anything much in terms of territorial gains but has the satisfaction of repulsing all attacks on the citadel".

This blocking game was clearly not going to suffice in the era of the peace process and the hope for bright new beginnings. This week, nearly three years after becoming leader, Trimble finally came up with a new unionist idea: partnership with nationalists, so long as they eschewed violence and were seen to be committed to peaceful means. The speech was studded with words such as diversity, inclusive, tolerance, constructive and respect for each other's traditions. It concluded with a vision of a future "when each may grasp his neighbour's hand as friend". This is not the normal stuff of unionist speeches; in particular it is not the traditional stuff of speeches made in election campaigns, with voters preparing to go to the polls tomorrow.

Appeals to tribal loyalty are more common than his evocation of a new Northern Ireland "in which pluralist unionism and constitutional nationalism can speak to each other with the civility that is the foundation of freedom". Cynics are already saying that this is rhetoric without substance: where, they ask, is the appeal to Orangemen to curb their marching instincts, where the explicit readiness to work with, or even talk to, Sinn Féin without the familiar blocking pre-conditions?

It is certainly the case that this was an astute election move. In last month's referendum on the Good Friday agreement well over 100,000 people turned out who had never voted before. Many of them came out because they believed a more constructive politics was on offer, and voted Yes. Trimble clearly wants to inspire them to come out again and to cast their votes for him. He is also looking for SDLP transfers which, under proportional representation, could help him win several valuable seats. Recasting unionism in a more constructive light makes sense in terms of electoral tactics.

Yet this is a course fraught with dangers. Unionism is confused and fragmented. His own party is a mess, largely because many of its important members have refused to follow the new Trimble line. His parliamentary party is a shambles, with 6 of his 10 MPs in open revolt against him. He has lost the support of almost all the "baby barristers", the up-and-coming younger members who seemed set to provide the next generation of Ulster Unionist MPs. Some senior party members are running against him in the election as anti-agreement independents.

To survive, and to prevail over all these opponents, he must make a successful appeal to the unionist electorate over the heads of those who cling to the old order. He is banking on the hope that a clear majority of Protestants are prepared to step into the political unknown. His judgement on this is probably right. Unionists are accused of being inward-looking, conservative, cautious and suspicious of change. But while this has been the traditional state of affairs, it is not necessarily a natural one. Some unionists actively relish and revel in bigotry, but many others plainly yearn to be rid of the sectarian yoke they have been lumbered with. Given half a chance, many would be hugely relieved to see tribalism superseded by a new civil society.

Some of that seemed to be in Trimble's mind on Monday. In the early phase of his leadership he attempted to compete with the Reverend Ian Paisley, but now he has struck out determinedly for the centre. At Malone House he had the air of someone engaged in something greater than a simple pitch for votes: he gave the sense of a man who had made an important psychological choice. Embracing the peace process, or even part of its philosophy of inclusiveness, cannot have been easy for him, for he has spent years opposing it at almost every point. But he and many unionists are making a journey from the negative to the positive, a journey all the more instructive for being so difficult and so painful.

One important turning point came in March when he and SDLP deputy leader Seamus Mallon went, together, to visit the relatives of two men, one Catholic and one Protestant, who were killed in the village of Poyntzpass. This was evidently a deeply moving experience. On Monday there was a lump in Trimble's throat when he spoke of shared suffering and of a force "which made us mark each other's bereavements, and feel for each other's losses as parents, sisters, husbands, wives and brothers".

There is so much mistrust in Northern Ireland politics that it will take a long time for nationalists to accept that this politician may have turned a new corner, and that unionism is capable of being refashioned to include the concepts of inclusiveness and partnership.

This was not a de Klerk-style conversion. But there was at Malone House a strong sense of a new personal outreach, of a political leader saying to his supporters that the era of the politics of trench warfare may be over, and that it is time to look to new horizons.

If David Trimble had come late to the idea of the peace process, John Hume was one of the designers of its underlying philosophy.

Architect of
the peace process

Nobel prizewinner John Hume, who helped transform northern nationalism

John Hume infuriates many academics because he is not just leader of a
political party but also a conceptualiser and thinker on a grand scale, not
just a politician but also the instigator of whole new theories of conflict
resolution. While some academics obviously believe that this sort of thing is
best left to them, it has excited the support and admiration of Irish nationalists.
Yesterday he received his electoral award for this from voters who clearly

155

regard him as the architect of the peace process. The idea of an inclusive process, with room in it for the extremes of both republicanism and loyalism, has come to be taken so much for granted that it is instructive to recall just how controversial a concept it was just a few years ago.

As the election results vividly illustrate, that notion has yet to take firm root within unionism, a movement which shows all the signs of being badly split and confused about the Good Friday agreement.

But the results also showed nationalists to be practically unanimous in embracing the new philosophy, many voting SDLP as a gesture of gratitude for John Hume's initiative in finding what many had feared did not exist: a potential exit route from the troubles. The great divide within Irish nationalism has always been between those, like the IRA, who believed that violence was the best way of achieving their aims and those, like Hume, who argued for politics.

The early part of his career, first as a civil rights activist on the streets and later as a politician, was about building power and influence for northern nationalism. This had traditionally been a community characterised by dolefully impotent isolation. Hume extended his influence by becoming a figure of note not just in Belfast but also in Dublin, London, Brussels and Washington. An odd situation developed in the Irish Republic in particular, where staunch supporters of southern parties looked for guidance on the north not to their own leaders but to Hume. As a result there is a fair amount of resentment against him among the political élite in Dublin.

In addition to the south, the American card lent a whole new dimension to northern nationalism, building up as it has to the point where Bill Clinton takes a strong personal interest in the peace process. Gerry Adams may command greater popular attention, but Hume has automatic access to the most powerful Washington decision-makers.

This process of empowerment of northern nationalism led to the Anglo-Irish agreement of 1985, when London and Dublin laid aside many of their differences and agreed to regard Northern Ireland as a common concern best managed jointly. Again, Hume was regarded as being among the accord's architects.

When later he came up with the idea of the peace process, however, it was seen as very much a solo run. In one sense the concept evolved out of the Anglo-Irish agreement, since this had recognised Irish nationalism as a legitimate identity, the accord standing in itself as a sign of what political lobbying could achieve. It showed Sinn Féin and the IRA that northern nationalism could make progress without killing people, but it very definitely did not invite them to participate in the political field. That came next, beginning in 1988, when Hume made a serious pitch to the republicans and opened talks with Adams. The republican worry had been that simply calling off their campaign of terrorism would leave their supporters without influence, a friendless and apparently vanquished community prey to ostracisation and discrimination by an unreconstructed unionism. Hume argued that abandoning violence would lead to more, not less, political clout.

All this can now be made to sound all very straightforward and logical: it is easy to forget just how much controversy those original Hume–Adams contacts were. They represented a spectacular violation of the general protocol that constitutional representatives should not speak to those associated with violence. When word of the contacts leaked out there was a furious fire storm of condemnation. This was maintained as the contacts continued, since as the talks went on IRA bombings and shootings continued. At many points the pressure on Hume to give up was intense, as many found it impossible to reconcile the idea of a peace process with the fact that the killing had not stopped.

His lowest moment probably came in late 1993 when an IRA bomb exploded in a Shankill Road shop, killing not only the bomber but nine Protestant men, women and children. The peace process seemed in ruins. Hume was lambasted by various senior southern Irish politicians for "using Provo-speak" and for making common cause with paramilitaries. A senior unionist leader said he had "sold his soul to the devil". A Dublin newspaper noted: "Mr Hume is on the highest of high wires, with no safety net and with a great many enemies who would only too happily see him plunge to his political doom." One columnist declared: "John Hume has been evasive and illogical. He is increasingly irrational. He is clearly intent on sucking us into an immoral relationship with active terrorists. Mr Hume and Mr Adams have nothing to offer."

One of the most poignant moments came when he attended the funeral of one of the victims of loyalist retaliation for the Shankill Road bombing. He was approached by the daughter of one victim, who told him: "Mr Hume, we've just buried my father. My family wants you to know that when we said the rosary around my daddy's coffin we prayed for you, for what you're trying to do to bring peace." The television cameras captured the scene as Hume nodded, held her hands, then turned away and broke down in tears.

The pressure took such a toll that he collapsed and was taken to hospital. There he received 1,169 letters, notes and get-well cards and other cards, most of them urging him to persevere. When IRA and loyalist ceasefires eventually came about, followed by the potentially historic compromise of the Good Friday agreement, most if not all the critics said Hume had been vindicated.

Of continuing concern within the SDLP, however, was the worry that Hume might have sacrificed the interests of the party to the extent that Sinn Féin could overhaul it to become the largest nationalist grouping in Northern Ireland. Many party members were worried sick that the republicans might take over.

Sinn Féin has certainly prospered electorally, its share of the vote rising from 11 per cent to 17 per cent in the last decade. The fear in SDLP ranks was that republicans, having failed to win their war, might instead manage to win the peace. Yesterday's result shows, however, that after all the risk-taking the SDLP has consolidated its position as the main nationalist voice.

But yesterday's success brings, as ever, fresh challenges. Hume is already a Westminster MP and a Euro-MP, party leader, and the SDLP's principal link to Washington and Irish-America. It remains to be seen how deeply he will wish to become involved in a new assembly. Whatever his choice, the history books will say he helped transform a northern nationalism which was friendless, fatalistic and apathetic into a vibrant political force. In the process he has made himself into by far the most powerful of Irish political figures.

The elections to the new Northern Ireland assembly produced strong showings for the SDLP and Sinn Féin, but again confirmed a divided unionism.

29 JUNE 1998   THE INDEPENDENT

Peace in Ulster may be on course but the champagne is still on ice

The trouble with the assembly election result is the same as last month's referendum on the Good Friday agreement: it was historic without being definitive. Perhaps that's the way it will always be, since this is a process and a long one at that: we never do get to the end of history, especially Irish history.

In any event it was another of those steps forward, another of those increments which mark real progress but which never quite set the champagne corks popping in Belfast. Northern Ireland has very little culture of celebration, puritanically considering it unseemly and superstitiously believing it to be tempting fate.

The main thing is probably that the peace process remains on course, and has come a long distance since the Good Friday agreement. It chalked up 71 per cent support in the referendum and has now delivered an assembly with more than three-quarters of its members who approve, either enthusiastically or tentatively, of the agreement.

Concern centres on the state of play within unionism, which may be in the process of tearing itself apart. All the other elements are solidly and indeed fervently in favour of the new deal offered by the Good Friday accord: Irish nationalism north and south, London, Washington and the world all regard it as Northern Ireland's political salvation and best hope for the future. But the agreement rests on several mutually dependent props, and its success depends on all of them taking the strain. Unionism is not solid; if anything it is in a state of barely suppressed trauma, split down the middle. Half of unionists are opposed to the deal either in whole or in part, and have now twice voted against it.

The pro-agreement unionists tend to accept the accord reluctantly rather than embrace it wholeheartedly; voting for it was an effort requiring the suppression of many of their basic instincts. Many of them view it as closer to a last resort than a golden opportunity.

David Trimble was applauded for last week's speech in which, critics said, he showed for the first time some sense of vision about Northern Ireland's future and how its people might live together as neighbours. But he only said it once: such a bold new message needs repetition and emphasis to sink in, and it has yet to do so.

The assembly will face many crises, the first of which may be when First Minister Trimble is required to accept Sinn Féin people as members of his new ruling executive. There will be Paisleyite pyrotechnics but there will also be much heart-searching, and possibly rebellion, within Ulster Unionist ranks.

Much will depend on the character, fortitude and political skills of Trimble. Although he has been around in politics a long time, he is relatively inexperienced at senior levels, having been an MP for only eight years and party leader for just three. Now he faces the Reverend Ian Paisley, with all his decades of guile and cunning, and the negative but highly effective skills which have helped dispatch more than one of Trimble's predecessors to premature political retirement. By the time Trimble was aged 27 Paisley had founded his own party and his own church, been elected to Stormont and Westminster and been to jail a couple of times. You can call him a dinosaur, say that he is 72 years old and point out that he has never managed to become number one in unionism. But the fact is that he speaks for a solid one-third of Northern Ireland Protestants. You can say he exaggerates their underlying fears, but the fact is that those fears are real enough, and that many unionists agree with him that the best tack is obstinate resistance rather than mutual accommodation.

We may now see the reappearance of the recurring themes of Paisley's three decades in politics, which is the formation of tactical alliances with dissident elements from the Ulster Unionist party. One of these, Trimble's heir-apparent Jeffrey Donaldson, broke ranks on Good Friday. He started out maintaining that his opposition was based on his objections to the agreement and not to the party leadership. This high-minded stand, however, degenerated on Friday into televised slanging matches with Trimble supporters.

The gloves having come off, we may now see the emergence of a unionist anti-Trimble coalition doing battle not only in the assembly itself but at Westminster and indeed throughout the structure of the Ulster Unionist party. That battle may also be fought on the streets on what could be a difficult Orange marching season.

How well-equipped is Trimble to cope with all this? Sometimes he wins the battles within the unionist family, sometimes not. To lose one MP may be regarded as a misfortune; to lose half a dozen might be deemed carelessness. He has, however, done well in his assembly team. It was first thought many of his back-benchers might be anti-agreement, but he has successfully ensured that nearly all of them are on his side.

He somehow managed to simultaneously win and lose this election: as winner of the largest number of seats he will become first minister in the assembly. But a delve into the statistics shows that it was the lowest-ever vote for his party. And Ian Paisley was only 3 per cent short of the Trimble total. Trimble has thus delivered enough seats to make the assembly workable but too few to instil confidence that the new arrangements are definitely going to last. He himself admits with slightly endearing frankness to feeling the pressure, telling the *Belfast Telegraph* the other day that he had thought of taking beta-blockers to help cope with the strain of it all.

In the old days nationalists might have taken some pleasure in his difficulties, reckoning that unionism's extremity could be nationalism's opportunity. But in the emerging new order of things the fortunes of all pro-agreement elements – even Sinn Féin – are to a greater or lesser extent bound up with the fortunes of the Ulster Unionist leader.

Even beginning to think in these terms is an important sign of the developing new civil society struggling to come into existence alongside the old tribal patterns. In the meantime there is still plenty of tribalism and ill-feeling out there, still plenty of people hoping to exploit the assembly and the marches to produce rancour rather than reconciliation.

This helps explain the lack of celebration and the prevailing sense that, though violence has fallen sharply and progress is being made, it would be rash to open that champagne just yet. Once again a milestone has been passed and once again it was momentous but not conclusive.

But while the peace process marched on, so too did the Orange Order, right into Drumcree 4. The new Parades Commission banned the return parade into Portadown, the RUC and Tony Blair said the ban would be upheld, and confrontation once again ensued. This time the Orangemen had laid plans aimed at bringing about disruption right across Northern Ireland.

7 JULY 1998   THE INDEPENDENT

A day of confrontation, a night of terror – the fear is back

The cold statistics convey the ugliness of it all: 384 outbreaks of disorder in 24 hours, 115 attacks on the security forces, 19 police injured, 1 suffering a fractured skull. Petrol bombs thrown on 96 occasions, 403 petrol bombs

The determination of loyalist Ulster: Orangemen at Drumcree, adamant that their heritage requires them to march down Garvaghy Road

seized, 57 homes and businesses damaged, 27 vehicles hijacked, another 89 damaged.

Northern Ireland is once again in the grip of widespread loyalist disorder as the Drumcree stand-off continues with no end in sight. And the impasse has only just begun: everyone expects it to get worse as the week goes on. But even those statistics, which cover the period until 6 am yesterday, do not tell the whole story.

For the fear is back, the apprehension which last night kept hundreds of thousands of people confined behind locked doors in their homes. The pattern is familiar in Belfast, though many had hoped the city had seen the last of it: hot spots of nocturnal burnings and rioting, surrounded by much larger areas filled with apprehension and fear. Loyalist disorder is proving again to be much more destabilising and unnerving than nationalist rioting. Republican ghettos, as the term implies, tend to be well defined, easily skirted and relatively manageable for the security forces to contain at times of unrest. But when loyalist Belfast takes to the streets, as is now happening, the disruption is far more widespread.

Loyalists live all over the city and can easily interfere with major thorough-fares. They also have the numbers to ensure that police and troops are kept at full stretch. As a result most of Belfast was last night virtually deserted as news spread that the roadblocks had sprung up again.

Even a simple car journey can take on a nightmarish aspect. A doctor said yesterday: "My 18-year-old daughter was out at a friend's house from early evening; I'd lent her the car. On her way home she came across a barricade blocking the road. She turned off into sidestreets, which she wasn't familiar with, and threaded through these streets, expecting to run into another barricade at any minute. She was okay, she eventually made it, but she was shaking when she got home."

Those manning the roadblocks are not polite men in suits: often they are belligerent teenagers spoiling for a fight. Sometimes they are drunk. At times like these many of society's normal rules go by the board, as youths with cudgels become temporary rulers of their districts and its roads. Thus people on a routine car journey can suddenly come face to face with the prospect of anarchy and mob rule, of beery threats, of the loss of their vehicle or worse. Many of the protesters believe in their cause and the Drumcree issue; but many are excitedly pouring out of the backstreets, revelling in the belief that their community has given the go-ahead for law-breaking.

The lesson from the many precedents is that there is no way of controlling and modulating widespread loyalist protests. The Orange Order calls for support for its Drumcree struggle, then condemns the violence that results and blames the disorder on the authorities. But the violence has come as a surprise to no one, for it invariably accompanies protests such as these. Once the loyalists take to the streets discipline disappears, cars get hijacked and torched, and the fear spreads. Not everywhere goes up in flames: the full-scale clashes between the youths and police are reserved for the real hot spots, which this time round are Sandy Row, Londonderry, and Carrickfergus in County Antrim. When places like these are seething sensible people go nowhere near them.

But the fear is everywhere: most people get to work in the mornings, but the charred vehicles shunted to the roadsides and the scars on the road where the tarmac has boiled serve as ugly reminders of the power of the mob, and of the dark forces that can be unleashed in times of Protestant crisis.

Behind the scenes efforts go on to find a way out. David Trimble, who was once identified with Drumcree but is now, as Northern Ireland's first minister, seeking a resolution, yesterday held meetings with political figures and church leaders. Urging people not to break the law, he declared: "This situation has the capacity to destabilise, and if the situation is not resolved satisfactorily, it could put at risk all the political progress we have achieved."

At Drumcree itself, where hundreds of Orangemen are camped out, the mood was one of determination rather than confrontation. The Order's leaders say they will stay there "as long as it takes" to get the parade down the Catholic Garvaghy Road.

Drumcree '98 could only end badly and it did, as one of the thousands of incidents of disruption and violence associated with it claimed three young lives. In the early hours of the Twelfth of July three small boys died in a fire caused by a petrol bomb through their bedroom window in Ballymoney, County Antrim. The Quinn children had a Catholic mother and a Protestant father.

A leading Orangeman, the Reverend William Bingham, called from his pulpit on the Twelfth morning for an end to the Drumcree protest. No march was worth a single life, he said. Faced with such horror, most Orangemen abandoned the attempt to get down the Garvaghy Road.

Is Drumcree
the Orangemen's Alamo?

DAVID ROSE, *Independent*

Croppies lie down: a 200-year-old slogan still in use today at Drumcree

The death of the Quinn children was the ghastliest of climaxes to an awful week in Northern Ireland. It provided the most horrendous illustration of what happens when civic responsibilities are ignored, when the hoods from the backstreets are let loose. The pathetic scenes at yesterday's funerals of the three boys would have melted the heart of a stone.

Ballymoney joins the long sad litany of places visited by death, where lives are taken and those of the survivors ruined. Nothing can bring the boys back, but it is possible to believe that their deaths will, unlike most killings, help to break down divisions rather than harden them.

Drumcree 1998 was awful in terms of death and damage to Northern Ireland's community relations, its economy and its image. But it was also a defeat for the forces of reaction, for those elements who oppose the Good Friday agreement, the new Belfast assembly, and the whole idea of a new partnership coalition aimed at bringing the two communities closer together.

This year's Drumcree had a double purpose. The Portadown Orangemen, for whom the adjective "single-minded" might have been coined, repeated their familiar clockwork Orange act, saying they would stay at Drumcree "for as long as it takes" to get down the Garvaghy Road. Others on the loyalist side supported them, as per usual, but this time they had the ulterior motive of undermining the new settlement. The Reverend Ian Paisley and his allies had lost in the Good Friday referendum and lost again in the assembly elections. But they figured they had a couple more cards to play.

One, which is at the advanced planning stage, is the creation of a loyalist rejectionist front combining the Paisleyites, the Orange Order, Robert McCartney's UK Unionists and those people in David Trimble's party who are unhappy about his political direction. Drumcree was supposed to act as a cement to bring these elements together. It was also supposed to isolate and weaken David Trimble, who as Northern Ireland's first minister, and as a former Drumcree man himself, was put under intense pressure by the stand-off.

One unionist observer said last week: "Paisley and company think they have Trimble on a spit, and they're giving him a real roasting." Much of his discomfiture arose from the fact that unionist opinion at first stayed eerily quiet about the controversy, waiting to see which way the wind was blowing. But by the end of the week a Protestant consensus seemed to be emerging that Drumcree had got out of hand with the widespread violence making Belfast a ghost town in the evenings. At Drumcree the Orangemen could not hold back what they called "the blue bags" – contingents of belligerent drunks who nightly brought along their Dutch courage in plastic bags.

Nor could they hold back the paramilitaries who, under cover of the Orange lines, threw nail-bombs and fired shots at police. Unionism was beginning to make up its mind that enough was enough when the Quinn murders took place and ended all indecision. The terrible denouement of the children's deaths has dealt a severe blow to the rejectionist unionists, for in the public mind there is a clear linkage between Drumcree and the No campaigners.

As a result David Trimble is in a much stronger position. This is not particularly due to any outstanding political talents he displayed during the crisis. Rather it is because the Orange Order, and various other loyalist elements, showed such a lack of leadership that he shone by comparison. Furthermore, the rejectionists have become identified in the public mind with the tactic of extra-political street activity; and that tactic has led to death, destruction and an unmistakable setback for the general unionist cause. It will be a foolhardy unionist leader who ever tries to order his people back on to the streets again in such a manner. This is important in that a menacing weapon has for the moment at least been removed from the extreme loyalist armoury. It will no longer be possible to argue to their people that political consensus can easily be trumped by determined action on the streets.

The leaders of Portadown District Loyal Orange Lodge Number 1, founded in 1796, have not yet absorbed this message. They are going to stay on at Drumcree, unaware that their marching cause is lost. Unionism is chastened, the Order is split, their movement more sundered and demoralised than ever: many Protestants simply wish they had never heard of Drumcree. But the Portadown brethren, immune to the broader picture, will stay there in what could turn into an Orange version of Greenham Common. Or perhaps the Alamo is a better metaphor, for many of the frontiersmen who made their tenacious but futile stand out there, people like Davy Crockett and Jim Bowie, were of implacably obstinate Ulster stock.

The Alamo's defenders could have staged a prudent retreat but instead stayed on and, hugely outnumbered, were wiped out. The Portadown men will probably still be there in the autumn when normal politics resumes, serving as a generally unwelcome reminder of an unsavoury and tragic episode. As their support dwindles away, as it seems bound to, we may see the emergence of a new formula which will stand a chance of doing away with the marching controversies which are so destabilising and so dangerous. The disaster of Drumcree '98 may lead some opponents of dialogue to conclude that it is the only way.

At the broader political level Drumcree will have important effects. The RUC, presently the subject of an intensive review, showed during the dispute that it was prepared to withstand the most intense pressure from lawless loyalists. This will stand to the force's advantage when its record is considered in the months ahead.

The new team of David Trimble and his deputy Seamus Mallon came through an intensely testing time. They appear to have mastered the knack of supplying mutual support: Trimble may have need of this, for it emerged in the course of the crisis that his back needs protection from unsheathed knives in the ranks of his own party. The sense of fledgling partnership they imparted was a powerful illustration that old adversaries can act in concert: Northern Ireland is badly in need of such models of the advantages of co-operation rather than conflict.

Drumcree '98 began as an attempt to re-establish the old pattern of one community being able, through force of numbers, to impose its will on another. It finished as a stark example of the dangers of that approach, showing what can happen when men try to overwhelm the politics of consensus with the politics of the street.

The battle between the two elements of unionism, old-style and new-style, is by no means over, but Drumcree '98 has in the last analysis weakened the hands of the rejectionists who are striving to turn the clock back. It has shown the dangers of anarchy and the importance of the rule of law. The pity of it is that these lessons had to be learned the hard way, and that the young lives of the Quinn boys were lost in the process.

In the wake of the Ballymoney tragedy tensions ebbed away and the sense of confrontation was replaced by a period of reflection. Drumcree 1998 was a deeply upsetting experience for almost everyone but the Quinn deaths had removed much of the poison from the air, and they were followed by a comparative lull in violence.

Then, on a sunny Saturday afternoon in a crowded shopping street in a busy County Tyrone town, came the Omagh bombing.

"If this is peace, what's war?"

The bomb was so devastating that most of the anger has not yet burst through. Omagh is still at the stage of shock, numbness and bewilderment about why such diabolical savagery should have been visited upon it on a sunny Saturday afternoon. The grief is in its early phase, for few in the town can really comprehend the scale of its loss. The grief will build over the coming days, accompanied by anger against the bombers and what they did.

They killed 9 children, 13 women and 6 men, snuffing out a total of 28 lives. Eleven people are still critically ill in hospital, which means their lives may still be in danger. Northern Ireland has had many bad days but this was the worst of them, a new record death toll, a new low.

Yesterday came the VIP visitors, including Tony Blair and Irish president Mary McAleese, to signal their sympathy and support. Next will come the full lists of the dead, reminiscent of the casualty lists posted up during the First and Second World Wars. Then will come the full details of how families have been affected, some losing more than one member, some suffering more than one injury. One of the women killed was pregnant. One family has lost a pregnant woman, her daughter and her mother.

And next will come the funerals, too many for one small town, too many for one community to bear, a day or days filled with nothing but burials. The sense of loss will be communal as well as personal: that shared burden may make the funerals slightly easier to get through. But after that will come everlasting loss for so many families: the chair where a mother used to sit, a father gone for ever, a child's empty room.

The recent emphasis on looking after victims of the troubles has brought to light just how many people never really get over the effects of violence, even decades after the event. Many who think they have recovered find that years afterwards they go through flashbacks and nightmares. The Omagh bomb has just condemned hundreds more people to the status of victims. Two hundred were injured and hundreds have lost loved ones; some will now go through life as orphans or amputees or bearing terrible physical and mental scars.

Until the bomb went off two days ago, at 3.10 pm on Saturday afternoon,

169

PACEMAKER

The tragedy of Omagh

Omagh might have been rated a reasonably lucky town by Northern Ireland standards. Like many towns it had its share of killings, and had residents killed elsewhere, but most of those deaths occurred back in 1973 and 1974, with another outbreak of killings around 1979. While not trouble free in the years that followed, it was only occasionally touched by violence. Most of the casualties have been members of the security forces killed by the IRA in or near the town. There are many republicans in the vicinity, but somehow they were never quite as active or as militant as those in comparable areas elsewhere.

It has its social problems, with a developing drug culture and its share of deprivation. As is the case almost everywhere in Northern Ireland, there is a degree of religious segregation: its residents talk, for example, about "the Protestant end of the town". It is around 60 per cent Catholic and 40 per cent Protestant, a balance reflected in the fact that the council has a Sinn Féin chairman with a unionist deputy. Relations between the two communities are not totally harmonious but nor are they poisonous. One Omagh man said: "Okay, it's not a shining example, but it's not the worst place either."

On Saturday, though, the centre of Omagh became the worst place imaginable for its people. The narrow street where the car-bomb had been parked was busy, housing as it does a coffee shop, a couple of clothes shops and a pub. It became even busier as police shepherded people towards it, a telephone caller having warned of a bomb at the courthouse some 250 metres away. The fact that the street was packed helps explain why the bomb caused the highest-ever death toll. The new school term begins in two weeks' time, and some of the women killed were in buying uniforms for their children, uniforms which some children will now never wear.

The explosion left little of the car and little of many of the victims. The blast, the disintegrated car, the glass from the shop windows, masonry from the buildings, scythed the people down, lacerating and dismembering. Shocked, those first on the scene told of the details we would rather not hear: of battered prams, of the blackened bodies of children, of detached legs, arms, hands.

The rest of Northern Ireland looked on in steadily growing horror. First came television newsflashes asking off-duty doctors to report urgently to Tyrone County Hospital in the town; then reports that several people might be dead; then rumours that 12 could have died. People could hardly believe it when the official death toll reached a dozen: why on earth should Omagh be attacked? Who would want to cause casualties on such a scale? Aren't the troubles supposed to be on the wane?

The focal point of horror had meanwhile shifted to the Omagh hospital, where wards and corridors were running red with blood. A surgeon described it as "a battlefield". A nurse said people were "running, screaming, crying". The hospital took in 96 women, 22 children and 30 men, some of them arriving in busloads. Patients were dispatched to five other hospitals. Distraught people spent many hours awaiting word of their relatives and friends: some had to wait all night, hoping against hope, only to hear eventually the news they had dreaded hearing.

The worth of the whole peace process will now be re-examined by the public. One tearful and upset woman in Omagh asked yesterday: "If this is peace, what's war?" London, Dublin and nearly all the major parties, north and south, were already doing their best yesterday to shelter and protect the political progress which has been made.

With the exception of the "Real IRA" and the Reverend Ian Paisley, few major figures in Ireland want to see the abandonment of the peace process and a return to the drawing-board. The process is a long and difficult road but, the body politic reckons, it is the only road ahead.

The Real IRA is held responsible for the bombing, though nobody can fathom what they hoped to achieve. Attacks which cause major civilian casualties are regarded by republican groups as counter-productive setbacks. The Real IRA has tried to kill soldiers and police before now with mortar attacks on security bases, but until Saturday it had never taken life. Its speciality has been attacks on town centres with large bombs, though it generally gives warnings and then depends on the efficiency of the RUC to clear the area. The police view is that Omagh was a deliberate effort to take life, but this leaves questions unanswered. If inflicting large-scale casualties was its intention, it is more likely to have targeted a Protestant town rather than a mixed one such as Omagh, where the dead were bound to include nationalists. Dead nationalists are bad for republican business.

The organisation has also left itself open to the most stringent police and army response, for the near-universal sentiment is that the security forces should go in after them, and go in hard. This sentiment is visible among nationalists as well as unionists, and in the south as well as the north. The Taoiseach, Bertie Ahern, has already spoken of "crushing" the group and of "ruthlessly" suppressing them. British ministers are talking in similar terms.

But it really hardly matters to the citizens of Omagh whether the Real IRA meant to kill all those people or whether the deaths flowed from some sort of foul-up. Everyone knows who is to blame for the carnage: the Real IRA is the cause of all this present misery and all the future suffering.

The buildings of Omagh can be replaced and repaired, but murdered people cannot be, and the injuries of many will never fully heal. The families of the dead have been left to salvage what they can from the ruins, to try to divine some meaning or purpose in it all, and somehow to try to make some sense of so much senseless murder.

The world looked on as the dead of Omagh were laid to rest.

Terrible beauty
as victims are buried

The churchyard where they yesterday buried Avril Monaghan, her daughter Maura and her two unborn twins, in the first of the Omagh funerals, must be one of the most beautiful in all of Ireland. The stone wall surrounding it does not block the view: the graves are beside St McCartan's church on a gentle slope on a little hill. It overlooks verdant Tyrone countryside, grass and trees and hedges lush from all this year's rain rolling off into the distance, as peaceful and restful a sight as you could hope to see.

The burials followed a simple soothing Catholic country ceremony conducted mainly by Avril's uncle, Father James Grimes. The business of burials is only just beginning, for the funerals of the other 26 victims of the Omagh bomb will follow this week.

Avril's mother, Mary Grimes, who was 65, will be buried today, as will at least four other people. Avril was 30 years old; her daughter Maura was aged 18 months; her twin girls were due to be born two months from now. Her surviving children are aged 6, 5 and 3.

Her husband Michael must have thought the next major event he would be attending in St McCartan's would be the christening of his baby twin daughters. Instead, yesterday he found himself burying them, together with their mother and their sister. Today he buries his mother-in-law.

The two coffins were brought from the handsome bungalow which Michael, a builder, had built for Avril and the children. One of Michael's old teachers described him a fine fellow, a hardworking man. He walked behind the coffins with his three children, none of whom understood the significance of the day. Avril was conveyed in a standard casket, sturdy countrymen shouldering the burden, but Maura was in a small white coffin signifying her tender years and her innocence. Too small to be carried by four men, too slight to be hoisted on shoulders, it was carried awkwardly at waist level by two relatives.

St McCartan's, a solid country church on a hill outside the village of Augher, was full when the coffins arrived. More neighbours, friends and sympathisers stood in the grounds and along the little road. With 28 in all killed in nearby Omagh, it was for some just the first of many funerals they will go to this week.

173

Inside, Father Grimes held his own grief in check as he tried to give solace to Michael and the rest of the bereaved. He said: "That terrible explosion in Omagh on Saturday has shattered not only our families, but many other families throughout the country. The reason for it we cannot explain.

"We must try and pray for forgiveness for those who carried out that most awful act of murder in Omagh. We ask the Lord to forgive those men, and women if they were involved, to change their hearts and that this may be the last of the terrible agonies our people have suffered during the last 30 years." The congregation went through the comforting rituals, reciting the Lord's prayer in Irish, filing up to take communion, and praying: "Grant us peace in our day."

The Bishop of Clogher, Dr Joseph Duffy, added that people must exorcise the evil behind the bomb, declaring: "We must all of us again honestly face the perverse insanity and deep-seated and deep-rooted nature of the evil that has caused all this suffering and pain."

But the phrase which most of the mourners will carry away with them was used by Father Grimes, who asked them to pray for Avril "as she takes her little angel with her to heaven". This echoed what the family had already said about Maura, describing her as "just a beautiful, curly-haired angel who was loved by everyone".

Then the coffins were carried out the short distance to the premature graves which had been prepared for Avril, Maura and the twins. Afterwards mourners stood together, generating a murmur of quiet respectful conversation, before drifting quietly away.

You could see for miles in most directions from that little graveyard: you could see trees and hedgerows, winding lanes and small woods. But no matter how hard you tried, you could not see why Avril and her three daughters should have died so horribly on the bloody streets of Omagh on a sunny Saturday afternoon.

Something as ghastly as Omagh, it might have been thought, could have put paid to all thoughts of peace. Yet the carnage only served to strengthen the aspiration for peace.

Can good emerge from the evil of the Omagh bomb?

Can anything good flow from evil, even something as obscenely evil as the Omagh bomb? The answer is yes, possibly, for part of the art of politics is the skill of harnessing the negative energies generated by atrocities and turning them against the terrorist perpetrators. It feels almost indecent, as the procession of funerals goes on, even to begin to ponder the longer-term political implications.

But London and Dublin are certainly doing so, as they must. The terrorists of the Real IRA have made a terrible, lethal mistake; now is the time to seize the moment and use it against them. For one thing, there has never been such a broadly based consensus against such violence. The bombing was an attack not just on the town of Omagh but also on the Good Friday agreement, and this week all the disparate supporters of that agreement stood together against it.

Those components span a large range, stretching as they do from David Trimble's Ulster Unionists to Gerry Adams's republicans. All coalitions have tensions, and such a broad spread is bound to have more than most. The two leaders have yet to actually speak to each other, but this week they conspicuously refrained from turning destructively against each other. Instead they have shown a sense of common purpose in condemning Omagh. Trimble has been, if not actually statesmanlike, then certainly calm and dignified in his reactions in a way which suggests he is growing in his new job as first minister. He and Gerry Adams have never even spoken directly, but in a curious way they found themselves on the same side this week.

Trimble used to say that bombings such as Omagh were carried out not by genuine republican dissidents but by proxies egged on by Adams and associates. This week he made no such allegation. Adams, for his part, used not to condemn acts of violence but this week he did it. In doing so, whether he meant to or not, he implicitly gave the authorities greater licence to move against the Real IRA.

The challenge posed by the Real IRA is very different to that posed in the past by the mainstream IRA and Sinn Féin, but there are many lessons to be drawn from the experience of the 1970s and 1980s. The first is that inflicting civilian casualties ultimately rebounds on the fortunes of republican groups. The key example here is that of the bombing of Enniskillen, a town not far away from Omagh, where on Poppy Day in 1987 an IRA bomb killed 11 Protestants waiting for a Remembrance Day parade. It generated a wave of anger against the IRA which, although huge, was actually smaller than that currently engulfing the Real IRA.

A few days after Enniskillen, in a small back room off the Falls Road, a senior IRA man told me: "Politically and internationally it is a major setback. Our support is in concentric rings. The centre is the republican movement, the next is the nationalist community in the north, followed by the south, then solidarity groups, left groups and finally international sympathy. Our central base can take a hell of a lot of jolting and crises, with limited demoralisation. But the outer reaches are just totally devastated."

Everything he said proved correct. The core held together but the outer reaches were extensively damaged and severe isolation resulted. Those outer reaches were only rebuilt, in fact, when the republicans took to professing an interest in politics and a move away from the bomb. It is arguable that events such as Enniskillen ultimately hurt the IRA as much as did the whole battery of security, legal and military measures deployed against them by the authorities. Enniskillen was a huge setback, and a self-inflicted one.

The Real IRA is now going through the same experience. It never has had widespread support: according to one estimate it consists of perhaps 30 seasoned ex-IRA veterans, together with a few score of young recruits, described by one source as "cubs".

Its political fig leaf, the 32 County Sovereignty Movement, is a bit of a joke, with maybe a couple of hundred supporters. A small number of activists in the United States, who used to fund-raise for Sinn Féin, seem to have switched their allegiance to the Sovereignty people. But all this is absolutely minuscule in comparison to mainstream republicanism. Its "central base" is tiny, and after Omagh is already showing signs of panic and disarray.

Even after Enniskillen Sinn Féin could count on a core vote of around 70,000 people. The Sovereignty Movement has never put forward candidates in elections and now it is a fair bet that it never will, for the revulsion felt against it is universal and enormous. The intelligent thing for London and Dublin to do now is to fashion a security response with a high level of political content. The people of Ireland and everywhere else want the Real IRA dealt with as quickly as possible, and there is a mood abroad which says that if the authorities cut a few corners in doing so, then go ahead.

The problem inherent in this, though, is the possibility of the Real IRA yet pulling off the old republican trick of transforming themselves from villains into persecuted martyrs. If the authorities use a sledgehammer, without regard for international legal standards, they might conceivably transform this little group into the real IRA. The Catholic and nationalist community places great emphasis on the concept of justice, and anything that is seen to depart from that concept could ultimately be counter-productive. The knack will be to deal with them effectively while preserving the standards of decency and dignity which they denied to the people of Omagh.

So where is the good which could flow from all this? The answer is that while these are the worst of times for the people of Omagh, they also appear to be the worst of times for the small but shockingly dangerous splinter groups intent on bringing down the Good Friday agreement and returning Northern Ireland to full-scale conflict.

The Real IRA has announced a suspension of bombings, while the political wing of the Irish National Liberation Army is publicly saying that the time for "armed struggle" is past. On the extreme Protestant side the Loyalist Volunteer Force says its war is over. All of these statements are being treated with caution and scepticism, for all of these groups have denounced the Good Friday agreement as a sell out.

It has also been a chastening time for the militants of the Orange Order, which during last month's Drumcree crisis thought it could paralyse Northern Ireland with impunity. But the organisation ended up taking a large measure of blame for the deaths of the three young Quinn brothers in a fire-bomb attack.

All these groups started out determined to use death or disruption to bring down the agreement. The disruption and especially the death toll since then have been awful, but the agreement has proved unexpectedly stable and the anti-accord groups are greatly weakened.

It is thus possible to hope that the political and moral illiterates are one by one realising that war has had its day, and to hope that Ireland is still moving in the direction of eventual peace. But other questions remain: Why do these slow learners have to learn the hard way? Why do they always have to be confronted with coffins before they understand? And how many more innocents may die along the tortuous path to peace?

As the days went by it became evident that the tentative judgement that Omagh could strengthen the peace process could be more confidently advanced.

The bomb that united them

And still there is hope, and even a stirring of optimism, even after the destruction, the deaths and the mutilations of Omagh; still there is the prospect of progress, even while the grieving and the sorrow remains sharp as a knife. There is good cause, based not just on a yearning for peace but on sound political reasoning, to believe that the bombers who inflicted such damage in Omagh have also inflicted huge damage on their own organisation and, indeed, on all those who would resort to terrorism.

During the course of the troubles relatives of many victims have voiced the hope that their deaths would have some meaning and would help prevent the deaths of others. Tragically that hope has not been realised: the killings have always gone inexorably on.

But Omagh is different. It will be a turning point because its terrible results have at a stroke swept away so much of the ambiguity about violence which lurked in so many Irish minds, nationalist and unionist. It has cemented an emerging coalition of democrats and those edging towards democracy; it has isolated the violent as never before.

The so-called Real IRA is about to face huge pressure from police north and south of the border. It has no credible political wing to make its case, no coherent theory to expound, no perceptible public support on which to fall back. There will be raids and arrests, and within weeks there will be new legislation specifically tailored to crush it.

But the sheer weight of public revulsion generated by Omagh poses if anything even greater challenges for the terrorists. Anyone even reputed to be associated with them is going to be ostracised. On Friday, for example,

Bernadette Sands-McKevitt, the voice of the 32 County Sovereignty Committee which has been linked to the Real IRA, could not open her print shop in Dundalk: the locks had been changed. Rallies are being held in Dundalk to dissociate the town from what it regards as deeply undesirable elements.

The May referendum on the Good Friday agreement demonstrated conclusively that nearly all republicans, north and south, endorsed the accord and were prepared to give the political path a chance. The Real IRA simply disregarded this, its mouthpieces dismissing the referendums as illegal and undemocratic. They maintained, ludicrously, that they had a mandate deriving from the last all-island elections of, wait for it, 1918. They drew on that dangerous little piece of old republican dogma which holds, with breathtaking arrogance, that the people have no right to be wrong.

This nonsense has been swept away by an Omagh fatality list which reads like a microcosm of troubles deaths, and which left no section of Irish life untouched. The dead consisted of Protestants, Catholics, a Mormon and two Spanish visitors. They killed young, old and middle-aged, fathers, mothers, sons, daughters and grannies. They killed republicans and unionists, including a prominent local member of the Ulster Unionist party. They killed people from the backbone of the Gaelic Athletic Association. They killed unborn twins, bright students, cheery shop assistants and many young people. They killed three children from the Irish Republic who were up north on a day trip. Everyone they killed was a civilian. The toll of death was thus both extraordinarily high and extraordinarily comprehensive.

The Real IRA will not make a comeback after this, for a number of reasons. One is the sheer scale of that death list, and its indiscriminate nature, which speak of either a completely murderous intent on the part of the bombers or of sheer incompetence.

Most mainstream republicans, it should be noted, do not believe the Real IRA wished to kill all those people, regarding the attack as a catastrophic foul-up rather than deliberate mass murder. But even with that belief, they do not go on to absolve the Real IRA of blame. So this time, possibly for the first time ever, mainstream republicans found themselves in the same camp as the rest of the body politic, reacting with revulsion rather than scrambling to find ways to excuse and mitigate.

This is an illustration of the strength of the Good Friday agreement as endorsed by referendum. In one sense the agreement and its endorsement can sound like little more than a combination of standard politics and a mathematical exercise, but the fact is that it has developed a mysterious appeal and power far in excess of its individual components. Some might have thought that Omagh might have blown the fledgling accord apart: instead it has fortified it.

On the day they buried Avril Monaghan, who died together with her mother, her daughter and her unborn twins, a family statement said: "She was looking forward to bringing up her family in a peaceful society following the Good Friday agreement and the recent referendum." Even on that day of unbearable grief the bereaved held out the agreement as a source of hope.

The stature of Adams and Trimble rose in their respective camps this week. The republican impressed some unionists with his unequivocal condemnation of the bombing; the unionist was warmly applauded by the congregation when he attended the funeral of three Catholic children in the Irish Republic.

The Omagh bombing has dissolved none of the political problems facing Northern Ireland but it has had a bonding effect. Many have taken from it the moral that the only alternative to the Good Friday agreement appears to be more violence. It is now pretty well inconceivable that any of the important elements supporting the agreement could think of walking away from it.

It has been a horrendous experience but it has also been a shared one, the bombers inflicting a parity of grief on the two traditions. All the signs are that it has had a devastating effect on the Real IRA and on some of the other violent splinter groups. While it cannot be said that the violence is over, the wave of revulsion has been so utterly overpowering that it is difficult to imagine any armed group, republican or loyalist, finding it possible to wage a sustained campaign of violence again.

If so, the attack on Omagh may turn out to be a watershed of truly historic significance. While nothing can bring back the dead, that thought may in future provide some little solace and consolation to the survivors and the bereaved in their terrible grief and pain.

The public pressure for peace brought political movement.

Omagh's legacy of sadness and hope

The sudden burst of activity in Belfast, centring on the statement from Gerry Adams that violence should be "a thing of the past, over, done with and gone" is a sure sign that the tragedy of the Omagh bombing will have a two-fold legacy. The attack, which caused 28 deaths and scores of ruined lives and shattered families, will go down in history as a day of infamy.

Yet within weeks of that awful event, unionists and republicans are publicly inching towards each other. Both sides are still mistrustful and still burdened by their own political baggage, but they are unmistakably edging towards each other rather than back into the trenches.

The Omagh effect has precedents in the South African peace process, as related by Allister Sparks in his book *Tomorrow is Another Country*. He wrote of one violent episode: "As with all the previous crises, this national trauma strengthened rather than weakened the political centre and spurred the negotiating parties to speed up their work."

A similar effect is now visible in Belfast. The past year has been an extra-ordinary one, marked as it has been both by violent convulsions and political progress. There was the killing of Billy Wright, followed by a spasm of loyalist violence; there were the deaths of Philip Allen and Damien Trainor in Poyntzpass. Then there was Drumcree '98, and the deaths of the three Quinn boys. Then there was Omagh.

In every case the immediate revulsion at the attacks was followed not by despair but by a sense of communal hope and political determination. Last autumn most of the parties got round the table together and refused to be dislodged from it by whatever violence was played out on the streets.

Eastertime brought the Good Friday agreement; May brought a 71 per cent endorsement of it in a referendum; June brought an assembly election with a similar result; July saw the first meeting of the assembly, with David Trimble and Seamus Mallon designated as first minister and deputy first minister of the executive. The executive itself has still to be formed, raising the question of when and whether David Trimble can bring himself to preside over what will in effect be a cabinet containing leading members of Sinn Féin. After that will come the establishment of new links with the south and a whole series of huge questions. The issue of future policing, for example, remains to be thrashed out.

The new institutions set up under the Good Friday agreement are obviously in their infancy, yet the sense that an important deal has been forged, and is worth preserving, has already lodged in the minds of almost everyone. Even at this early stage the institutions and structures are providing a political coherence which Northern Ireland has never known before. The ultimate aims of unionists and republicans are as far apart as ever, but the agreement has already delivered an unexpectedly firm area of common ground.

It was this new sense which made Omagh seem, in addition to being simply murderous, so politically incoherent and meaningless. And it was this sense which has made those involved in the peace process opt not for mutual recrimination but for what has been in effect a negotiation.

That negotiation was perhaps hastened by Omagh, but its exact timing was most of all determined by the fact that Bill Clinton's plane today touches down in Belfast. This US president has invested a lot in the peace process: this week he called in his markers, insisting he had to have something upbeat to take back to Washington. The general communal desire for progress was thus reinforced by American insistence on flexibility, though to be fair to David Trimble and Gerry Adams neither seemed opposed in principle to the idea of a session of give-and-take.

Adams wanted a public handshake with Trimble and an assurance that he would not attempt to block Sinn Féin members taking their place on the new executive. Trimble wanted IRA arms de-commissioning, a republican declaration to the effect that the war was over, and movement on the issue of "the disappeared". This last refers to the dozen or more people the IRA is believed to have abducted, shot and buried in the 1970s. The plight of their families, who in the absence of their bodies have never been able to grieve properly, has been increasingly recognised in recent years.

Neither side got exactly what it wanted, but each got something. Trimble has called together assembly party representatives for a meeting on 7 September. This is ostensibly to discuss how the assembly proceeds, but everyone believes it has been designed to be the first direct contact between the Ulster Unionist leader and Gerry Adams. The two were in the same room together on numerous occasions in the negotiating sessions in the lead-up to the Good Friday agreement but did not speak to each other. This is to be the first occasion when they will have personal engagement: others are expected to follow.

On the republican side the IRA said last week that it is taking the question of the disappeared seriously. The republicans have clearly concluded that the issue will not go away, and that the grisly business of disinterring bodies and laying them to rest properly should be tackled sooner rather than later.

On 1 September Adams said violence must be a thing of the past, taking Sinn Féin full circle from the time when the party simply acted as propagandist cheerleaders for IRA violence. Gone are the days when the Sinn Féin paper had a column headed "War News" with the purpose of recording and commending the latest bombings and shootings.

Then yesterday Martin McGuinness was appointed as Sinn Féin's representative to meet the international commission on de-commissioning. The arms issue is the most problematical of all, as is evident from conversations with grassroots republicans. The Adams statement presents no problems, since it is regarded as little more than a reflection of the near-universal hope and belief among republicans that the major republican and loyalist campaigns of violence are over for good. At the same time, however, even the most dove-ish disapprove of de-commissioning, partly on grounds of principle but largely because, as the events of the last year have shown, Northern Ireland is a most unpredictable political entity and no one knows what the future might bring.

So it is not clear whether there will ever be actual de-commissioning, just as it is not clear whether Trimble will seek to block Sinn Féin from the executive. It is also not known yet whether the IRA will cease the savage "punishment beatings" of alleged miscreants in the republican ghettos.

Progress may be taking place, but it is not doing so on the basis of an increase in mutual trust. Rather, the sense is that things are moving along because powerful elements – London, Dublin, Washington – are there first to apply pressure and then to act as guarantors and witnesses of deals which are being worked out at one remove, since face-to-face contacts have yet to take place.

To set out the many problems which lie ahead is to formulate an agenda daunting in both its size and its difficulties. No one can be sure that all this will work and eventually deliver a settled peace. The hope for success lies, however, in the fact that so many obstacles have already been surmounted, and that even something as vile as Omagh has not extinguished the common determination to press ahead in the cause of peace.

POSTSCRIPT

The Omagh bombing claimed a 29th victim on 5 September, when a 61-year-old man died of his injuries.

President Bill Clinton visited Belfast, and Omagh, saying of peace: "Do not let it slip away. It will not come again in our lifetimes. Give your leaders the support they need to make the hard, but necessary, decisions." Spurred by such pressure, David Trimble agreed to his first-ever direct contact with Gerry Adams. The meeting, held in September behind closed doors well away from the media, was, by all accounts, civil, if not conspicuously productive. Then a few days later, less than a month after the devastation of Omagh, the new assembly met for its first substantive session in the old Stormont parliament chamber.

---

14 SEPTEMBER 1998   THE INDEPENDENT

A new home
for old foes

They were all there yesterday for the first meeting of the new Belfast assembly in the old Stormont: the good, the bad and the ugly, those who incited violence, those who used it, those who have suffered from it. Yesterday they all seemed to have found a political home together in the chamber of the old Stormont parliament which was deliberately shut down in 1972 and accidentally burnt down in 1994.

The old chamber has, like some of its new members with dubious pasts, now undergone a process of rehabilitation and has reopened for what some yesterday declared to be the new politics and the new disposition for Northern Ireland.

The old issues were still there, UUP leader David Trimble repeating his warning that Sinn Féin would not be welcome in government until the IRA was "prepared to destroy the weapons of war". But he said he would welcome those who were genuine about "crossing the bridge from terror to democracy". In a speech which caught something of the day's largely positive tone he declared: "We are in the fortunate position of struggling with democratic constitutional arrangements rather than struggling with the politics of the latest atrocity."

There were, however, some bridges which looked like they would never be crossed. The Reverend Ian Paisley may have sat only 15 feet away from Martin McGuinness of Sinn Féin but the inclusive philosophy of the peace process looks unlikely to pervade their relationship. Paisley denounced Gerry Adams as "the leader of IRA/Sinn Féin in this house"; a Sinn Féin member retorted that some unionists might have their own paramilitary associations.

There was also verbal swordplay on the question of the use of the Irish language in the chamber, which Adams wants and Paisley does not, and on the question of whether the Union Jack should fly over Stormont, where their positions are the opposite.

Most of the rhetoric about looking to the future came from Trimble and his deputy Seamus Mallon. Mallon, referring in friendly fashion to "David and I", said the Omagh bombing and other violence meant it had been a cruel summer, but one which had given them a greater sense of purpose to create something absolutely new. "A new politics has begun," he said. "It's time for responsibility and commitment, for taking responsibility for our own lives."

There was humour too, as Trimble's party deputy, John Taylor, said they should congratulate the Northern Ireland team who had won a shooting competition at the Commonwealth Games. "I'm glad to see Mr Adams laughing," he added jovially, "because it was with legal firearms."

The reconstructed Stormont chamber provided a sumptuous backdrop for the new politics with its blue leather seats, gorgeous wood panelling (Spanish walnut) and stately columns topped with much gilt. Everyone gets a seat, the more prominent members having a desk as well.

After this splendour the basement canteen proved a great leveller. Men who had just been jutting their jaws at each other across the chamber were suddenly reduced to people looking for their lunch, queueing together in uneasy proximity before dispersing with their trays to separate tables.

Then it was back upstairs for more politics. The Ulster Unionists are anxious to move ahead on a number of fronts, in particular sorting out the number of departments, and thus ministers, the new administration should have. But they want to move slowly on actually forming an executive, demanding arms de-commissioning as the price of Sinn Féin entry. Sinn Féin, however, want an executive formed as soon as possible, with their party taking two seats on it. Their urgency on this front is in contrast to de-commissioning, where they want a slow-motion approach.

Paisley, meanwhile, is saying he wants two executive seats. His party should run two departments, he argues, but it would do so as free agents, not sitting down with Sinn Féin. Most other parties believe the executive should be, in Mallon's words, a single, coherent, consistent body. The question of what to do with Paisley has thus joined that of what to do with Sinn Féin.

New dispensation or not, nationalists and unionists are arrayed on opposite sides of the chamber. In the middle, where the two sets of benches converge, some independents and small parties form a *cordon sanitaire* between the two big blocs. Perhaps this will loosen up as time goes by, if and when this new assembly makes progress in the long slow business of building new political arrangements and eventually new relationships and, perhaps, trust in place of the enmity of the past.

As time passed with no sign of de-commissioning by the IRA or the major loyalist groups, the Conservative party and other elements stepped up calls for a halt to prisoner releases. The government resisted this. In Belfast, meanwhile, one businessman turned his thoughts to the question of life after prison.

The man who puts terrorists back to work

Surely, you'd think, his friends in the business community must think him mad. Surely, the smart thing for Ken Clelland to do, with a thriving Belfast printing business, is to conform to the middle-class norm, by keeping his head down, raising his family and making money. Yet here he is, chairing a committee including republican and loyalist representatives, one of whom has done time for a double murder, a committee dedicated to finding employment for IRA, UVF and UDA ex-prisoners.

Ken Clelland has, passionately, voluntarily, and for no financial reward, immersed himself in a world which most of Northern Ireland's business class has avoided like the plague: the world of released prisoners, many of whom retain paramilitary attachments. That is the first surprise. The second is the reaction he reports from others in business: "In the three years I've been quietly doing this I have not met one employer who has said to me, 'What are you doing, are you mad, do you think I'm going to take those guys in here? Catch yourself on.' Every single person has said they believe in it, it's the right thing to do. They are happy to participate but they don't want any publicity. Since I did TV and radio interviews recently I've been contacted by a number of leading industrialists who've said they will offer places in their companies. All they want is an assurance that they're not going to have any more difficulty than they would with a normal employee, and I can assure them of that."

All this speaks to a more open and pragmatic attitude among Protestant business people than is evident among unionist politicians, many of whom are against the early release scheme established by the Good Friday agreement.

Apart from the idea of giving a man a second chance in life, Ken Clelland reports that there is a sound practical reason for business to take this approach. He explains: "The business community have a difficulty filling vacancies at the moment. There is a general skill shortage, and if we have a potential labour force of guys who can do a good day's work, wouldn't we be foolish to turn it down?

"We have people coming out of prison who believe it's important to get to work at eight o'clock, who genuinely believe it's important to do a good day's work. I have to say that many young people do not display those characteristics. These are mature people who've gone through a learning experience – a very heavy learning experience."

Hundreds of prisoners, loyalist and republican, are now getting out because of the Good Friday agreement, but they represent only a small part of the problem. The calculation is that over the 30 years of the troubles no fewer than 20,000 men have been behind bars for paramilitary offences. Many of these have joined Northern Ireland's particularly large army of long-term unemployed. Some have found work, but they are not welcome in the public sector, which in Northern Ireland provides an inordinately large part of the workforce. Clelland says he wants not preferential treatment for them but a level playing field: "I do not believe that prisoners should be given anything better than anyone else. All I believe is that they should have equity and fair treatment, but I've learnt that society continues to punish them long after release. We want to provide within the private sector meaningful, well-paid jobs. It's all about self-respect and family respect. There are young children who've grown up with the father away in prison for 10 years, and that's a hard thing to come to terms with. You need family units to be brought together again and kept together," he says.

Clelland himself has family roots in the loyalist Shankill Road area, which has had more than its fair share of paramilitarism. His committee does not however differentiate between loyalist and republican, and he has watched fascinated as republican and loyalist representatives have worked well together on it. He started with a general interest in training, but he has of late zeroed in on released paramilitaries. The committee he heads has representatives from a training agency and the probation service, but is completely independent from government and statutory bodies. Asked what the committee actually does, he explains: "We are a mentoring group. We want to help one person get into a job; two people to start a little business on their own; a group of them to start a company of their own – whatever it takes to get people working and making money, that's what we're about, so they don't have to rely on the dole."

So what has made him put his head above the parapet in this way?

"It has to be said," he replies, "that there were concerns about personal safety. For an east Belfast Prod to be travelling up the Falls Road to meet republicans – it has been a journey of faith. I believe in social justice. I suppose that goes back to my student days when I was a bit of a socialist. Now I'm the arch-capitalist but I still maintain social justice is right.

"Does the journey we've come through in the last 30 years teach us nothing? I don't want a society of people who feel they've nothing to offer. We've been down that road. I believe passionately that if we don't do this that the seeds of future conflict would be sown. The bottom line in all of this is that I don't think of myself as being altruistic. I'm doing it for very selfish reasons because I want Northern Ireland to be a place where everybody feels there's a future for them."

T hen came news which in many other countries might have been regarded as a breakthrough and a spur for progress: John Hume and David Trimble were jointly awarded the Nobel Peace Prize. The reaction in Northern Ireland, however, said much about the rift in the community that had helped perpetuate the troubles, and that now made peace-making so slow and difficult.

---

10 DECEMBER 1998   THE INDEPENDENT

The prize fighters

"My political career has had a lot of downs as well as the occasional up," David Trimble mused the other day. "And actually I think that's a good thing – it's important for politicians to have known failure as well as success. I think those who have not experienced failure are then less able to cope with problems when they arise."

The words of the Ulster Unionist leader said much not only about his own career but about the general course of the peace process. It has been a real rollercoaster – a white-knuckle ride, as he has described it – replete with violent death, long periods of stalemate, and occasional exhilarating breakthroughs.

And both David Trimble and John Hume will be only too well aware, as they step onto the Oslo stage today to receive their Nobel Peace Prizes, that it is not over yet. Failure, or at least severe setbacks, remain real possibilities, and continuing political controversy is a certainty.

The Nobel Committee, in making the award in the form it did, clearly wished not only to mark the achievements of the peace process but also to hearten and inspire all the disparate elements to keep working for its eventual success. So far, however, it has had no such effect. The peace process is currently in difficulties, the irony being that the business of negotiation and movement this week is being held up as various party leaders travelled first to the US to receive other awards, and then as Messrs Trimble and Hume went on to Norway.

They left behind them in Belfast a process which is, if not in real crisis, then indisputably in the doldrums. The actual Nobel ceremony may somehow produce a surge of momentum, but if there is a Nobel spirit, last week's difficulties show that it has yet to infuse Belfast's political circles. This is partly due to the fact that the awarding of the prize produced very different reactions within the two communities, nationalist and unionist. There was certainly an element of celebration, particularly on the nationalist side, but for many unionists the news was received with caution and even suspicion.

On the nationalist side, John Hume's award was generally regarded as warmly deserved recognition for a three-decade career based on a non-violent search for accommodation. There is now an expectation that he will pull back from the front line of politics, having named his party deputy Seamus Mallon as deputy to David Trimble in the planned new administration. The prize thus had the appearance of acknowledging a long and distinguished career, the crowning achievement of which was Hume's role in mapping out the peace process which produced the Good Friday agreement. The award will take its place in his Donegal home with the other tributes, dozens of them, which he has acquired over the years in the form of scrolls, citations, honorary degrees and doctorates. These are both an indication of his high international standing and a measure of how successfully he has marshalled and deployed world opinion in support of his goals. They are a visible sign of the network of powerful friends, allies and admirers who helped him make it all possible.

The only real argument to be heard going on among some nationalists, and especially among republicans, is whether Gerry Adams should have received a share of the prize as well as, or indeed instead of, David Trimble. Sinn Féin supporters would contend that Adams helped launch the peace process bandwagon, while Trimble only recently and reluctantly clambered on board. But even among those nationalists who believe that Adams is leading his people on a laudable migration from violence to politics, the prevailing feeling seems to be that it is too soon to reward an odyssey which is as yet unfinished. Besides, the feeling goes, putting Adams on the Nobel ticket would have destroyed its symmetry and balance and, disastrously, could even have led to Trimble refusing the honour.

Nationalists have also been debating whether David Trimble deserves his honour. One faction thinks he has not earned it, while another endorses the view of the columnist who wrote: "Credit where credit is due – having been pulled screaming and protesting into the peace process, Trimble has put his head on the political block." Another section, perhaps the largest, agrees with Nobel laureate Seamus Heaney, who gracefully commended the unionist leader for having "the intellectual clarity and political courage to know that 1998 was the time to move unionism towards an accommodation".

Viewed from a unionist perspective, however, all this looks very different. Just as unionism remains deeply divided about the Good Friday agreement and the peace process, so too is it divided over the Nobel prize. Many unionists regard it as a mixed blessing, and indeed quite a few see it as no blessing at all. In the past, international recognition has been the preserve of John Hume and sometimes of Gerry Adams: Ulster Protestants have grown accustomed to being viewed as the bad guys, and to watching their opponents being fêted abroad. International recognition is such an unusual phenomenon for unionists that when the Nobel landed in Belfast many regarded it as a sort of Trojan horse.

So far it has been of no obvious benefit to David Trimble in his daily struggles with the Reverend Ian Paisley and the sizeable faction in his own party which opposes the Good Friday accord. In anti-agreement quarters it is projected as clear evidence of a sellout. Paisley's deputy Peter Robinson acidly described it as "a vivid example of the rewards offered to those who are prepared to jettison principle and reward terrorists. Better by far to be scorned by the world."

Trimble may well echo the sentiment of Shimon Peres who, after winning the peace prize with Yitzhak Rabin and Yassir Arafat in 1994, noted: "It is not enough to negotiate with your enemy. You also have to negotiate with your own people and that can be the most difficult of all." The fate of Rabin, and the present problems besetting the Middle East peace process, present a stark illustration of the fact that the Nobel prize brings with it no guarantee of success.

Within a divided unionism, in other words, the whole thing has seemed problematic rather than a help. At the Ulster Unionist party conference, held a week after the announcement, the prize was barely mentioned. More recently Trimble noted: "In certain sections of the unionist community people have felt uncertain, uneasy about the developments, worried about whether they will be for real, whether they really will deliver what they promise or whether it's all simply a con job. The prize doesn't change anything except it changes the atmosphere and it generates confidence and I think people feel easier with things as a result."

It will, however, take some time for traditionally xenophobic Protestants to become accustomed to viewing the international community as friendly, or even neutral, rather than as pro-Irish nationalist. But some of the Good Friday agreement's more far-sighted architects fervently hope that the accord, together with gestures such as the peace prize, will offer new horizons and new perspectives on the outside world.

Many will regret, even as they congratulate the prize-winners, that the work of others involved in the peace process will not go down on the Nobel list. George Mitchell, the former US Senator who chaired the talks with sometimes superhuman patience, is often mentioned as a possible recipient; so too are Tony Blair, Mo Mowlam, Taoiseach Bertie Ahern and various others.

In the meantime, at the mundane level of everyday politics, the daily, and of late unproductive, slog continues. Last week Tony Blair thought he had set up another increment of progress, only to have the deal fall apart within hours of his departure. Arms de-commissioning is as difficult and dangerous an issue as ever. Last week's exercise was intended to clear the decks for a new assault on the problem by dealing with the less highly charged issues of how many new government departments and cross-border bodies there should be. These are important but essentially administrative details which a modicum of horse-trading should have settled. Most sides thought it would be good to have some progress to show, before the Nobel presentation and the Christmas recess, but in the event a general unionist trepidation about the pace and direction of events prevented even this modest advance.

This raised several disturbing points. For one thing, Trimble seems to have decided to proceed only at the speed of the slowest ships in the unionist convoy, which is to say that he will be governed largely by the most nervous of his assembly back-benchers. For another, Blair's authority was undermined, at least temporarily. The moment seemed right for progress and the prime ministerial presence has often been enough, at strategic points, to help bring about movement. But last week the Blair touch did not work as envisaged: he will be reviewing what went wrong and attempting to ensure it does not happen again.

In Oslo today the air will be filled with high-minded rhetoric, but back in Belfast last week's setback has amply replenished the old reservoirs of mistrust and suspicion. No solution is in sight to the years-old de-commissioning problem; Trimble and Mallon are not getting on; tensions abound; trust is in short supply. Yet for all that, the overall mood, among both the politicians and the public at large, contains much more hope than dismay. Although no one has been able to show just how the de-commissioning issue can be resolved, there is nevertheless a widespread expectation that somehow it will be.

The Nobel prize has had no appreciable effect on this mood, and has created no new good will among the politicians. To many members of the general public, however, it has great meaning as an award which reflects their profoundly held aspiration for peace. If the present drama should escalate into crisis, it is they who will probably rescue the peace process from collapse. As voters they of course care about the fortunes of the parties they support; but as citizens they put the preservation of peace far above party advantage. If need be, they will be there to give their representatives the same message as that of the Nobel Committee: that from now on failure is no longer an option.

After the Omagh bombing the killing rate dropped dramatically. It did not, however, stop altogether. There were two deaths in October, both the work of loyalists: the random killing of Catholic man Brian Service in north Belfast, and the death of RUC Constable Frank O'Reilly, who during Drumcree-related disturbances had been hit by a blast bomb.

Then late January brought another brutal killing.

Defiance that led to death

Eamon Collins, who met a violent death on a road at Newry, County Down, in the early hours of yesterday, was a man who in his 44 years took the most reckless risks with his own life and those of others. A former IRA volunteer, he turned against the IRA and other republicans in the most open and public of ways, developing his own brand of the "naming and shaming" of alleged activists and relentlessly criticising republicanism.

He was not unique in doing so, since recent years have produced up to half a dozen former IRA members, who have now foresworn violence and who regularly criticise the IRA and Sinn Féin in the media and in books of memoirs. But he was remarkable in that he returned to live openly in a hardline republican area in Newry, a town which holds hundreds of IRA supporters and thousands of Sinn Féin voters. Hundreds of ex-prisoners and activists live within a 10-mile radius of his home, and all of them detested him for his behaviour and regarded his presence as a standing affront. There he was constantly intimidated and abused, suffering a number of attacks. With hindsight, perhaps the surprise lies not in his death but in the fact that he stayed alive as long as he did.

His body was found at 6 am yesterday on a country road a few hundred yards from the house where he lived for the past two years. He had a terrible death, having been stabbed and severely beaten.

The IRA are assumed to be the prime suspects for his death. The security forces and the government will be keenly searching for confirmation of mainstream IRA involvement, since there is already heated criticism of the organisation for its continuing use of violence in the form of "punishment" shootings and beatings. If the IRA was responsible, the timing of the killing is difficult to fathom, given this background.

There are other possibilities. Collins last year made a particular denunciation of the Real IRA, the breakaway group which carried out the Omagh bombing in August. In a lengthy newspaper article he all but named the Real IRA's alleged leader, claiming he had also been responsible for the killing of 18 soldiers at Warrenpoint, County Down, in 1979. There is also the possibility that the attack on Collins was carried out by republicans on what might be called an unofficial or semi-official basis. Last year, in an open letter to Gerry Adams complaining of intimidation, Collins wrote: "The people that are carrying this out are former Provisionals, former Sinn Féin people, and are now playing dual roles of being tied in with Sinn Féin, tied in with the republicans and tied in with the dissidents."

During his IRA career Collins was clearly a valuable asset to the terrorist organisation, being involved in at least 5 murders and possibly 15. From the late 1970s until the mid-1980s he functioned as an intelligence officer, helping to gather information through his job as a customs officer in the Newry area. In 1985 he cracked under RUC interrogation and made confessions which led to him being charged with five murders. He also initially agreed to act as a "supergrass", promising to go into court to give evidence against alleged former associates. But afterwards he refused to testify and subsequently disowned his own statements. He was acquitted by a judge who accepted his claims that the RUC had used unacceptable methods to extract his alleged "confessions".

At that point Collins disappeared from the scene for almost a decade before suddenly reappearing on a television programme speaking about the killings. In doing so he relied on the legal provision that, having been tried and acquitted, he could not be prosecuted for them again. One of the deaths was that of an 11-year-old Protestant schoolboy who died when a bomb went off in the County Down town of Banbridge. He said he had "scouted in" the bomb. Another was that of Ivan Toombs, a customs service official who was also a part-time member of the Ulster Defence Regiment.

In the 1997 book *Killing Rage* Collins described in meticulous detail how he carried out the surveillance and planning involved in the Toombs killing and other murders. He wrote: "When I set out to kill Ivan Toombs I was setting out to kill a UDR uniform. What was brought home to me was that you can never kill a uniform, you can only kill a person." He added: "By exposing myself to the anger of my former comrades and the families of my victims, I wanted to show that I had thought long and hard about what had happened and that it is possible to become a different person – as we all have to become different people if we are to live together in Northern Ireland without political violence. I truly believe that only by confronting our past actions, by understanding the forces which drove us to carry them out, can we hope to create the possibility of a society in which these actions do not occur again."

His return to the dangerous town of Newry appears to have been part of a personal odyssey undertaken as he attempted to grapple with his conscience and come to terms with his past. In his case this led him not to introspection but to literally broadcasting his thoughts, and contributing long articles to newspapers. In 1998 he accepted payment from the *Sunday Times* for appearing as a witness in a libel case heard in Dublin. In court he claimed the plaintiff was a senior member of the IRA. His high profile in the media continued despite intimidation which included being struck by a car in a hit-and-run incident and a serious fire at the family home he was renovating.

Last year he said he was leaving Newry with his wife and children, but at another level it seems he wished to stay there and continue with his intense self-analysis. At that time he asked, with terrible prescience: "What's the next stage? Does my house get burnt? Do I get executed on the street?"

The funeral of Eamon Collins was a sombre affair.

30 JANUARY 1999   THE INDEPENDENT

Collins is borne past the graffiti of hate to his grave

It struck a chord with more than one at the funeral of Eamon Collins yesterday when a young woman read from the Bible about a time to keep silent, a time to speak, a time to be born, a time to die. The lines from Ecclesiastes helped explain why the funeral was taking place: ex-IRA man Eamon Collins had, for his own complex reasons, decided simply to ignore the republican rule that a man in his position should keep silent.

Some 50 people, silent, downcast, some with red-rimmed eyes, followed his coffin from his home in Barcroft Park to St Catherine's church. Barcroft Park is a tough republican area of the town of Newry, a tight-knit hilly estate: few gathered to watch, and those who did looked on impassively.

The splashes of colour on yesterday's grey day came mostly from the plentiful republican paraphernalia. As the mourners shuffled down the hill they passed the graffiti which had threatened Eamon Collins and in some cases predicted his death. He used to go out with a paintbrush and paint over the slogans or alter them: he changed one which labelled him "RUC Tout" to "RUC out". But he could not extinguish the hatred of those who regarded him as a traitor to the republican cause, and those who carried a personal grudge against him.

Thus it was that the body inside the coffin was not just dead but mutilated, stabbed and battered in an attack which, as one police officer graphically put it, could have been carried out by primitive cavemen.

The sad little procession, which seemed to be mostly family, walked past a tricolour, past a poster glorifying an IRA man with a machine gun, and past an elaborate granite monument erected in memory of locals "who were part of Ireland's struggle for freedom". Further down they walked slowly past small knots of people who, wiser and more discreet than Eamon Collins, plainly knew the value of silence. They said little or nothing, even to each other, giving the impression that they were simply observing rather than being in the business of paying their respects to the dead.

But there was a surprisingly large representation inside the church, perhaps 200 people listening to Father Peter McParland chide politicians who did not wish to know Eamon Collins when he was alive but who now "use his death to suit themselves". Father McParland produced no extravagant anathema against the killers, contenting himself with remarking in general terms that they had all seen too much of war, hatred and injustice, and the hope that this pointless killing would be the last.

And then in a local graveyard they buried Eamon Collins, the man who helped the IRA kill so many people but who in the end refused to obey the republican rules, and paid the price for it with his life. He will be remembered as the latest of the more than 3,600 victims of the troubles. But there at the graveside was a wreath from his four children – "In loving memory of Daddy from Lorcan, Aoife, Sorcha and Tiarnach" – to serve as a reminder that he was also somebody's father, somebody's husband, some mother's son.

The de-commissioning dispute dragged on apparently endlessly. The LVF handed over a token number of its weapons, but there was no sign of the larger groups following suit. David Trimble and Gerry Adams held a series of meetings but no

sense of breakthrough emerged; the peace process was very much alive, but everything had slowed to a crawl.

The vacuum created by the apparent lack of political progress was filled by a firestorm of media interest in the persistence of "punishment attacks", the beatings and shootings maintained by both republicans and loyalists. Although within Northern Ireland it was clear that these grabbed the limelight only because the ceasefires had so greatly reduced more deadly violence, the near-daily recital of injuries began to create a sense in Britain that the peace process was unravelling.

---

7 FEBRUARY 1999   THE INDEPENDENT

Does peace have a chance?

People are being assaulted in Northern Ireland almost on a nightly basis, as IRA and loyalist toughs burst into their little backstreet homes, hold them down and fire shots into their legs or smash their limbs with baseball bats. Peace process or no peace process, the paramilitary enforcers still go about their barbaric business. It was ever thus: in the 1970s their predecessors used to tar and feather "soldier dolls", young girls accused of fraternising with soldiers.

After all the years and all the horrors of the troubles many thought they were beyond shock, yet the sight on their televisions of Andrew Peden, victim of one such attack, caused some to wince and to weep. Loyalists shot him so badly nine months ago that both his legs had to be amputated. An infection in one of his stumps will not heal. He cries often when he gives interviews. He looks smaller than his children; his wife says that when she cuddles him in bed it is like cuddling a child. His life is ruined.

The continuation of such barbaric practices has caused many to question the worth of the peace process and the value of the efforts to lead former paramilitaries on a journey away from bombs and into the democratic processes. Many in Britain, horrified at the unending catalogue of brutality, ask whether things are as bad as they seem. With typical northern Irish complexity, one answer is that in some ways it is better than it seems, while in others it is actually worse.

It is probably worse than many in Britain imagine, in that their newspapers and televisions do not convey to them a comprehensive picture of the scale of what might be called low-intensity violence. At the moment they are hearing much about the punishment attacks, but these are just one type of incident.

Although many parts of Belfast remain disfigured with high peacelines designed to keep sectarian factions apart, there are still places where youths gather to clod stones and bricks at each other. Much more seriously, an organised campaign of loyalist intimidation is under way, with Catholic homes the target for petrol-bombings a couple of times each week. Petrol-bombings, though terrifying for the families attacked, are rarely lethal, but every so often they take life: last year, for example, a loyalist attack claimed the lives of three young brothers. They are one of the reasons why the authorities are forced to maintain a busy emergency rehousing scheme, as intimidated families beg to be taken out of danger. Those availing of the scheme include many police families. In a reversal of the usual pattern of the troubles the police now have more problems with loyalists than with republicans. Most of the RUC families who move home do so because of loyalist threats or attacks.

In Portadown, which has become Northern Ireland's heart of sectarian darkness, loyalists continue to protest against the banning of last year's Drumcree march. Just this week, for example, a 200-strong mob attacked police lines with bricks, bottles, stones, fireworks and ball bearings fired from powerful catapults. The RUC says that 70 of its officers have been injured in protests since last year's Drumcree march. One of them, Constable Frank O'Reilly, lost his life, dying two months after being hit in the face by a blast bomb. He was a victim of the Red Hand Defenders, the latest lethal group to emerge from the loyalist underworld, who also seem to be responsible for most of the sectarian petrol-bombings.

The persistence of such incidents is very familiar in that it is highly reminiscent of pre-troubles Belfast. There never was a tranquil golden age back then, as a trawl through the newspaper archives quickly reveals: the newspapers for even the supposedly quiet years teem with disturbances, riots,

199

arson and street clashes. The unpalatable fact is that Northern Ireland has never been at peace and at ease with itself, and that the settlement of all the destabilising political and territorial issues, and the healing of the scars left by the troubles, is going to take decades.

The widespread perception is that things in Northern Ireland are as bad as ever they were, that the peace process must be a hollow sham and that it is all back to square one. The cold statistics tell a different story, a story which offers some comfort. In the 53 months leading up to the first IRA ceasefire of August 1994, 420 people died violently. In the 53 months since then 115 people have been killed, a substantial reduction. To make another comparison: deaths at the beginning of this decade were running at an average of 92 a year while the annual average is now 28.

A number of the 115 killings in the last four and a half years are difficult to classify. But 40 were killed by loyalists, 20 by the IRA, 29 by the Real IRA in last August's Omagh bombing, and 12 by the INLA. One encouraging sign is that since Omagh ceasefires have been declared by three previously active groups, the Real IRA, the INLA and the LVF.

The killing rate of the IRA is tailing off dramatically. It has carried out fewer than one-fifth of the killings of the last four years, and it was responsible for 3 of last year's 55 deaths. Violence is also down on an overall level: since the Omagh bombing three people have been killed, two by loyalists and one by republicans. On a human level this represents three tragedies, three families plunged into grief, three question marks over peace. But on a statistical level it represents possibly the most pacific period Northern Ireland has enjoyed in more than three decades.

It may surprise many to learn that loyalists have been responsible for so much of the violence, but this is part of the familiar phenomenon that IRA violence will always receive more attention than that from other quarters. At the moment this is additionally due to an odd but highly effective tactical alliance which includes former republicans, unionists and the Conservative party. This plays up republican violence and plays down that from loyalists.

Ulterior political motives do not, however, negate the heart of the issue, which is whether republicans should now be admitted into a new Northern Ireland administration. One stance is to hold that anyone even suspected of associations beyond the strictly political should be excluded from the political system. One problem with such a purist approach, however, is that the previous Conservative government had protracted dealings with the IRA even as it was setting off bombs in London and in Warrington. Another is that quite a few unionist representatives have past associations with some highly dubious organisations and individuals. On the unionist side, politics can be a rough old trade, as Ulster Unionist MP Ken Maginnis and others found this week when they were kicked and punched by crowds of protesters who included members of Ian Paisley's party.

The goal of the present administration is to get Sinn Féin into government, but to do so by securing the assent of unionist leader David Trimble. This is a difficult proposition, given his insistence that the IRA must first de-commission weaponry, and the matching republican insistence that they will not. The search for a middle way in all this is expected to take the form of an intensive negotiation, perhaps beginning later this month and reaching a conclusion by the target date of 10 March. If it fails, nobody really knows what might happen; if it succeeds, the peace process will have survived yet another apparently insurmountable hurdle, and will move on.

Either way the backstreets will continue to be the scene of barbarities. Even if there is progress, it will provide only marginal consolation to those such as Andrew Peden who are suffering so grievously. But although violence may be endemic to Belfast, the good news is that the killing rate is falling and that lives are being saved. While the peace process offers no magic solutions, it seems incontestable that without it many people who are alive today would be in untimely graves. It is not a perfect peace: if it were, there would be no need for a peace process.

March brought another high-profile killing. Just as Eamon Collins had been a hate figure for republicans, human rights lawyer Rosemary Nelson held the same status for loyalists in County Armagh, where she championed the cause of Portadown nationalists both in the courtroom and in the public arena.

She paid for her advocacy with her life when loyalists placed a boobytrap bomb under her car. It exploded just as she was leaving home, inflicting terrible injuries, and within a few hours she was dead.

Brave children's farewell to mother

The funeral yesterday passed over the very spot where the bomb went off on 15 March, mutilating Rosemary Nelson's body, sending her silver BMW careering into a stone wall and creating a new martyr for Irish nationalists.

The cortège started off from her Lurgan, County Armagh, home, taking the same route as she had on the last journey of her life. The relatives who bore her coffin and the mourners who trudged after it passed over the small hole which had been gouged out of the roadway by the downward blast of the bomb. Scorch marks were visible on the tar around the indentation. Then they wheeled slowly out of her oddly English mock-Tudor housing estate, Ashford Grange, past the remains of the stone wall where the firemen had carried out the terrible task of cutting her dying body out of her mangled car. Little bunches of flowers have been deposited at the wall. More bouquets were left at her office, one of them proclaiming: "A beautiful woman with a beautiful vision – peace, equality, justice." Another said: "Murdered by the enemies of justice, equality and freedom."

From Ashford Grange the funeral passed by Tannaghmore primary school where Sarah Nelson, aged eight, heard the explosion which left her without a mother. Outside the school, Sarah's classmates lined both sides of the road as the mourners shuffled past in the cold morning sunshine.

Next along the route came black flags, hung out by residents of the working-class Kilwilkie estate in tribute to the lawyer who represented so many of them in their skirmishes with officialdom. Rosemary Nelson was seen not just as a highly effective solicitor but also as one prepared to go beyond the orthodox legal role and speak for them in the public arena. Which is probably why that bomb was placed underneath her car with such care and such hate. It is almost certainly true that in targeting her, the loyalist assassins thought they might strengthen the Orange cause in the annual Drumcree marching dispute in neighbouring Portadown. It is also true that they oppose the Good Friday agreement and want to bring it down. But at heart the primary motivation of the attack was probably raw sectarianism, the desire to strike at the local Catholic and nationalist community by removing a woman who was fast becoming one of its foremost advocates.

In the face of such hatred Rosemary Nelson's sons displayed real character and something close to heroism when, inside St Peter's church, they held their shock and grief in check to speak of their mother. Eleven-year-old Gavin said proudly: "My mum was a brilliant solicitor and friend, and whenever you were in need of help she was right there by your side. However, we her family know her as the best mother, wife, daughter and sister anyone could ever wish for."

The priest described her as a tireless worker and called for an independent inquiry into Rosemary Nelson's death. Outside, those unable to get into the church, standing talking in the cold, had no need of such an investigation: they nearly all firmly believe the RUC must have had something to do with it.

Overall the mood was stoical and sombre, with no evident thirst for vengeance in the air. But there had already been overnight rioting and petrol-bombing in Portadown, involving nationalists, loyalists and the police, and one of the mourners, Councillor Breandán Mac Cionnaith, bore a conspicuous wound. He was without his usual glasses and instead had one eye covered by a large surgical patch. He had earlier been pictured with blood streaming from his eye, telling the cameras a policeman had struck him: "I was smashed in the face with a baton. He smashed the glasses right into my eye."

RUC Assistant Chief Constable Tom Craig said one of his officers had reported accidentally striking Mac Cionnaith as he sought to defend himself against a person attacking him. Saying the incident would be investigated, Craig blamed the night of violence on "sheer drunken aggression and demonstrations of tribalism". Thirty-eight officers were injured in disturbances, though only one was hospitalised.

Ill-feeling against the police is nothing new here. A plaque on a wall just around the corner from St Peter's church commemorates two people "murdered on the 15th August 1879 when police opened fire on a Catholic procession".

Many of Northern Ireland's most senior politicians are now on their way back from the St Patrick's Day festivities and political exchanges in Washington, where they took part in many meetings but achieved no breakthroughs. There were two killings while they were away, that of Rosemary Nelson and the renegade loyalist Frankie Curry.

The next few weeks will bring crucial talks aimed at making the Good Friday agreement work. The hope will be that Rosemary Nelson's death will not send them back into their trenches, but will spur them on to cement an agreement which might prevent more funerals like hers.

CONCLUSION

So what are the prospects for the future? A glance back at the events of the years covered by this book shows the perils of prediction, for no writer of fiction would have dared to construct a plot filled with such incident and commotion. No one could have forecast all the high spots and low points, all that hope and all that tragedy.

At the time of writing, the various political elements remain locked in debate over de-commissioning and the formation of an executive. Such talks have become wearisome to almost everyone, and they have gone on for so long that the European election campaign is now looming, together with the marching season and the prospect of yet another Drumcree. Late summer is expected to bring the Patten report on policing, which is bound to generate fierce argument. And in the meantime the splinter groups on both the republican and loyalist sides have not gone away, with loyalists in particular staging potentially lethal petrol bomb attacks on Catholic homes.

It is all too easy to imagine political or security crises being produced by any or all of these: the question is whether they might singly or in combination hold the capacity to wreck the peace process. No one can answer that question with complete certainty, yet it is clearly the case that this process has absorbed and survived the most fearful buffetings and attacks on its existence. It has lived on through arctic stalemates, through oceans of mistrust and through crescendos of violence. The fact that it has survived so much implies that for all the bitterness and division, a large majority of people fervently want a new era in which differences and disputes can be dealt with by political argument rather than violence. If this were not the case the process would have collapsed long ago.

It is obvious enough that many crises and difficulties lie ahead, but the fact that unionists and republicans both want an executive established probably means that it will sooner or later come into being. After that will come more crises of various types, for learning to live together, and govern together, will not be a smooth experience.

It will never be possible to relax, for fringe republicans or loyalists will always retain the ability to take life; marching disputes could flare up at any time; and, most dangerous of all, one or other community might conclude that the new arrangements are operating unfairly. The level of violence has already dropped dramatically, but Northern Ireland politics will continue to be a minefield. The hope is, however, that enough people have learned enough lessons to realise that even an imperfect politics is infinitely preferable to a return to the tragedy of the troubles.

INDEX

Adair, Johnny ("Mad Dog"), 109, 117–18, 119
Adams, David, 122
Adams, Gerry, 4, 8, 13, 15, 17, 18, 19, 25, 48, 56, 70, 130, 133, 136, 181, 182
  condemns Omagh bombing, 175, 180
  demands entry to talks, 20–1
  election as MP (1997), 59–60, 67
  and Good Friday agreement, 138, 139, 140, 142, 144–5
  negotiations on new institutions, 182–3
  and new IRA ceasefire (1997), 83
  and Nobel Peace Prize, 190, 191
  political path, 2, 6, 7
  and Republic's presidential election, 106
  violence should be "a thing of the past" statement, 181, 183
Ahern, Bertie, 130, 133, 136, 172, 192
  political background, 133
Ahern, Julia, 133
Aintree bomb threats, 54–7
Alderdice, John, 37
all-party talks. see political talks
Allen, Philip, 126–8, 181
Alliance party, 16, 37
Amnesty International, 66
Ancram, Michael, 51
Andersonstown (Belfast), 13
Anglo-Irish agreement (1985), 34, 88, 129–30, 156
Anglo-Irish approach, 66
Anglo-Irish treaty (1921), 100–101
Annesley, Sir Hugh, 31, 33
Apprentice Boys, 36
Arafat, Yassir, 191
Ardoyne (Belfast), 7
arms de-commissioning, 5, 8, 9, 10, 12, 37, 51, 76, 182, 185, 201, 204
  Good Friday agreement, 137
  LVF token handover, 197
  removal of talks proviso, 76, 77, 78, 83
  SF representative to international commission, 183
assembly. see Northern Ireland Assembly
Attlee, Clement, 62–3, 64, 65

Augher (Co. Tyrone), 173
Averill, Liam, 111, 117

B Specials, 30
Balcombe Street gang, 140, 142
Ballygomartin (Belfast), 13
Ballymena (Co. Antrim), 12, 13
Ballymoney (Co. Antrim)
  murder of RUC officer, 73–4
  Quinn murders, 164, 165, 166
Ballymurphy (Belfast), 13
Ballynafeigh (Belfast), 82
Bates, Robert "Basher", 74–5
Begley, Thomas, 75
Belfast, 2, 28
  religious riots in 19th century, 29
Belfast assembly. see Northern Ireland Assembly
Belfast city council, 10, 71
  Book of Peace, 122
  largest parties, 71
  unionists lose control of, 71
Belfast Telegraph, 160
Bellaghy (Co. Londonderry), 57, 58
Benn, Tony, 64
Bessbrook (Co. Armagh), 54
Bingham, Rev. William, 164
Birkenhead, Lord, 100
Black and Tans, 133
Blair, Tony, 62, 66, 67, 71, 76, 87, 89, 130, 136, 169, 192
  authority of, 92
  at Balmoral Show (1997), 68–9
  general election landslide (1997), 67
  and Good Friday agreement, 141, 143, 144
  political initiative (June 1997), 76, 77–8
  reopens direct contacts with Sinn Féin, 68–9
  and Trimble, 130–1
Bloody Sunday (1972), 123–5
Bono, 143
Boyne, battle of (1690), 26, 30
Bradwell, James, 47
Brennan, Larry, 118

British government, 12, 16, 18, 34. *see also*
Blair, Tony; Major, John
communications with IRA and Sinn Féin,
5
double standards for terrorists, 50–3
neutrality questioned, 53
and peace process, 5–6
republican suspicions of, 5, 8
strategic military interests, 64–5
British withdrawal, 65
Brooke, Peter, 134
Brookeborough, Lord, 63
Brown, Gordon, 141
Bruton, John, 8, 19, 20, 106, 130
BSE, 69

CAC (Continuity Army Council), 90
Callaghan, James, 44, 62, 65–6, 67
Canary Wharf bomb (Feb. 1996), 1–7, 17, 48,
55
Carson, Edward, 34
Catholicism, 44
Catholics
and Good Friday agreement, 139, 144
increase in Catholic population, 70
loyalist attacks on, 118–21
and peace process, 121
centre-out approach, 18
Churchill, Lord Randolph, 29–30
Churchill, Winston, 99, 100
civil rights campaign, 34, 64, 87
civil society, 143–4, 154, 160–1
Civil War, Irish, 133
Clare, Anthony, 106
Clelland, Ken, 187–9
Clinton, Bill (US president), 7, 9, 48, 78, 141,
144, 156
visit to Belfast and Omagh (1998), 182,
184
Collins, Eamon, 194–6
funeral of, 196–7
IRA career, 195
Collins, Michael, 99–101
Conservative party, 66, 150, 186, 200
Cookstown district council, 70
Copeland, Eddie, 51
Corrigan, Fr Desmond, 127
Craig, Bill, 64, 87, 88
"shoot-to-kill" speeches, 87
voluntary coalition idea, 88
Craig, James, 30, 34, 98–9
Craig, Tom, 203
Crumlin Road jail, 113
Curran, Fr Anthony, 82–3
Currie, Austin, 104

Curry, Frank, 203

de-commissioning. *see* arms
de-commissioning
de Valera, Eamon, 98–100
Democratic Unionist party, 9, 10, 40, 41, 42,
46. *see also* Paisley, Rev. Ian
demographic changes, 70–3
Derry city council, 150
Devlin, Bernadette, 10
Dillon, Seamus, 118
disappeared, 182–3
discrimination, 64
Doherty, Pat, 56
Donaldson, Jeffrey, 133, 160
Downing Street declaration (1993), 4
Drumcree dispute, 26, 29, 76–7, 89, 110, 151,
161–3, 165–8, 204
Drumcree 1 (1995), 25–6, 89
Drumcree 2 (1996), 31–5, 49, 66; moral
dimension, 33–4; intimidation and
boycotts, 36–7; reactions in Republic
and Britain, 38; nationalist and unionist
reactions, 38–9, 73; RUC role, 148;
Trimble meeting with Billy Wright, 110
Drumcree 3 (1997), 79–81, 89
Drumcree 4 (1998), 161–8, 193; killing of
RUC constable, 199; loyalist protests,
199; murder of Rosemary Nelson,
202–3
Dublin–London relationship, 129–30
Dublin–Monaghan bombings (1974), 104
Duffy, Rev. Dr Joseph (Bishop of Clogher),
174
Dundalk (Co. Louth), 179
DUP. *see* Democratic Unionist party

elections, 10
1996 Forum elections, 9–18; justification for,
15–16
1997 Westminster election, 56–61, 67, 69;
Mid-Ulster, 56–9; West Belfast, 59–60;
Labour landslide, 67
1997 local government elections, 70–2
1998 assembly elections, 158–61
demographic changes, 70–3
personation and vote-stealing allegations,
59–61, 72
Enniskillen bomb (1987), 176
Enright, Terry, 118
Ervine, David, 12, 16, 51, 94
Evans, Estyn, 152
executive, 159, 186, 204

Falls Road (Belfast), 7, 84, 176

Fermanagh district council, 70, 71
Fitt, Gerry, 66
FitzGerald, Garret, 65
Flanagan, Ronnie (Chief Constable, RUC), 51, 82
Foot, Michael, 64
Framework Document (1995), 68
Free Presbyterian church, 44–5

Garda Síochána, 24
Garvaghy Road (Portadown), 26, 32, 33, 80, 148; see also Drumcree dispute
general election (1997), 56–61, 67, 69, 70
gerrymandering, 60, 64
Gladstone, William Ewart, 4, 29
Good Friday agreement, 136–48, 153, 182, 188
  negotiations on new institutions, 182–3
  new political order, 150
  No campaign, 139, 141, 142, 145, 146
  Omagh bomb and, 175–7, 179–80
  outline for, 134–5
  policing reform, 150
  preliminary talks process. see political talks
  prisoner release scheme, 187, 188
  reactions to, 138–9
  referendums, 141, 146–9, 153, 158–9, 179, 181
  Stormont talks, 132–6; see also political talks
  Yes campaign, 139, 141
Gould, Matilda, 118
Gould, Tracey, 14
Grand Orange Lodge of Ireland, 77
Grimes, Fr James, 173, 174
Grimes, Mary, 173

Hackett, Fr Brian, 128
Hammersmith, 48
Hartley, Tom, 84–5
Haughey, Denis, 57–9
Hayes, Maurice, 44
Healey, Denis, 64, 65
Heaney, Seamus, 58, 191
Hillsborough (Co. Down), 46
home rule, 29–30, 34, 63
Hughes, Ben, 118
Hume, John, 4, 9, 10, 17, 48, 57, 70, 78, 133–4, 139
  architect of the peace process, 154–8
  Nobel Peace Prize, 189–93
  and Republic's presidential election, 104
Hume–Adams contacts, 4, 17, 48, 130, 156–7
hunger strikes (1981), 112, 117

Independent, 84
INLA (Irish National Liberation Army), 82, 90, 119, 122, 200
  internal feud, 3
  murder of Billy Wright, 107, 109, 111, 113
intimidation, 199
IRA (Irish Republican Army), 3, 4, 5, 12, 15, 37–8, 46, 49, 52, 68
  army council, 23–5
  ceasefire (1994), 4, 5, 15, 16, 18, 48, 53, 56, 106; effects of, 24, 84
  ceasefire breakdown (1996), 1–9; "Sinn Féin's fatal dilemma", 6–9; republican reaction, 17–18; IRA's strategy, 37–8, 54–7; reinstatement hopes – Blair initiative, 76, 78, 79, 83
  ceasefire resumption (1997), 83–4, 89–93
  disappeared, 182–3
  killing rate, 200
  military discipline, 23–4
  prisoners, 115, 116; hunger strikes, 112; Maze breakout (1983), 112, 117; peace process, 113
  punishment attacks, 183
  violence – specific incidents: Kingsmills murders (1976), 109; Enniskillen bomb (1987), 176; Shankill Road bomb (1993), 75, 157; Canary Wharf (1996), 1–7; Garda McCabe killing (1996), 22, 24; Manchester bombing (1996), 22–5, 48, 55; Lisburn bombings (1996), 47, 48; Stephen Restorick killing (1997), 54; Aintree bomb threat (1997), 54–7; killing of 2 RUC constables in Lurgan (1997), 76; suspected of involvement in Eamon Collins killing (1998), 194
Irish-America, 7
Irish Republic
  concerns about Sinn Féin, 106
  declaration of, 62–3
  Good Friday agreement referendum, 146
  presidential campaign (1998), 105–7
Irish Republican Army. see IRA

Jenkinson, Norman, 36–7
John Paul II, 44
Jones, Baptist, 57

Kelly, Gerry, 105
Kingsmills (Co. Armagh)
  IRA killing of 10 Protestants (1976), 109
Kissinger, Henry, 65

Labour party, 55. see also Blair, Tony
  Attlee administration, 62–3, 64

Callaghan administration, 65–6, 67
espousal of Irish unity, 64, 65, 66
general election landslide (1997), 67–9
and Irish question, 62–7
sponsor of unionist interests (1976–9), 65–6
Wilson administration, 64–5, 66, 67
Lavery, Bobby, 11–12
Ligget, Noel, 82
Limavady (Co. Derry), 81
Lisburn bombings (Oct. 1996), 47, 48
Liverpool, 64
Lloyd George, David, 4, 100
local government elections (1997), 70–1
demographic changes, 70–2
London
Canary Wharf bomb (Feb. 1996), 1–7
Londonderry, 36, 81, 123, 150
Londonderry, Lord, 99–100
Longford, Lord, 63, 64
Lower Ormeau Road, 81, 82–3
loyalist ceasefire. see loyalist paramilitaries
loyalist general strike (1974), 34, 65, 66, 88
loyalist marches, 73. see also Drumcree
dispute; Orange Order
loyalist paramilitaries, 12, 16, 25, 32, 45, 49,
50, 90, 94, 95, 200, 204. see also LVF;
Red Hand Defenders; UDA; UVF
ceasefire (1994), 37, 50; conditional nature
of, 51, 90; "partially intact", 50–1
commitment to democratic means
questioned, 51
"counter-terrorism", engaged in, 119
disorder at Drumcree. see Drumcree
dispute
government's double standards towards,
50–3
intimidation, 36, 199
numbers killed by, 53
punishment attacks, 37, 51
republican violence, contrast with, 118–19
sectarian motivation, 118, 120–1
violence – specific incidents: Dublin–
Monaghan bombings (1974), 73–4;
Shankill Butchers, 74–5; attacks on
republicans, 50–3; murder of John
Slane, 54; murder of RUC officer in
Ballymoney, 73–4; attacks on Catholics,
118–20; Poyntzpass murders (1998),
126–8; Quinn murders (Ballymoney,
1998), 164, 165, 166; murder of
Rosemary Nelson, 202–3
loyalist parties, 37, 42, 51, 119. see also
Progressive Unionist party; Ulster
Democratic party
electoral mandate, 51, 72

and loyalist violence, 51
talks participants, 133
Loyalist Volunteer Force. see LVF
Lucas, Kyle, 68
Lundy, Alan, 97
Lurgan (Co. Armagh)
IRA killing of 2 policemen (1997), 76
loyalist killing of Rosemary Nelson (1998),
202–3
LVF (Loyalist Volunteer Force), 80, 90, 109,
119, 122, 200
token handover of arms, 197

McAleese, Mary, 105, 169
career of, 101–4
and Catholic hierarchy, 103
presidential campaign, 105–7
McCabe, Cormac, 96
McCabe, Garda Jerry, 19, 22, 24
McCartney, Robert, 16, 17, 50, 52, 166
Mac Cionnaith, Breandán, 203
McCrea, Rev. William
general election campaign (1997), 57–9
McCrory, Sam, 116, 117
McCusker, Fergal, 118
McCusker, Harold, 60–1, 88–9
McGlinchey, Dominic, 109
McGoldrick, Michael, 32
McGuinness, Martin, 6, 21, 56, 183
election campaign (1997), 57–9, 67
McKeague, John, 109
McMichael, Gary, 16, 51, 94, 96, 119, 122
McMichael, John, 94, 96, 97
McNamara, Kevin, 64, 66
McParland, Fr Peter, 197
McVeigh, Jim, 116
McWilliams, Monica, 40–1
Maginnis, Ken, 88, 94, 95, 96, 135, 200
IRA target, 95
Maguire, Harry, 116
Major, John, 3, 8, 9, 12, 15, 19, 20, 33, 39, 45,
48–9, 55, 68, 78, 92, 93, 122, 134, 138,
140, 144
handling of peace process, 4–6
UDA killings, and, 122
Mallon, Seamus, 154, 167, 181, 185, 190,
192
Manchester bombing (June 1996), 22–5, 48,
55
Mandela, Nelson, 129
Markethill (Co. Armagh)
IRA bomb (Sept. 1997), 95
Maskey, Alex, 97
Mason, Roy, 65–6
Maudling, Reginald, 45

Mayhew, Sir Patrick, 15, 20, 33, 134
  double standards towards loyalist terrorists,
    50–3
Maze (prison), 111–17
  conditions for inmates, 114–17
  hunger strikes (1981), 112, 117
  IRA breakout (1983), 112, 117
  killing of Billy Wright (Dec. 1997), 107, 111,
    113
MI5, 56
Mid-Ulster
  general election campaign (1997), 57–9
Middle East peace process, 191
Milltown cemetery (Belfast), 114
mistrust, 79, 83–5
Mitchell, George, 19–20, 129, 192
Mitchell principles, 51, 122
Mogg, Martin, 115, 116
Molyneaux, James, 34, 89, 152
Monaghan, Avril, 173, 174, 180
Monaghan, Maura, 173, 174
Monaghan, Michael, 173
Monday Club, 87
Morrison, Herbert, 63
Mosley, Oswald, 87
Mowlam, Dr Marjorie ("Mo"), 62, 66, 68, 71,
    76, 122, 136, 192
  meeting with UDA prisoners (1998), 114, 117
multi-party talks. see political talks
Murphy, Lennie, 75

nationalism, 38
  alienation, feelings of, 143
  demographic increases, 70
  electoral share, 70
  and Good Friday agreement, 143–5, 148,
    156
  new nationalism, 148
  and Nobel Peace Prize, 190–1
  pan-nationalist front, 130
  and peace process, 17; Hume as architect
    of peace process, 153–8
  political talks, philosophy in, 135
  process of empowerment of, 156
Nelson, Gavin, 203
Nelson, Rosemary, 202–3
New Lodge (Belfast), 11
Newell, James, 69
Newry (Co. Down), 194, 195, 196
Nixon, Rev. Joseph, 128
Nobel Peace Prize, 189–93
Normanbrook, Lord, 63
north–south bodies, 135
Northern Ireland Assembly, 135
  election results, 158–1

first meeting, 181, 184–6
  negotiations on new institutions, 182–3,
    185–6
Northern Ireland Forum, 39
Northern Ireland Office, 21
Northern Ireland Women's Coalition, 39–41

Ó Conaill, Dáithí, 46
O'Hare, Dessie, 109
Omagh bomb (Aug. 1998), 168–80, 182
  can good emerge?, 175–7
  Clinton visit, 184
  funerals, 173–4, 180
  and Good Friday agreement, 175–7,
    179–80
  legacy of sadness and hope, 181–3
  and peace process, 171–2, 180
  reactions, 178–80, 181, 182
  turning point, 178, 180
  victims, 169, 179, 183
O'Neill, Terence, 60, 64, 87, 141
Orange marches, 73, 89, 149
Orange Order, 26–31, 34, 35, 39, 76–7, 80,
    81, 161–3, 166–7, 177
  and Good Friday agreement, 139, 141
  historical development, 28–30
  parading disputes, 27–8, 29, 31, 204. see
    also Drumcree dispute
  decision on 4 contentious marches
    (July 1997), 80, 81–3
  unionist governments and, 30–1
O'Reilly, Frank, 193, 199

Paisley, Rev. Ian, 8, 9, 10, 19–20, 21, 26, 38,
    40, 52, 57, 64, 71, 78, 82, 85, 86, 134,
    146, 154, 166
  and Drumcree dispute, 166
  Forum election campaign (1996), 12, 13,
    14, 16, 17
  and Good Friday agreement, 139, 141,
    145–6
  and Northern Ireland Aassembly, 185, 186
  and peace process, 95
  and Trimble, 85–6, 159, 160
  "25 years of Ireland's Dr No", 42–7
Paisley, Ian Junior, 13, 41
pan-nationalist front, 130
pan-Protestant front, 27
Patten, Chris, 149–50, 204
Patten commission, 148–51, 204
Patton, Joel, 82
peace process, 24, 25, 38, 49, 159. see also
    Good Friday agreement; political talks
  and 1996 elections, 15, 17, 18
  Good Friday agreement and, 143–6

Hume as architect of, 153–8
important relationships in, 129–31
initial development, 4–5, 91–2; Hume–
	Adams contacts, 4, 17, 48, 130, 156–7
John Major's handling of, 4–6
nationalist support, 17
Omagh bomb and, 171–2, 178
prisoners and, 113
Protestant attitudes to, 91–2
punishment attacks and, 198–9
southern suspicions, 106
unionist political denunciation of, 91
Peden, Andrew, 198–9, 201
Peep o' Day Boys, 28
people power, 17–18
Peres, Shimon, 191
personation, 59–60, 61, 72
policing, 37; *see also* RUC
Patten commission, 148–51
political talks
	1996–1997: 2, 3, 8, 15, 16, 19–21, 25, 37,
		48, 55; Forum elections, 9–10; fruitless
		wrangling, 49; loyalist presence, 51–3
	1997–1998: reconvening, 73; Blair initative
		(June 1997), 76, 77–8; removal of
		de-commissioning proviso, 76, 77, 78,
		83; resumption of IRA ceasefire, 84;
		Protestants favour talks with Sinn Féin,
		92; "Unionist standard-bearers square
		up to Sinn Féin", 93–5; "...behind every
		seat ... stands a ghost", 96–7; "...how
		blood enemies learned to talk", 132–6;
		temporary exclusions, 123; "Ulster
		moves towards its Mandela moment",
		129–31; outline for settlement, 133–5;
		Good Friday agreement, 136–40
	philosophical differences, 135
	talks building, 135–6
population changes, 70–3
Portadown (Co. Armagh), 29, 32, 109. *see
	also* Drumcree dispute
loyalist violence, 119
Portadown District Loyal Orange Lodge
	Number 1, 167
powersharing, 65, 85, 88
Poyntzpass murders (1998), 126–8, 154, 181
Price, Vincent, 44
Prior, James, 45
prisoners
	employment of released prisoners, 187–9
	Maze prison, 111–13, 114–17
	and peace process, 113
	releases, 75, 187, 188
Progressive Unionist party (PUP), 51, 72, 94
	election campaign (1996), 12, 14

Protestant–Catholic relations, 49
Protestants
	and Good Friday agreement, 139, 142,
		145–6
	population decline, 73
	power of, 65, 66
proximity talks, 92
punishment attacks, 37, 51, 84, 183, 198–9,
	201
PUP. *see* Progressive Unionist party

Queen's University Belfast
	"Protestant university", 103
Quinn murders (Ballymoney), 164, 165, 166,
	168, 181

Rabin, Yitzhak, 191
Real IRA, 176–7, 178, 200
	and murder of Eamon Collins, 194
	Omagh bomb, 172, 175, 179
rebellion of 1798, 28–9
Red Hand Defenders, 199
Redemptorist Order, 106
Rees, Merlyn, 65
refugee tourism, 77
Reid, Fr Alex, 106
religious riots, 29
Republic of Ireland. *see* Irish Republic
republicans, 6–8, 12, 15, 16, 38, 39, 130. *see
	also* INLA; IRA; Sinn Féin
	and breakdown of IRA ceasefire, 17–18
	effects of Enniskillen bomb (1987), 176
	and Good Friday agreement, 138
	hunger strikes (1981), 112
	IRA's grand strategy, 54–7
	and Manchester bombing (1996), 22–4
	Real IRA, 172, 176–7
Restorick, Stephen, 54
Reynolds, Albert, 4, 130
Robinson, Iris, 41
Robinson, Mary, 101, 105
Robinson, Peter, 41, 71, 191
Roosevelt, Theodore, 34
Rowley, John, 57
RUC (Royal Ulster Constabulary), 30, 31, 38,
	80, 133, 195, 203
	composition, 151
	credibility problem, 148
	and Drumcree dispute, 34–5, 148
	ethos of, 151
	interrogation, 66
	Orange lodge in, 30
	Patten commission, 148–51, 204
	size of, 151
rule of law, 33

St MacCartan's church (Augher), 173
St Malachy's Catholic church (Belfast), 82–3
Sands, Bobby, 117
Sands-McKevitt, Bernadette, 179
SAS, 65
Second World War, 63
sectarianism, 36–7, 41, 143
 loyalist violence, 118–19, 120–1
security forces, 91; *see also* RUC
Service, Brian, 193
Shankill Butchers, 74–5
Shankill Road bomb (1993), 75, 157
Shaw, George, 96
Shiels, Eric, 96
Sinn Féin, 2, 3, 4, 5, 6, 10, 13, 15, 16, 17, 39,
 52, 53, 68, 135. *see also* Adams, Gerry
 ard-fheis 1998, 138, 140
 Belfast city council seats, 71
 Blair reopens direct contacts, 67–9
 desire for new peace process, 72
 election campaigns, 67, 70; 1996, 11–14,
 15; 1997 general election, 56, 57–9
 electoral base, 72
 electoral mandate, 17, 18, 24
 electoral share, 72, 158–9
 and Good Friday agreement, 138
 and IRA army council, 24–5
 and Manchester bomb, 24
 personation and vote-rigging allegations,
 59–61, 72
 and political talks. *see also* political talks;
 "Sinn Féin's fatal dilemma", 6–9;
 demands for entry, 20–1; Blair initiative
 (June 1997), 78; Protestant population's
 willingness to talk, 92; "Unionist
 standard-bearers square up to Sinn
 Féin", 94–5; temporary exclusion, 123
 southern concerns and reservations, 106
 and unionists, 92, 94, 96, 97, 131
Slane, John, 54
Smyth, Rev. Eric, 14
Social Democratic and Labour party (SDLP), 4,
 10, 17, 39, 48, 66. *see also* Hume, John
 election campaigns, 67; Mid-Ulster (1997),
 57–9; West Belfast (1997), 59–60
 electoral share, 70, 72; consolidation of
 vote, 158
 personation allegations against Sinn Féin,
 59–60, 61
Somme, battle of, 30
Soper, Donald, 44
South Africa, 10, 129, 181
Sparks, Allister, 181
Spirit of Drumcree, 82
Springfield (Belfast), 13

Stone, Michael, 114, 116
Stormont Assembly. *see* Northern Ireland
 Assembly
Stormont system, 63–4
Stormont talks. *see* political talks
Strabane district council, 70
Straw, Jack, 55
Sunday Times, 195

talks process. *see* political talks
Taylor, John, 88, 94, 107, 185
terrorist attacks, 50, 54, 96–7, 109, 118–19,
 120–1, 134, 164–6, 193, 198–9, 200,
 202–3, 204. *see also* INLA; IRA; loyalist
 paramilitaries
 British government's double standards,
 50–3
 Canary Wharf bomb (1996), 1–7
 Dublin–Monaghan bombings (1974),
 104
 Enniskillen bomb (1987), 176
 Kingsmills massacre (1976), 109
 Lisburn bombings (1996), 47, 48
 Manchester bomb (1996), 22–5
 Omagh bomb (1998), 168–80
 Shankill Butchers' killings, 74–5
Thatcher, Margaret, 5, 45, 144, 150
32 County Sovereignty Movement (later
 Committee), 176, 179
Toombs, Ivan, 195
Trainor, Damien, 126–8, 181
Treanor, Edmund, 118
Trimble, Daphne, 89
Trimble, David, 8, 9, 10, 16–17, 18, 26, 38,
 39, 46, 52, 64, 71–2, 81–2, 85, 130, 134,
 136, 181, 182
 anti-Trimble coalition, 160, 166–8
 challenges for, 78–9, 160
 and Drumcree dispute, 34, 110, 163, 167
 election campaigns: 1996, 12, 14, 16
 and Good Friday agreement, 138–42
 and Mary McAleese, 103
 negotiations on new institutions, 182–3
 new personal outreach, 154
 new unionism, 148, 152–4, 159–60
 Nobel Peace Prize, 189–93
 and Omagh bombing, 175, 180
 political career, 85–8; membership of
 Vanguard, 86, 87, 88; joins Ulster
 Unionist party, 86, 88; wilderness years,
 87; elected leader of UUP (1995), 89
 and Sinn Féin, 92, 185–6, 201; talks with
 Sinn Féin (1997), 93–5; first direct
 meeting with Adams (1998), 184
 and Tony Blair, 130–1

troubles, 48, 49. *see also* terrorist attacks;
    victims of the troubles
Tyrone County Hospital, 171

UDA (Ulster Defence Association), 45, 87, 97.
    see also loyalist paramilitaries
  killings of Catholics (1998), 121
  political wing, 119
  prisoners, 113, 114; meeting with
    Mo Mowlam (1998), 114, 117
UDP. *see* Ulster Democratic party
UK Unionists, 16, 41, 166
Ulster Clubs, 88
Ulster Defence Association. *see* UDA
Ulster Defence Regiment, 95, 96, 124, 195
Ulster Democratic party (UDP), 13–14, 51, 72,
    119
  temporary exclusion from talks, 123
  and UDA violence, 121–2
Ulster Unionist Council
  Good Friday agreement, ratification of, 138
Ulster Unionist party (UUP), 9, 10, 14, 16, 34,
    39, 40, 41, 46, 66, 86, 106–7, 131, 137.
    see also Trimble, David
  Belfast city council seats, 71
  English politicians and, 94
  meeting with republicans, 98
Ulster Volunteers, 63, 64
unionism, 16–17, 38–9, 130, 131
  anti-Trimble coalition, 160, 166–8
  divisions within, 16–17
  electoral share, 70–1
  and Good Friday agreement, 138–9, 141–2,
    145, 148, 156, 159–60
  and Mary McAleese, 106–7
  new unionism, 148, 152–4, 159–60;
    Trimble's "big idea", 152–3

and Nobel Peace Prize, 191–2
  political talks, philosophy in, 135
unionist governments
  and Orange Order, 30–1
united Ireland
  Labour's consideration of, 64, 65, 66
United Irishmen, 28–9
UVF (Ulster Volunteer Force), 14, 30, 37, 80,
    109. *see also* loyalist paramilitaries
  death threat against Billy Wright, 110
  mid-Ulster brigade, 37, 109, 110
  prisoners, 113

Vanguard Unionists, 86, 87
Vatican, 43, 44
victims of the troubles, 75, 96–7, 198–9
  mental scars, 169
  Omagh bomb (1998), 169, 179, 183
voluntary coalition idea, 85, 88
vote-stealing, 60, 61, 72

West Belfast, 13
  general election campaign (1997), 59–60
Westminster election (1997), 56–61, 67, 69,
    70
Wheeler, Sir John, 50–1
Whitelaw, William, 45
Wilson, Harold, 62, 64–5, 66, 67
Wilson, Paddy, 97
Wilson, Paudraig, 116, 117
Woodvale (Belfast), 14
Wright, Alan, 88
Wright, Billy ("King Rat"), 32, 42, 59, 80,
    108–10, 113
  and Drumcree dispute, 110
  killing of, 107, 109, 111, 113, 134, 181
  UVF death threat, 110